ST. MARY'S COLLEGE OF MARYLAND
ST. MARY'S CITY, MARYLAND 20686

NEOCOLONIALISM AMERICAN STYLE, 1960–2000

Recent Titles in
Contributions in Political Science

Cautious Revolution: The European Union Arrives, Second Edition
Clifford Hackett

The Kingfish and the Constitution: Huey Long, the First
Amendment, and the Emergence of Modern Press Freedom in America
Richard C. Cortner

Unions and Public Policy: The New Economy, Law, and Democratic Politics
Lawrence G. Flood

U.S. Foreign and Strategic Policy in the Post-Cold War Era:
A Geopolitical Perspective
Howard J. Wiarda, editor

Comparing State Polities: A Framework for Analyzing 100
Governments
Michael J. Sullivan III

Federalism and the Environment: Environmental Policymaking in
Australia, Canada, and the United States
Kenneth M. Holland, F. L. Morton, and Brian Galligan, editors

Public Enterprise Management: International Case Studies
Ali Farazmand, editor

Mainstream(s) and Margins: Cultural Politics in the 90s
Michael Morgan and Susan Leggett, editors

The European Union, the United Nations, and the Revival of
Confederal Governance
Frederick K. Lister

The Leviathan in the State Theory of Thomas Hobbes: Meaning and
Failure of a Symbol
Carl Schmitt
Translated by George Schwab and Erna Hilfstein

On Ruins of Empire: Ethnicity and Nationalism in the Former
Soviet Union
George Mirsky

Ethnoregional Conflict in Democracies: Mostly Ballots,
Rarely Bullets
Saul Newman

NEOCOLONIALISM AMERICAN STYLE, 1960–2000

William H. Blanchard

Contributions in Political Science, Number 372

GREENWOOD PRESS
Westport, Connecticut • London

Library of Congress Cataloging-in-Publication Data

Blanchard, William H.
    Neocolonialism American style, 1960–2000 / William H. Blanchard.
        p.   cm.—(Contributions in political science, ISSN
    0147–1066 ; no. 372)
        Includes bibliographical references (p.   ) and index.
        ISBN 0–313–30013–5 (alk. paper)
        1. United States—Foreign relations—1961–1989.   2. United States—
    Foreign relations—1989–   3. United States—Foreign relations—
    Iran.   4. Iran—Foreign relations—United States.   5. United
    States—Foreign relations—Nicaragua.   6. Nicaragua—Foreign
    relations—United States.   7. United States—Foreign relations—
    Philippines.   8. Philippines—Foreign relations—United States.
    I. Title.   II. Series
    E840.B58   1996
    327.730172′3—dc20   95–49673

British Library Cataloguing in Publication Data is available.

Copyright © 1996 by William H. Blanchard

All rights reserved. No portion of this book may be
reproduced, by any process or technique, without the
express written consent of the publisher.

Library of Congress Catalog Card Number: 95–49673
ISBN: 0–313–30013–5
ISSN: 0147–1066

First published in 1996

Greenwood Press, 88 Post Road West, Westport, CT 06881
An imprint of Greenwood Publishing Group, Inc.

Printed in the United States of America

The paper used in this book complies with the
Permanent Paper Standard issued by the National
Information Standards Organization (Z39.48–1984).

10 9 8 7 6 5 4 3 2 1

To

Jess and Tobi

CONTENTS

PREFACE

This book is a follow up to a study of mine called *Aggression American Style,* published in 1978. In the earlier book I described what I felt was a typically American style of aggression, dominated by two important drives which both conflicted with and complimented one another. First, there was the desire for success which had pushed us into the position of one of the major nations of the world. Second, there was the desire for virtue which made it necessary for us to deny the aggressive implications of the first motivation. We did not admit to a struggle for power. Instead, we believed power came to us because of our goodness. In the early history of our country we saw ourselves as a people of high moral principle and we assumed that our foreign policy was not inconsistent with the morality of the Bible. Parson Weems, an early biographer of George Washington, described our first president as a man who could not tell a lie. Few people still believe the naive tale of Parson Weems, but the myth of American virtue and honesty continues to this day. It influences the public statements and behavior of our national leaders.

In *Aggression American Style* I examined, in some detail, ten cases or incidents that I felt illustrated the American style in aggression. We Americans have not been reluctant to engage in aggressive acts, but we have been quick to deny aggressive intent. In the current book, *Neocolonialism American Style,* I have changed the focus from single incidents to a long-term look at the consistency of American foreign policy toward individual nations over an extended period of time. Instead of exploring all the major instances of American neocolonialism I decided to examine three in some detail with an analysis of the historical background to illustrate how these neocolonial relationships developed.

Both the United States and my personal opinion about the American character have changed a great deal since the first book was written. I have described some of the changes in the first chapter of the current volume. However, enough has remained the same that the first chapters of both books bear a strong resemblance. In the first chapter of *Aggression American Style* I devoted several pages to the role of religion in American policy. Tocqueville has remarked that there is no country in which the Christian religion has a greater influence on the souls of men and that this control is reflected in American political life with a power that extends beyond the narrow interests of any one party. This role of religion is something that has been noted by several observers from France, England, Israel, Germany, Turkey—all over the world. From the inaugural address of George Washington to the speeches of Jimmy Carter and Ronald Reagan the influence of religion and morality has had an inevitable effect on the development of policy.

Jimmy Carter told reporters that he would never lie to the American people and he seemed puzzled when they expressed doubt that this would be possible. His human rights policy turned out to be a disaster because he felt he should never tell a lie and yet he could not face the fact that he might need to overlook a bad human rights situation to get the help he needed from a foreign leader. To the last day the shah of Iran remained in power Mr. Carter persisted in maintaining that the human rights of Iranian citizens had improved under the shah. This was not a deliberate lie, but an act of bad faith. He first lied to himself and then told what he thought was the truth to the American people. A deliberate lie would have been much easier. It would have preserved his flexibility. He could have changed his attitude when the evidence of the shah's dictatorship became overwhelming.

Even though we know, at one level, that the CIA has falsified documents, sabotaged the facilities of sovereign governments with which we are not at war, and made plans to assassinate foreign leaders, at another level the myth persists that American leaders are "honest" in the conduct of foreign policy. On March 3, 1981, in an interview with Walter Cronkite, President Reagan remarked that the Communist leaders in the Soviet Union "have said that the only morality—remember their ideology is without God, without our idea of morality in the religious sense—their statement about morality is that nothing is immoral if it furthers their cause, which means they can resort to lying or stealing or cheating or even murder if it furthers their cause."

Today, while we often hear statements that imply that the United States has no national interest that is in conflict with the good of all mankind, the long self-searching that followed the Vietnam War has made us more aware of the complexity of motives behind American foreign policy. Our leaders often make use of the myth of American altruism as a justification for policy. It was used most recently by President Bush when he announced the American mission in Somalia. But it is more generally recognized as the kind of obligatory "boiler-plate" that must be a part of our public statements.

In a military intervention in response to a crisis situation it is easier to disguise intent. It becomes more difficult in a long term relationship with another nation in which the United States plays a dominant role. It is for this reason that I have selected these cases of sustained intervention, to examine the erratic nature of American policy in more detail.

While myth plays an important role in American policy, we are not prisoners of our myths. With a rational approach to administrative organization it is possible to change policy. I have come to the conclusion that we need some ongoing organization in the government hierarchy that will serve the function of bringing realism to American foreign policy and preserving its consistency. At the present time, the Department of State, with its many deficiencies, has had to serve in that role. State has inherited the task by default. I maintain that we need a more conscious and deliberate shifting of policy responsibility to the State Department or some other agency that is organized for that purpose. Clearly, the National Security Council, with its closeness to the president, is unsuited for such a role.

I am indebted to Professor Eugene Dvorin for advice and criticism on the manuscript for this book. He has helped on the content as well as tightening up the writing. The comments of Bijan Rafailzadeh and his doctoral dissertation, *The Economics of Bribery in Less Developed Countries with Special Reference to Iran*, have provided insights into the political situation in Iran during the reign of the shah. Dr. Joseph Fink, Director of the Planning, Analysis and Research Institute, where I have been a senior fellow for the past decade, has helped with review and suggestions, as have other members of the staff. My wife, Hitchie, has been an invaluable critic and a great companion during the long creative process.

I am also indebted to the Kennedy, Reagan, Carter and Roosevelt Presidential Libraries for help in locating manuscripts and providing copying services for important materials. I am particularly grateful to Susan K. Forbes, Archivist at the John F. Kennedy Library for her help in locating documents on the Kennedy policy toward Iran.

ACRONYMS

ARDE	Democratic Revolutionary Alliance (Eden Pastora's contras)
CIA	Central Intelligence Agency
FAO	Broad popular front of parties opposed to the Somoza regime
FDN	Nicaraguan Democratic Force (contras sponsored by U.S.)
FSLN	Sandanista Liberation Front (including the military and political wings)
INR	Bureau of Intelligence and Research in the State Department
NATO	North American Treaty Organization
NEPL	A right wing fund-raising group managed by Carl R "Spitz" Channell
NSC	National Security Council
OAF	Spanish acronym for the Organization of American States
OAS	English acronym for the Organization of American States
OPEC	Organization of Petroleum Exporting Countries
OSS	Office of Strategic Services
PLO	Palestein Liberation Organization
PROFS	Professional Office System (a computer network in the White House)
SAVAK	The secret police of the Shah of Iran
UDEL	Pedro Joaquin Chamorro's democratic opposition group (against Somoza)
UN	United Nations
UNO	An umbrella anti-Somoza organization with members from the ARDE & FDN

1

THE ERA OF AMERICAN INTERVENTION

On November 4, 1979 the American Embassy in Tehran was attacked by Iranian student militants and the staff taken captive. At first it was assumed that this was merely a student demonstration that had gotten out of hand. Once government officials were informed, our people would surely be released. After all, this was U.S. government property. The people inside had diplomatic immunity. On the morning of November 5, crowds surrounded the embassy and speakers began to talk to them from improvised wooden stands. The crowds were wildly enthusiastic and seemed to support everything the students had done.

The students had one demand. The shah of Iran had been admitted to the United States for treatment of cancer; the students wanted him sent back to Iran and turned over to the government. The U.S. government rejected the demand of the students and continued to insist that the provisional government of Iran honor the assurances of Prime Minister Bazargan, made shortly before the attack, that the Iranian government would do its best to provide security for the embassy.

As the days dragged on, no one could quite believe that the Americans would not be released. The word *hostages* was studiously avoided. It was unthinkable, and everyone hoped it was unthinkable to the Iranians as well. But Iranian officials remained obdurate in spite of patient explanations, the movement of American ships and carriers into the Arabian Sea, and President Carter's various economic sanctions.

On November 17, when the Ayatollah Khomeini ordered the release of female and black hostages, it was clear that he was in control of the situation and that the students obeyed him. Later information that the students had been bused into Tehran just days before the attack on the embassy suggested that the taking of U.S. hostages was a deliberate and calculated act engineered at the highest levels of the Government of Iran.

In all, the hostages remained captive for 444 days. Their treatment was brutal and inhumane, including physical and psychological torture. At last they were released only after the inauguration of President Reagan.

OUR SHAH OR THEIR SHAH?

The arrow has been removed, but the memory of the hostage crisis in Iran remains a grievous wound that still festers in the hide of our country. The humiliation of a world power that has had its embassy sacked, and its citizens captured and mistreated, is not easily forgotten. It was an outrage, an act of war. But why did it happen? Have we ever done anything that would justify such an act of aggression?

There is, of course, no justification for the kidnapping and imprisonment of innocent people, but terrorism is the weapon of the weak. It is never justified in the legal sense. It occurs because the terrorists feel they must avenge an injury and they cannot reach the party they believe to be guilty. They are frustrated by a sense of anger and impotence. They attack innocent victims simply because they are available.

But why would they attack us?

In the 1960s and early 1970s the view of the shah of Iran from the United States, as portrayed by newspaper accounts and television interviews, was that of a benevolent despot who was trying to improve the life of a very primitive people. He wanted only the best for them, but he had to go slowly and carefully, hauling them into the 20th century for their own good. He improved transportation, education and health care. He stamped out revolution and made the streets safe so a woman could walk in comfort in the evening. He raised the status of women and reduced the role of religion in the secular life of his people.

In the television interviews with the shah, he was, to be sure, a bit distant, formal, attached to pomp and ceremony, and he sometimes shocked us with remarks that seemed to justify repression in his country. But, after all, he was a monarch. He never claimed to be running a democracy. He would always smile and remind us that his people had not lived for two centuries under democracy, as we had. In their present state they needed discipline. Once they were educated and fed enough democracy to civilize them, he was sure he could relax his iron grip.

At times we would have terrible demonstrations from the Iranian students in this country—usually when the shah arrived for a visit. They said mean things about him, claiming his secret police had torture chambers in the prisons and had discovered hideous means of getting information from his subjects. But then, students were always protesting something and they were known to exaggerate.

After all, it was obvious that his people adored him and they all loved America. Whenever an American president visited Iran, people swarmed into the streets to cheer the shah and his visitor, waving small American flags. Nobody ever asked where they got all those American flags on such short notice.

In the late 1970s we began to hear more of religious protests and student riots in Iran. The puzzling thing about these demonstrations was the anti-Americanism that accompanied them. On January 16, 1979, after over a year of riots and revolution, the shah left Iran on a "vacation" from which he would never return. In the subsequent seizure of the American embassy and the parade of hostages we discovered that the Iranian people had hated us all the time. We had thought that he was *their* shah, but now they said he was *our* shah. He was called a tool of American interests, a traitor to his own country.

Americans were accused of imperialism and colonialism, when everyone knew we had never coveted the territory of another nation and we had even given the Philippines their freedom after our trusteeship. They said we were an aggressive world power that had placed the shah on his peacock throne against the will of the Iranian people and had used him to enslave the people of Iran and deliver its resources into our hands. Our policy, they said, was one of neocolonialism, like the British, the Germans, and even the Soviet Union.

Is it possible that this nation, which began its history as a rebel against colonialism and which had always supported the ideals of democracy, could be guilty of repressing another people in order to exploit their resources? If this were true, would we not be aware of it?

THE AGE OF INNOCENCE

When the Revolutionary War ended and the United States gained its independence as a nation, we tried to avoid entanglements with the European powers. This policy was closely tied to the belief that there was something special about the United States, that our geography, our distance from the intrigue of Europe made it possible for us to be a better, more honorable people. The notion of a virtuous mission, particularly a religious mission, was evident in President George Washington's first inaugural address. There were frequent supplications to the "Almighty Being who rules over the universe" and the "Great Author of every public and private good." In every advance of the United States, Washington saw the hand of providence. He contrasted the "tranquil deliberations" and "voluntary consent" by which the various states decided to join the union, with the violence by which other governments had been established. He spoke of the "indissoluble union" that exists between virtue and happiness.[1] In his farewell address he warned that we must preserve this uniquely American virtue by avoiding foreign entanglements. If we involve ourselves in the affairs of Europe, we would risk losing this peaceful virtue.

Europe has a set of primary interests which to us have none or a very remote relation. Hence she must be engaged in frequent controversies, the causes of which are essentially foreign to our concerns. Hence, therefore, it must be unwise in us to implicate ourselves by artificial ties in the ordinary vicissitudes of her politics or the ordinary combinations and collisions of her friendships or enmities.[2]

During the early stages of World War I, Woodrow Wilson was praised because he kept us out of the war. Our final involvement in the war brought about the end of American isolationism, but the attitude remained that we were, as a nation, above the narrow and short-sighted attitude of Europeans. The power of this myth is evident in the pronouncements of Wilson at the close of World War I. He had the conviction that the United States' policy was not influenced by the narrow concerns of national interest but by the broad principles of world justice. He concluded, therefore, that we had no need to recognize the claims and counterclaims of the various European states, but that the Europeans, once they understood that we had nothing to gain, would be "converted to America."[3] It was as though the Europeans were to be converted to a religion.

You can see that the representatives of the United States have laid down for them the unalterable lines of principle. . . . They [Americans] came as crusaders, not merely to win a war but to win a cause; and I am responsible to them, for it fell to me to formulate the purposes for which I asked them to fight. And I, like them, must be a crusader for those things, whatever it costs and whatever it may be necessary to do, in honor to accomplish the object for which they fought. . . . I do not mean any disrespect for any other people when I say that America is the hope of the world. And if she does not justify that hope results are unthinkable. Men will be thrown back on bitterness of disappointment not only but bitterness of despair.[4]

In the years that followed, the United States continued to grow in status and power. With the end of World War II we were one of the two most powerful nations in the world. The European powers had found the reach for empire too costly and had begun to retreat from their major possessions throughout the world. The age of our innocence had ended, but we were not quite aware of it yet. We continued to believe in our virtue and our innocence. While there was much inconsistency in American policy, the myth continued that we had no national interest, but only wanted to do what was best for the world as a whole. When an American intervention began to go wrong some congressman would ask for withdrawal and complain that the policy was not in our "national interest." But the myth of international responsibility persisted as a general explanation of American foreign policy. If we had a number of colonies or territorial possessions, our stated goal was to grant them independence, to "let the people decide." If we did not want to act on that goal, we could always maintain that the people were not yet ready for independence. In any event, the deliberate conquest and holding of colonial territory was not considered a proper goal of American policy.

The British were proud of their empire, and that pride was not confined to the nobility. At the time of the Boer War, Joseph Schumpeter remarked that there was not a beggar in London who did not speak of "our" rebellious subjects.[5] Of course it is not acceptable for the leadership in a democracy to give voice to the satisfaction expressed by Schumpeter's beggar. The thirst for power in a democracy must be experienced as a painful necessity. It must be cleansed of any obvious libidinal satisfaction. Americans have always been proud of being strong. Children in our country are taught to be tough, to defend themselves. But the notion of a deliberate, conscious struggle to dominate others is foreign to our national ethos. Of course we do it, in both our domestic and foreign policy, but it is characteristic of the American style that it must happen without conscious intent.

NEOCOLONIALISM

In a previous book[6] I have covered the type of American intervention in which we invade another nation to "protect it" from communism or to "save the lives" of Americans who are presumably in danger. These are short-term incidents of intervention. It is relatively easy to disguise our intent in such cases. The American notion of global management by putting out fires in various parts of the world, ill-advised as it is, is not as deliberate as the instances of sustained intervention. In the current study I examine the slow development of a long-term relationship of dominance over another nation on the part of the United States. Our critics have termed this phenomenon *neocolonialism*. The problem with this word is that it conjures up an image of Americans owning property and living an easy "colonial" life, with servants taking care of our daily needs while we place our own governor general in charge of the nation and work the native population to produce goods for us. The history of our relationship with the Philippines, Santo Domingo, South Korea, Iran and Nicaragua makes such an image incongruous. The term *neocolonialism* is a bit like *genocide*. If we are angry at the failure of the government to help the poor, we may decide that government policy is one of deliberate genocide. The problem is that terms such as this confuse the issue, degrade the language and make the accusation easier to deny.

However, *neocolonialism* has caught on and has become a part of our language. As it is much more easily recognized than *sustained intervention*, it would be best to have an understanding of what it means. I prefer Stephen Shalom's definition of the term.

Colonialism is traditionally regarded as the rule of one country over another. But when defined in this way, strictly in terms of nation-states, the concept becomes hopelessly narrow. What does it mean to say that Britain ruled Jordan or India? Surely not that all the citizens of Britain ruled over all the citizens of these colonies. The factory workers of Manchester and Liverpool not only did not rule over the Hashemite monarch or the Indian rajahs, they lived under incomparably worse conditions. . . . In 1907, in areas of India encompassing 17.5 million people, there were only twenty-one British civil servants and twelve police officers. This was possible only because the British had the cooperation of the Indian elite. The latter collaborated with the British—as junior partners to be sure, but as partners nonetheless—in ruling over the mass of the Indian population.

The alliance was a symbiotic one. The Indian elite was able to maintain its position of local dominance, and the British elite acquired its greatest outlet for trade and investment. The interests of the two elites were not identical, but they were close enough to permit the mutually beneficial relationship to last for ninety years. Colonialism, then, must be viewed in class terms as well as in national terms.

Neocolonialism follows the same pattern. It shall be defined here as an alliance between the leading class or classes of two independent nations which facilitates their ability to maintain a dominant position over the rest of the population of the weaker of the two nations.[7]

This definition describes our relationship with the Philippines, South Korea, Iran, and most of Central America—as well as Santo Domingo under Trujillo. Our shadow also falls upon South America, but our domination is less complete. In addition, there are smaller territories such as American Samoa and Puerto Rico. Hawaii is a special case. It is the only occupied territory that has been completely absorbed by the mother country through colonization. Alaska, of course, was an outright purchase.

Modern neocolonialism has less chance of lasting ninety years. Much has changed in America since the 1960s. While we are still a major military power, we no longer have the economic muscle to back it up. Hunger and homelessness, which were not really visible in the 1950s, are confronted daily on the streets of this nation. Not only the press, but the people are more ready to criticize the president and Congress. We have become more aware of the rest of the world and we no longer have the naive faith in our own goodness and in the inevitable justice of American institutions that we had at the close of World War II. All over the world, the political awareness of members of the oppressed classes and their international mobility make a neocolonial relationship increasingly difficult to sustain. For that reason we need to take a hard look at this phenomenon. The United States has never had the great monolithic culture that was sometimes attributed to it. Criticism of our country that refer to it as an example of "imperialism" fail to take into account the divergence of opinion, the frequent changes of administration, and the strange mixture of innocence and arrogance, good will and greed that form the distinguishing feature of inconsistency in the realm of U.S. foreign policy.

Our history books tell us that we supervised the development of the Philippines, educated the people and, when they were "ready," we "gave" them their freedom. How generous of us! How could anyone accuse us of neocolonialism? We were once an association of colonies ourselves and we fought for our freedom against England. We have served as an example to oppressed people all over the world. Our leaders have offered our behavior in the Philippines as an example of a policy that allows other nations to develop toward independence, the assumption being that we only want to protect them long enough for the people to develop some political maturity and learn to determine their own form of government. But in our "protective" role, we train their armies, give and sell them American military equipment, organize and supervise their trade and commerce, and educate them about our form of government. As long as the "people" decide on a pro-American government, make a place for our corporations in their economy, and allow us to keep our military bases on their territory all goes well. If there is some doubt about our welcome, there may be trouble.

After all, it is natural to want governments in other parts of the world that are friendly to the United States. We are only exercising our influence. However, when this influence extends to the overthrow of elected governments, it may well be perceived as domination. Moreover, the notion of influence and control goes beyond the U.S. Government to the actions of large American corporations—large enough to become small governments in themselves. This influence extends in both directions. Dictators such as Trujillo in the Dominican Republic and Somoza in Nicaragua have learned that the award of lush mining and food-processing contracts to major American firms can buy our silence on human rights abuses.[8] In this way the initial step toward neocolonialism may be taken by the subject nation itself.

But just as they have us figured out, we seem to change again. If the American press reports human rights abuses, describes death squads or wholesale arrests and executions over an extended period of time, the sleeping giant slowly stirs itself to protest these abuses. The American people do not want to feel that their foreign aid is going to support repression. They do not want to *knowingly* exploit others, which really means that there are some of us who want to profit by the exploitation without knowing about it and there are some who really, genuinely, do not want to exploit others. The latter will raise a protest with our government when they discover that we are profiting from the misery of others. Blatant election fraud or the slaughter of protestors in a dependent nation may arouse their anger and a demand that the United States cut its ties with an oppressive regime.

STUMBLING INTO A FOREIGN POLICY

There is every reason to believe that our foreign policy should be designed to support American interest rather than some mythical good for all mankind. However, we can only act in our interest if we are clear about two questions: (1) What actions and alliances are in our long range interest? and (2) What do we hope to achieve by our current policy? We have to be able to explain this policy to the American people in such a way that it makes sense. This means much more than having a president who is determined to be honest about his own motivation. No one sought honesty with more fervor than President Carter, but his personal friendship with the shah of Iran made it impossible for him to see that our support of the shah was detrimental to American interest. Carter's public statements during the years before the fall of the shah demonstrate that he had convinced himself that the shah was leading Iran toward democracy and that he had a human rights policy that was continuously improving.

There is a legitimate question as to whether U.S. influence (through friendship) is desirable in a severely repressive regime. If we do not respect their policy on civil rights, we will not change their domestic policy by threats or incentives. Instead, it is best to maintain a formal and correct relationship. This is a matter of degree, but dictatorships and repressive regimes are inherently unstable. It relates to our long-range national interest, whether we should encourage the favorable treatment of U.S. corporations by totalitarian powers, or if we should seek our influence among the members of the democratic opposition. The answer to this question may change over time. In the early days, an autocratic leader may still allow the rule of law and permit a free press. In the later stages he may be a dictator. At what point American policy must change will depend on many factors, but it should not depend on habit, the long association between two countries and the friendships their leaders have developed for one another.

Foreign policy needs to be reexamined at regular intervals and the president of the United States should subject his policy to a critical review. The president's advisor must be someone as close as possible to his own stature, who has the role of questioning his assumptions.

If a symbiotic relationship develops between the United States and a foreign dictator, he may be regarded as our "puppet," but this picture could be misleading. A puppet remains quiet until his master pulls the strings. Our dictator may have the goal of diverting foreign aid and amassing a fortune for himself. If this involves the seizure of property, false arrest, imprisonment, torture of his citizens, censorship of the press, and the suppression of political dissent, he is not merely our puppet. He is in business for himself and may be working against our long- range interest. We are paying a very high price for our military bases and our influence over his foreign policy. If he is protected by an American-trained army, surrounded by uniformed and beribboned American officers and civilian advisors, receiving large amounts of American aid and American weapons—in short, if he is perceived by his people as an American agent, he is doing us a serious disservice. Whether we like it or not, he represents the United States to his people. His deeds are our deeds. When he falls, we fall with him. When this happens, our influence has vanished and we have made an enemy of his successor.

In the following chapters I examine our neocolonial relationship with three nations: Iran, Nicaragua, and the Philippines. These are not our only neocolonial relationships. We have made trouble for ourselves in other areas as well. The examples in this study have been selected over a large and diverse part of the globe and they illustrate our good will as well as our folly.

Although the American desire to save the world from chaos and misery seems, on the surface, to be a very positive quality, there is a darker side to this image that manifests itself from time to time. Most behavior is really overdetermined, that is, people act not for one reason alone but with a variety of motives. Therefore, it is not surprising that an American involvement with another nation, that begins as a generous and unselfish desire to help others, can become mixed with motives of national aggrandizement, without anyone intending that it should happen that way.

NOTES

1. D. J. Boorstin, *An American Primer* (Chicago: University of Chicago Press, 1966) pp. 172-175.

2. Ibid., p. 205.

3. W. Wilson, *Messages and Papers of Woodrow Wilson, vol.2* (New York: George H. Doran, 1924) p. 642.

4. Ibid. pp. 622-644.

5. J. Schumpeter, *Social Classes and Imperialism* (New York: World Publishing, Meridian, 1966) pp. 72-73.

6. W. H. Blanchard, *Aggression American Style* (Santa Monica, California: Goodyear, 1978).

7. S. Shalom, *The United States and the Philippines: A Study of Neocolonialism* (Philadelphia: Institute for the Study of Human Issues, 1981) pp. xiv, xv.

8. In the Eisenhower administration both Alan Dulles, head of the CIA and John Foster Dulles, secretary of state, owned stock in the United Fruit Company which dominated the economy of Central America. John Foster was also the attorney for United Fruit before he accepted his position in the Eisenhower administration.

2

THE AMERICAN RELATIONSHIP
WITH IRAN

The development of anti-Americanism in Iran did not happen suddenly. Before the United States became a major world power our relationship with Iran was quite different. We began in an honest effort to help protect Iran from the colonial powers of Great Britain and Russia. But the responsibility of world leadership and a growing, almost frantic fear of the Communist menace played a central role in our search for a single, reliable, pro-American leader who would welcome our military bases and look after our interests in that part of the world. Our policy toward Iran is a long, torturous and erratic one, full of direct reversals. We have done much good and even more harm in Iran and both are well remembered by the people.

During the early part of this century the United States remained aloof from the struggle between Tzarist Russia and Great Britain for the control of Iran (which was then called Persia) and its oil resources. The conflict subsided in 1907 with the Anglo-Russian Convention dividing Iran between Great Britain and Russia for the purpose of commercial exploitation. In 1909 a constitutional government was reestablished in Iran with an active Majlis (Parliament). However, the countryside was in chaos. Tribesmen claimed control of several rural areas. Azerbaijan and much of Khorasan were occupied by Russian troops. Taxes could not be collected. The Majlis, suspicious of both Britain and Russia, turned to the United States for help. The U.S. sent Morgan Schuster, a New York banker to help them with their financial problems in 1910.

Problems in Iran at that time went far beyond financial difficulties, but Schuster proved to be an unusual individual who had abilities sufficient to meet the complex challenges. At the time the Majlis, though nominally in charge, had no capacity to govern. Iran was being strangled by foreign domination. Schuster organized a gendarmerie to collect taxes and enforce the law. He encouraged the development of Iranian nationalism by appropriating the estates of Shoa-el-

Soltaneh, the brother-in-law of the former shah, who was in debt to the Russian bank and in exile in Russia. The estates were guarded by Russian troops, but Shuster ordered his force to seize the property. The Russians sent an ultimatum demanding Schuster's dismissal and threatened an advance on Tehran. The Majlis refused and prepared for confrontation. This action was regarded by the people as a patriotic struggle in which the United States was their ally. Russian goods were boycotted and fighting broke out against Russian troops in several cities. A demonstration of women in Iran soon brought forth others, and the streets were filled with protesters demanding that the Majlis hold firm against the Russians. There was widespread enthusiasm for the United States and the memory of Schuster's work is still alive in Iran today.[1]

But the British, in accord with their 1907 agreement, supported the Russian move, and a coup d'etat by the regent, Nasir al-Mulk, resulted in the dissolution of the Majlis. The Russians were notified of the British action. As a result of the long period of British and Russian domination and this final suppression of the surge of Iranian nationalism, the people developed an attitude that everything that happened in Iran was the result of some great foreign power, working either directly or behind the scenes through some local tyrant.

In 1921, following invasions by both Russian and British troops during World War I, the government of Iran was close to bankruptcy. Riots and famine were endemic. Reza Khan, a peasant who had risen to the rank of colonel in the Russian forces, marched into Teheran and proclaimed himself minister of war and commander in chief. In order to secure the loyalty of the people he called himself a nationalist, and he justified much of his brutalization on that ground.

In the same year, the Majlis asked the United States for another financial mission. This one was headed by Arthur Millspaugh, who was given a contract with wider powers. By 1926 he had, as he says,

reorganized and reintegrated a financial structure that had fallen apart in a dozen directions and in a dozen ways. We centralized revenues, expenditures and accounting. With better administration and new tax laws, revenues increased. These laws abolished the road tolls that had delayed and vexed movement over the highways and the medieval duties collected at the city gates that had burdened internal commerce. . . . The government with our assistance balanced the budget, started payment of claims and provided for the financing of new constructive undertakings.[2]

Several American engineers and agricultural experts were employed, supervising farming methods and building the Trans-Persian Railway and the highways.

THE RETURN OF DESPOTISM

Reza Kahn soon declared himself shah and began looting the treasury. Slowly the country returned to its ancient and primitive absolutism without a protest from the many new leaders in the Majlis. In the following year the shah dismissed the American mission and took full control of the country. He was determined to make improvements, but in his own style. In 1936 he ordered women to put off their veils and the Moslem clergy was stripped of its power and prestige. He completed the Trans-Persian Railway and added many new roads. He was interested in education and he reduced illiteracy. But he also instituted a regressive taxation policy, shifting much of the burden to the middle class and poor, exempting landlords from taxation and restoring medieval duties collected at city gates. He created a new class of capitalists among the merchants, government contractors and political favorites. He neglected agriculture. Famine, caused by crop failure, began to appear in the country again. Says Millspaugh,

The practice of terror came naturally to Reza Shah. While I was still close enough to observe, instances of his brutality came to my attention; but after the first years of his reign, the terror intensified. . . . I was informed on my return to Persia that he had imprisoned thousands and killed hundreds, some of the latter by his own hand. Several prominent men, I was told, were poisoned in prison. . . . Fear settled upon the people. No one knew whom to trust; and none dared to protest or criticize.[3]

Despite the return of despotism in Iran, the United States had the reputation of a disinterested advisor, and Americans were very popular with prominent Iranian leaders and members of the Majlis. However, in 1942, when Reza Shah was suspected of collaboration with the Nazis, the United States played a prominent role in deposing him. Along with forces of Great Britain and the Soviet Union, U.S. troops marched into Iran and replaced Reza Shah with his more tractable son. However, we did not remain in the country as an occupying force. We recognized the British interest in the region and avoided open conflict by withdrawing our military.

At this time the Majlis again requested the services of Millspaugh. The shah's son (Mohammed Reza Pahlavi) had been appointed as a constitutional monarch, but there was little central authority and general anarchy prevailed. Regional tribes were arming themselves and robbing the citizens. Government officials were stealing revenues, agriculture was in a mess, and famine was once again a common experience. In the north, the Russians had occupied the country and the British were in control in the south.

The Majlis authorized Millspaugh to hire up to sixty Americans, and experts from a variety of fields were called on to help put the country together again. This time things did not work as smoothly. Many of the new arrivals had no experience with a foreign culture. It was difficult to adjust the pay scale. Some, it turned out, were underpaid for the task they were assigned, while others were overpaid. The larger number of Americans in this mission made them more noticeable and heightened the xenophobia of the Teheran press. Sometimes individuals were singled out and sometimes all Americans were condemned.

In addition, there was the problem of a corrupt Iranian government and a Parliament with a philosophy of each man for himself. Millspaugh remarked, at the time of his arrival, that the Iranian government had always been one of the most corrupt in the world, but it was now even worse than in 1922.

In the Persian government of 1943 dishonesty had become almost universal and practically a matter of routine. Merchants, landlords and all who had dealings with the government suffered from it, but they had come to accept it, to accommodate themselves to it, and thus to encourage it. Employees exacted bribes for the doing of anything that benefited anyone else; and they conveniently lost files when bribes were not forthcoming. . . . The men who were now engaged in comprehensive robbery were mostly those who had learned their lesson from the ex-shah, taken part in his commercial operations, or served as his accomplices.[4]

There were, of course, a few conscientious deputies who wanted to serve the interests of Iran. One of them was Dr. Mohammed Mossadegh, who referred to the Majlis as a den of thieves, in his public speeches. There were others who were part of the thievery, but who would have followed a strong, ethical leader if he could assume command. The young shah was an unlikely prospect for national leadership. Officially he was the head of government, but his power was sharply limited and he was surrounded by military advisors who had served his father. They reminded him that Iran was not ready for democracy and they regarded all current problems as due to a "weak," that is, nonabsolute, monarchy.

OIL AND UNITED STATES POLICY

Millspaugh felt that his mission might have succeeded if he had been backed by the American embassy, but the embassy was now focused on maintaining good diplomatic relations with Iran. Millspaugh began to see that he was increasingly isolated and that he could no longer represent the position of the United States. He resigned on February 15, 1945.

The embassy may have been acting on instructions from Washington. The world had changed a great deal from the situation in 1910, when the first American mission was undertaken. At that time the United States was in the early stages of consolidating its industrial potential. Oklahoma had just become a state. New Mexico and Texas were preparing for statehood. Taft was president and the tradition of isolationism was still a strong force in national politics. Oil was used primarily as a source of kerosine to fuel lamps. The American leadership supported the financial mission to Iran, the goal of which was to advise the government of Iran concerning necessary changes to improve its financial situation, to support the democratic forces in Iran and to oppose domination of Iran by any foreign power.

However, after World War II, the United States emerged as a world power. Oil was now the primary source of fuel for American strategic forces, which had land, sea, and air, bases all over the world. Before the war was over, we had already begun to assess our future oil needs. The first reports indicated that the Persian Gulf was the new center of gravity for the world's oil. American scientists estimated that U.S. reserves would be exhausted in ten to twelve years.[5] Further, Great Britain, one of the two major powers on the scene in Iran, was no longer a formidable world power. British diplomats in Washington were telling the administration that they could no longer oppose the Russians in Iran without American help. It seems clear that the concern of the American leadership was now to avoid offending the "sovereign power" of Iran, whatever form of government it might take, rather than to face its leaders with certain unpleasant truths about its fiscal policies and financial organization.

DEMOCRACY IN IRAN

After Millspaugh's departure, production in Iran sank below the prewar level. More than 80 percent of the population suffered from malnutrition and there were frequent outbreaks of famine. Oil production was in the hands of the British Anglo-Persian oil company, which consistently ignored the terms of its contract (for example, the training of Iranian specialists, and the provision of schools and hospitals). The Iranian leaders and the press of Tehran were outraged by this humiliation. The National Front party developed under the leadership of Dr. Mohammed Mossadegh, a courageous nationalist leader who had been sent to prison in the 1930s for his opposition to Reza-Shah. Mossadegh, now the elected representative from Tehran, advocated a parliamentary democracy with a monarchy controlled by the constitution. He demanded nationalization of Iranian oil, regardless of the financial consequences—even if the Anglo-Persian Oil Company had to be shut down and Iran were to lose this important source of foreign capital. The British countered with an offer of a 50 percent share of the profits, but a special committee headed by Mossadegh voted to reject the offer.

On April 30, 1951, Mossadegh was elected prime minister, and one day later the nationalization order went into effect. The British protested this breach of their 1933 contract with Iran and offered to negotiate, but since all meetings began with a British declaration that nationalization was an illegal act, no progress was made. The U.S. ambassador, Henry Grady, supported Iranian independence and Mossadegh. This dismayed the British. British efforts were directed toward an alliance with the United States and a joint approach to Iran on the matter of nationalization. The pressure of American oil companies was directed at the Truman White House, and a British-American alliance was finally concluded. This alliance was not forged without protests from Congress, but it soon became clear that the oil corporations could effectively control Congress through lobbying efforts and the prospect of money for future political campaigns. Great Britain began the imposition of an oil boycott against Iran supported by the United States.

Mossadegh was determined to restructure the economy of Iran so it could function without oil revenue, while the British, convinced that they could never make use of Iranian oil as long as Mossadegh was in power, began to work with political forces within Iran for his overthrow. At first the United States refused to support this approach. Ambassador Grady witnessed the crowds in front of the Majlis shouting their support for Premier Mossadegh and reported to Washington that 95 percent of the Iranian people supported him.

Encouraged by American friends, Mossadegh visited the United States in the fall of 1951. He was a passionate man and he made a number of speeches, many of them quite critical of the British and the Anglo-Iranian oil company. He did not get a good press. British interests succeeded in portraying him as a fanatic. Mossadegh was quite upset by the newspaper articles and Justice William O. Douglas, who admired him, tried to give him some perspective on the situation:

There may be disappointment in your heart as you leave [the U.S.]. But much good has been done. I think the great body of American sentiment will grow and grow in favor of you and your wonderful people, as the ugly and greedy British policy under [Winston] Churchill's management becomes as plain to everyone as it is to you and me.[6]

Justice Douglas was well-connected with government leaders and he spent much time trying to promote the cause of Mossadegh with his friend, President Truman (who had once offered Douglas the vice presidential spot on the Democratic ticket) and other Washington officials. But when Truman left office he was succeeded by Eisenhower and a complete change of administration. Douglas soon found himself frozen out. Eisenhower had worked closely with Churchill during the war. Secretary of State John Foster Dulles and his brother, Allen Dulles, who became head of the CIA, were both pro-British.

In 1953 the British, already worried about American support for Mossadegh, sent C. M. Woodhouse of British Intelligence to brief the U.S. commission in Iran. Eisenhower was informed of the danger of Communist influence through people close to the premier. Churchill put it rather directly to Eisenhower: The British Empire was at the end of its tether. From a financial and military point of view Great Britain was no longer a major world power. The Soviet Union was a chronic threat to British power everywhere in the world. The British could not meet this threat without American help—a great deal of help. In fact, it was an invitation for the United States to assume the British role in Iran.

The U.S. commission in Iran made several contacts with the shah, who was encouraged to defy Mossadegh. But when the shah made conciliatory gestures toward the British, Mossadegh was outraged. He dissolved the Senate and obtained special powers from the Majlis. He insisted that the shah remain within the authority granted to him by the Iranian Constitution and demanded that the monarch return the lands illegally seized by his father or turn them over to the government for redistribution. On February 24, 1953, the shah, badly frightened, offered to leave the country until some of the tension between himself and the government subsided.

However, it was clear that the U.S. government and the press were turning against Mossadegh. Many press reports suggested that his supporters were

Communists. Actually, Mossadegh declined support of the Tudeh (the Iranian Communist party), because of his desire for American support. The Tudeh press attempted to smear him and maintained that they were the true nationalists. But the charges served to convince many professional anti-Communists in both parties that Mossadegh must go. Many of the merchants, religious leaders, and members of the court had turned against him. Even within his own party, the National Front, some of the members had come out against him. Finally, Ambassador Henderson, the new American ambassador under Eisenhower, gave public support to the shah. Mossadegh became increasingly worried, but Henderson assured him that the United States would never interfere in the internal affairs of Iran.

Nevertheless Mossadegh, who was familiar with the long history of foreign powers dominating the politics of Iran, did not really believe the ambassador's assurances. He felt he had to do something to turn aside U.S. support for the shah. He was aware of the almost paranoid fear of communism in the Eisenhower administration and perhaps he thought he could make use of this fear to enhance his own position. He gave blatant encouragement to a street demonstration of the Tudeh party and, on May 28, 1953, he sent a letter to President Eisenhower implying that there could be a Communist takeover if he did not receive financial and possibly military aid from the Americans. Of course it had the reverse effect.

THE CIA ARRANGES A COUP

In early August, 1953, General H. Norman Schwarzkopf of the CIA arrived in Teheran. (This is not the commanding general in the Gulf War, but his father.) He was a personal friend of General Zahedi as well as the shah and, from 1942 to 1948, he had been in charge of recruiting and training police troops for the shah. Before that, he had organized the New Jersey state police. After Schwarzkopf met with Henderson, the ambassador decided to take a trip to Switzerland where he had a conference with Allen Dulles, chief of the CIA, and Princess Ashraf, sister of the shah who had been exiled by Mossadegh. Immediately after this meeting the shah made his move against Mossadegh. He gave the order for Mossadegh's dismissal and appointed General Zahedi the new premier. Zahedi sent troops to present Mossadegh with the order for his dismissal, but Mossadegh's house was guarded and the officers of the shah could not get through. They foolishly left the order with the guard commander. The shah, now very uneasy that he had tipped his hand but could not carry out the order for Mossadegh's dismissal, left the country to avoid retaliation.

The following day Mossadegh arrested the commander of the shah's bodyguard, Colonel Nasseri. Then he took to the airwaves announcing the attempted coup and the fact that the shah had fled the country. Most of the press published the attacks on the shah. It appeared, for a few days, that Mossadegh had won. But on the morning of August 19 the American CIA led a countermove. CIA officers, with satchels full of Iranian rials, distributed money to the street people through the Mullahs. A mob rushed into the streets of Tehran calling "Down with Mossadegh." Pro-Mossadegh citizens, hearing the cry, joined in the opposition and violent streetfighting followed. In the ensuing conflict over 250 people were killed.

General Zahedi went to Mossadegh's house with his officers, in a tank at the head of the CIA-sponsored mob. When the mob could not keep up with the officers, the CIA hired taxis for them. This time the guards were shot and Mossadegh fled, but he was soon captured and put on trial for treason before a military court. At his trial he presented a document showing that the day before the mob riot Iran Bank had cashed a check for $390,000 made out to Edward G. Donally, an American.[7] But his evidence was ignored.

Thus, Shah Mohammed Reza Pahlavi, who assumed all the power and pomp of his dictatorial father, was placed on his peacock throne by the CIA.[8] The change of leadership received the full support of the United States. In a few months there were over 900 American troops in Iran to support the shah and to train his army.

NOTES

1. R. W. Cottam, *Nationalism in Iran* (Pittsburgh: University of Pittsburgh Press, 1964) pp. 107-172. See also A. A. Saikal, *The Rise and Fall of the Shah* (Princeton: Princeton University Press, 1980) pp. 1-123.

2. A. C. Millspaugh, *Americans in Persia* (New York: DeCapo Press, 1976) pp. 12-19, quote, p.23.

3. Ibid, p. 37.

4. Ibid., p. 83

5. B. Nirumand, *Iran:the New Imperialism in Action.* (New York: Monthly Review Press, 1969) p.39.

6. W. O. Douglas, *The DouglasLetters: Selections from the Private Papers of Justice William O. Douglas,* edited by Melvin I. Urofsky (Bethesda: Adler and Adler, 1987) p. 282.

7. Nirumand, *Iran*, pp. 83-88.

8. See Saikal, *Rise and Fall,* pp. 1-123 for more details on the coup. In an interview with Amin Saikal, Loy Henderson, the American ambassador, confirmed the central role of the CIA in this coup and put the cost at "Millions of dollars." Those were pre-inflation dollars. Even John Foster Dulles, (Eisenhower's secretary of state and the

brother of Allen Dulles, head of the CIA) admitted to a House Foreign Affairs Committee that the "non-communist forces" were encouraged "by our aid and friendly interest." See Saikal, pp. 44, 214-15.

3

IRAN: THE RISE OF THE SHAH

In the previous chapter we examined the early relationship between the United States and Iran and the reversal of American policy that moved us from a position of support for a nationalist democratic government, having the enthusiastic backing of the people, to the sponsorship of an absolute monarchy. The American people were, for the most part, completely unaware of the popularity of Mossadegh in Iran. Our press portrayed him as a man who held meetings in his pajamas from his bedside. They took pictures of him weeping at public meetings, describing him as a fool. Mossadegh was not blameless. While he began his career seeking a democratic government and the independence of Iran, in his later years he became involved in the manipulation of elections and the bribery and corruption so common in the Majlis. However, he is remembered in Iran as a major figure in the struggle for independence, and there is no doubt among Iranian politicians regarding the central role played by the United States in his demise. A detailed account of the American-sponsored coup was reported in the *Saturday Evening Post* of November 6, 1954, and, while it is almost unknown in the United States, it has been widely read in Iran.[1]

American public officials have rationalized the U.S. role during the post-Mossadegh era as one of "friendship" for Iran, by which they generally mean friendship for the shah. The Eisenhower administration, which would not send aid to Mossadegh, sent over $600 million to the shah. The Iranian government passed a law to protect foreign investors, and money poured in from abroad. A special United States military mission was appointed to supervise the expansion and training of the Iranian armed forces. In 1957 the CIA helped to organize and train the Iranian State Intelligence and Security Organization, which became notorious under the acronym SAVAK. Mossad (Israeli intelligence) also acted in an advisory capacity. SAVAK, which was under the direct control of the shah, was developed into a brutal organization for repression and torture.

Meanwhile, Justice Douglas, the friend of Mossadegh, was distressed by the many changes he saw in Iran. In 1950 he had taken a pack trip into the back country of Iran, climbed into the mountains, and met the leaders of several local tribes. In 1955 he sent a respectful letter to the shah concerning the persecution of the Baha'i religious sect. He pointed out that the Baha'i problem was very much in the American press and that it could affect the "great prestige" of Iran if it continued. There is no record of the shah's answer. He continued arresting and imprisoning Baha'is.

In January 1957, Douglas heard from his friends, the Ghashgais, a confederation of nomadic tribes with branches all over Iran, that the shah was arresting and torturing their people. They were a prominent ethnic group in Iran and they had resisted the shah's attempt to bring them under the direct control of his government. Douglas, who now felt there was no way to get a message to the shah, wrote to the American ambassador, Selden Chapin, telling him about the persecution of this tribal group with a strong democratic tradition who are "true friends" of the West. He urged the ambassador to do what he could to let the shah know that the Gashgais were willing to pledge their support for the shah and promise not to interfere in the government if they could be left alone to govern themselves.   In all of his correspondence with the Eisenhower administration he continued to point out that if this persecution and torture were allowed to continue, revolution and civil war would result and no one would gain from this but the Communists. He made the same point in March 1957, when he wrote to Thomas E. Dewey that someone needed to go to Iran and "talk turkey" to the shah. In June of that same year he sent a long letter to Secretary of State Christian Herter, advising him that if the administration wanted to stop communism in Iran and build a secure government it should try to do something about the actions of the shah who was persecuting, jailing, and exiling anti-Communists, many of whom had saved the lives of Americans. The shah was attacking the very people who were needed to form a democratic government, which might serve as a source of support to a just monarch.[2]

The shah was often described as a "progressive" monarch by American officials. Certainly he favored the westernization of Iran and he did much to develop the oil resources as well as new financial, educational, medical, and military institutions. But after the fall of Mossadegh, he suppressed dissent, imposed censorship on the media, and forbade any form of political opposition. The Majlis was reduced to a body for the ratification of the shah's decrees and its members were elected from those who met with his approval. While he directed the formation of two political parties, both supported the government and both were controlled by his favorites. The followers of Mossadegh in the National Front were excluded from the ballot and, when they resorted to street protests, they were arrested and tortured. The result was a precarious system in which the shah, along with his brothers and sisters and a few chosen ministers, formed the ruling elite of Iran.

The failure to encourage public participation led to political apathy, punctuated by street demonstrations and riots. The shah had no real basis of political support from the people and, perhaps equally important, he had no way of knowing the attitude of his people. When he was visited by an important dignitary from abroad, SAVAK rounded up a few "volunteers" to line the sidewalks, wave flags, and attend the official reception.

THE KENNEDY ADMINISTRATION

The administration of John F. Kennedy did not look kindly on an imperial Iran. Its reliance on the personal power of the shah made Kennedy uneasy. The situation was brought to a head by the elections of August 1960, which were marred by such obvious bribery and intimidation that the shah was criticized by the foreign press, including the newspapers of friendly governments. In 1961 another attempt was made to hold elections and some of the seats in the Majlis were filled, but in May the police fired on students demonstrating outside the Majlis. The prime minister was forced to resign and the shah dissolved the Majlis. Kennedy felt that if the shah did not institute democratic reforms, his government could not survive.

It was at this time that the religious opposition, led by the Ayatollah Ruhollah Khomeini first came to the attention of Washington. Khomeini was a central figure in the 1961 disturbances. He was opposed to all the projects of the shah: land reform (in which religious property was confiscated), removal of the veil from women, Western cinema, modern education, and the legal Code Napoleon (as opposed to Moslem law). Even at that time he had a powerful influence over the people, particularly the poor and devout.

President Kennedy saw Khomeini as a serious threat to the stability of the shah's government. The only other political force in Iran was the nationalist-democratic element, many of whom belonged to the National Front, the old Mossadegh organization. While there were several conflicting factions in this organization, many of its members were pro-Western and approved the shah's program of modernization. Like the mullahs they were suspicious of foreign influence, but Kennedy saw them as potential allies of the crown, if they could feel they had a stake in the government. Without that political power, the shah stood alone with only the brute force of his army and SAVAK to stifle dissent.

To make matters worse, the current prime minister of the shah, Sharif Emami, had close ties to the right-wing religious groups. President Kennedy used the occasion of the street riots in Tehran to pressure the shah to accept a new, more democratically inclined, prime minister. Kennedy had met Ali Amini when he was the Iranian ambassador and he was favorably impressed. However, the shah was reluctant. Amini was now the leader of the Independents in the Majlis and a popular figure, one who might prove a potential source of opposition. On May 4, 1961, when police fired on students demonstrating outside the Majlis, members of the National Front were prepared to join the crowds on May 5. The shah was reportedly so upset that he was ready to flee the country and, at Kennedy's urging, he had another conference with Amini. He finally offered Amini the post of prime minister on the evening of May 4. When Amini passed the word of his acceptance, the following morning the National Front cancelled its plans to join the demonstration.

With this crisis behind him, Kennedy called a special task force on Iran on May 19, 1961. It was recognized that support of the shah would have no value unless he agreed to accept a constitutional role based on the development of broad political support. Reliance on the personal power of the shah was considered and rejected:

The United States could, at considerable expense, keep the shah in a position of personal power for several years by affording him uncritical and unlimited support. This would involve, among other things, providing greatly increased military assistance and pinning U.S. prestige and hopes for future influence irrevocably on a doomed political entity.[3]

The goal was to gain increasing support for the new Amini government on the assumption that no regime could survive without the acquiescence of a broad segment of the urban community. "In this connection the U.S. must actively seek to widen its contacts with nationalists and encourage those who give promise of providing firm and responsible leadership against those who have developed extremist anti-western tendencies."[4]

While it is nowhere stated in the unclassified portions of the task force report, it seems clear that Kennedy and his team planned to support Ali Amini as a possible democratic alternative to the shah. They saw the future role of the shah as a constitutional monarch, reigning but not ruling. Intelligence reports at the time had already indicated that "profound political and social change in one form or another is virtually inevitable; this, we believe, is the most important estimate to stress in regard to Iran."[5]

The task force concluded that U.S. policy "would be directed toward the support of the Iranian government rather than support of the shah personally." And further, "The goals which we envisage and which we believe to be in the long-term interest of Iran and the Iranian people are wholly consistent and almost identical with those which the new prime minister has publicly declared as his program. It is recommended that our purpose be to give full encouragement and support to the government of Iran in carrying out this program."

The Task Force Report was followed by a meeting of the National Security Council on May 19, 1961. The notes for this meeting, which have recently been declassified (10-2-95), reveal that the Kennedy administration planned to make a major effort to back the new Amini government. This would include military and financial support as well as a clear indication that the US would not favor a coup against the Amini Regime. In this connection, it was understood that Amini might have to make certain anti-American pronouncements in order to gain the support of Iran's nationalists. The US would adhere to previous agreements of the Eisenhower administration regarding the proficiency of Iranian military forces, but avoid further additions to the shah's military capability. Instead the US would make plans for active military intervention in case of a Soviet attack on Iran.[6]

Many of these decisions, if implemented, might have saved the shah by knocking him down a peg, but giving him the political support he needed. Clearly Kennedy saw the danger inherent in the growing power of the Ayatollah Khomeini and discouraged the appointment of a prime minister with close ties to the religious right. If he had lived he would have reigned in the shah and avoided giving him personal access to major US weapons systems, at the same time maintaining the option of US military support in the event of an attack on Iran by the Soviet Union or other powers in the region. If he did not succeed in pressuring the shah into accepting the role of a constitutional monarch, at least he would have increased the power of the democratic nationalists—the only group in Iran which could have confronted the Ayatollah.

THE SHAH HAS A FREE HAND

After John Kennedy was assassinated the shah began his own "white revolution" in 1963. Kennedy's recommendations for financial support to Iran were never implemented. Amini resigned in 1962 after a failure of the U.S. to supply a special aid package for Iran. He was replaced with a more tractable minister. The "revolution" of the shah was a major attempt at economic and social reforms, but without the necessary political freedoms. When Khomeini called his people into the streets to oppose these reforms, there were bloody clashes with SAVAK and the armed forces. Finally Khomeini was exiled, first to Turkey and then to Iraq, where he began sending taped cassettes of his anti-shah speeches into Iran, labeled as "Oriental Music," to be played in the mosques or sold in the shops of Qom and Tehran.

As the white revolution continued, it gained increasing credibility in the West, largely because many of the changes tended to westernize Iran. In 1965, critics dropped their complaints about the lack of political freedoms. The Johnson administration classified Iran as a developed country and made plans to discontinue American aid. The shah, less dependent on Washington, was able to strengthen his ties with the Soviet Union through oil and gas agreements. The diplomatic negotiations surrounding these agreements reduced the threat of domestic unrest from the Tudeh (Communist) party.

With the rise of OPEC, the shah skillfully exploited his position as leader of a non-Arab, pro-Western country. He supplied oil to the West at the time of the Arab oil boycott. The wealth of Iran increased dramatically as did the power and influence of the shah. He was courted, not only by the United States, but by Europe and Japan as well. In the early 1970s Iran was well on its way to becoming a major power in the region and the shah sought the aid of the United States in further increasing that power.

According to Professor Reza Baraheni, the shah had always been somewhat grandiose. As a child he claimed to see angels who talked only to him. As an adult he maintained that he had been instructed by God to lead his people. He gave himself an elaborate list of titles and conducted a coronation ceremony in 1967 for which the preparation took two years. He had his courtiers watch the film of Queen Elizabeth's coronation over and over again and practice their roles carefully to make sure he had produced an exact duplication.[7] Before the Persipolis celebrations of 1971, he had 10,000 suspects arrested to make sure there were no disturbances to mar the ceremony. At that time one of Baraheni's students told him there was no room left in the prisons. Inmates were sleeping in the corridors, the rest rooms, and even the torture chambers.

But the shah was not content with the mere symbols of power. From the beginning of his reign he had an almost obsessive urge to acquire advanced American weapons. He persisted in his requests from one president to the next.[8] Some American presidents raised doubts about his needs but to others, conscious of their own short term at the helm of state, the shah seemed an enduring source of power. Forgetting that he had been created by their predecessors, they were flattered when he favored them with a royal smile.

THE NIXON ADMINISTRATION

The shah's aspirations for regional power were given major support by the Nixon Doctrine of the early 1970s—in which Nixon sought to place more responsibility for military defense on regional Middleastern and Asian powers.[9] It was further solidified in the meeting with Nixon and Kissinger in May 1972. When the British announced their plans to withdraw from the area east of Suez and the Persian Gulf, President Nixon proposed to make the shah responsible for Western interests in the region. The shah agreed on condition that the U.S. assist the Kurds in their revolt against Iraq and give him unrestricted access to the more sophisticated American weapons. Nixon accepted his conditions.[10]

Amin Saikal describes this event with documentation of the enormous increase of economic and military aid to Iran during the years that followed.[11] Henry Kissinger denies the shah was given *carte blanche* to order whatever he wanted, but his denial is, at best, ambiguous. For example, when the shah wanted to buy F-14 aircraft, both the State Department and Defense Department objected, because these aircraft contained advanced technology. In his account of the controversy Kissinger defended Nixon's behavior: "Nixon overrode the objections and added a proviso that in the future Iranian requests should not be second-guessed. To call this an 'open-ended' commitment is hyperbole."[12] The charges and countercharges on this issue have been so numerous that it is pointless to add to them. In any event, Nixon's own comments suggest that he planned to make Iran into a regional power through an extensive military build-up.[13]

In the four years that followed, the shah ordered $9 billion in arms from the United States (and these were preinflation years). The Defense and State Departments continued to object, but without significant effect. The White House directive of 1972 was interpreted as a direct order to sell the shah whatever military weapons he wanted, except nuclear arms.[14]

The effect of this largess on the shah is widely debated. As might be expected, those responsible for the decision tend to characterize it as a continuation of support for a friend of the United States. "It is not obvious," says Kissinger, "that self-assurance in an ally is a bad thing."[15] Others felt that it induced not self-assurance but overconfidence bordering on megalomania. George Ball, a former undersecretary of state, says the Nixon administration's blank check on weapons procurement was "like giving the keys to the world's largest liquor store to a confirmed alcoholic."[16] Fereydoun Hoveyda, who was prime minister at the time of the Nixon visit, believed it went beyond a mere increase in military power.   Nixon, he says, encouraged the shah's authoritarianism by urging him to ignore the complaints of American liberals and by his open envy of the monarch's ability to silence student dissent.[17] The shah was told he had cancer just three weeks after the Nixon visit. All at once he was given enormous power, but told that he had a limited period in which to develop and use it. This could have provided a stimulus to the frantic rush to create an empire, a frenzy that characterized his behavior in the 1970s.

Following the oil price increase the Americans saw weapons sales as a means of getting back some of the money that was spent on oil. The Grumman Corporation was already deeply involved in bribing Iranian officials to get a contract to produce the F-14 aircraft for the Iranian Air Force. The F-14 was designed for the Navy and was not as safe or reliable as the F-15. But the F-15 was sold by McDonnell Douglas and Grumman had better connections with Iranian officials. Thus the Iranian Air Force bought an aircraft that was not as safe or suitable for their purposes. There is evidence that in 1974 the US Department of Defense deliberately increased the price of the F-14 fighter aircraft to Iran in order to recoup some of the money spent on oil.[18]

The aid received by the shah from Washington involved a requirement for U.S. technical advisors and instructors to help the Iranians operate and repair the more sophisticated weapons. This massive increase in U.S. personnel may have been a necessary consequence of the Nixon Doctrine, but it made the American presence more visible at a time when anti-Americanism was growing in Iran.

THE REVOLT AGAINST THE SHAH BEGINS

George Ball reports that during the middle 1970s, on one of his many visits to Iran, his Iranian friends told him that the shah was becoming increasingly repressive.[19] Iranian students in the United States attempted to contact the press and publicize the instances of torture and arrest without trial in the shah's regime. When they felt they were not being heard, they began demonstrations on

university campuses and in front of the White House. The shah's response was
to send SAVAK abroad to dispose of these protestors. Iranian students began
wearing masks when they joined a rally, so their faces could not be
photographed. Amnesty International, in its report for 1975-76, indicated that
"there has been an identifiable increase in the repression of opposition within
Iran and an extension of the activities of SAVAK . . . to countries in which
Iranians are living abroad. . . .   The torture of political prisoners during
interrogation appears to be routine practice."[20]

On September 8, 1976, Reza Baraheni was invited to testify in Washington
before a congressional committee. He told the committee that an average of
1,500 people are arrested every month and that on June 5, 1963, 6,000 people
were killed by the "American-trained" counterinsurgency forces and SAVAK.[21]
On August 1, 1976, the Senate Committee on Foreign Relations issued a report
"strongly critical of the level of U.S. weapons sales to Iran." It warned that this
increasing entanglement in Iranian affairs could end up dragging the United
States into a military conflict in the region.[22]

The group that profited most by the modernization program of the shah was
the Iranian business and industrial elite, perhaps 15 percent of the population.
These people, while they had little direct influence at court, were able to live a
luxurious Western lifestyle. In a more open society they might have become a
nucleus for political support. But in the mid-1970s, inflation became a serious
problem in Iran, in the face of a general slowdown of economic activity. The
poor were increasingly restless as the cost of their basic staples began to rise
beyond reach. The shah, instead of modifying his expensive military program,
sought foreign loans and called on the people for sacrifice.

In 1972, Justice Douglas wrote his last known memo on Iran. We do not
know for whom it was intended. As it is not a personal note, he may have
intended it for publication in a newspaper or magazine. He begins,

It is authoritatively reported to me through my Iranian friends that there are at least
20,000 dissidents in jail in Iran. These people have protested various actions of their
government either while abroad or at home and have been apprehended. Many of them,
although I do not have the exact number, have been tried and executed. The trials are
uniformly before military courts, not civilian courts. The executions take place
immediately, without any appeal, and they are done secretly. Even the closest relative of
the condemned man is not allowed to see his remains nor is the family ever apprised as
to the place of burial or other disposal of the body.[23]

He continues with an account of the routine torture in the prisons of Iran and
concludes with a call for all those who prize liberty to let their voices be heard.

NOTES

1. R. W. Cottam, *Nationalism in Iran* (Pittsburgh: University of Pittsburgh Press, 1964), pp. 226-27.

2. W. O. Douglas, *The Douglas Letters: Selections from the Private Papers of Justice William O. Douglas,* edited by Melvin I. Urofsky (Bethesda: Adler and Adler, 1987), pp. 283-287.

3. "A Review of Problems in Iran and Recommendations for the National Security Council," May 15, 1961, p. 1 of Recommendations section. Unpublished document, John F. Kennedy Library, partially declassified August 9, 1982.

4. Ibid.

5. Ibid., section on Basic Facts, p. 1.

6. Record of Actions by the National Security Council at its Four Hundred and Eighty-Fourth Meeting held on May 19, 1961. (Approved by the President on May 24, 1961). NSC Action nos. 2426-2428. Unpublished document, John F. Kennedy Library, declassified October 2, 1995.

7. R. Baraheni, *Crowned Cannibals: Writings on the Repression in Iran* (New York: Vintage, 1977), pp. 98-100.

8. G. Sick, *All Fall Down: America's Tragic Encounter with Iran* (New York: Random House, 1985), pp. 8-9.

9. H. Kissinger, *The White House Years* (Boston: Little Brown and Company, 1979). The doctrine arose from some informal comments Nixon made on Guam, which Kissinger describes as follows, pp. 224-25.
These comments from widely separated parts of an informal briefing were a sensation, dominating his [Nixon's] conversations everywhere he went in Asia. Surprised at first by their impact, Nixon soon elevated them to a doctrine bearing his name. . . .
--The United States will keep all its treaty commitments.
--We shall provide a shield if a nuclear power threatens the freedom of a nation allied with us, or of a nation whose survival we consider vital to our security and the security of the region as a whole.
--In cases involving other types of aggression we shall furnish military and economic assistance when requested and as appropriate. But we shall look to the nation directly threatened to assume the primary responsibility of providing the manpower for its defense.

10. G. Ball, *The Past Has Another Pattern* (New York: Norton, 1982).

11. A. Saikal, *The Rise and Fall of the Shah* (Princeton, N.J. Princeton University Press, 1980), pp. 205-206, 11.

12. Kissinger, *The White House Years,* p. 1264.

13. R. Nixon, "U.S. Policy for the 1970s: A New Strategy for Peace." Monday, February 23, 1970, *Weekly Compilation of Presidential Documents* (Washington: U.S. Government Printing Office, 1970).

14. Sick, *All Fall Down,* p.16.

15. Kissinger, *The White House Years,* p. 1263.

16. Ball, *The Past,* p. 455.

17. F. Hoveyda, *The Fall of the Shah* (New York: Wyndham, 1979), pp. 76-77.

18. B. Rafailzadeh, *The Economics of Bribery in Less Developed Countries with Special Application to Iran,* Doctoral Dissertation in Economics, University of Michigan, 1984, pp. 182-198.
"Subsequent to the oil price increase, the U.S. Government sought to maximize recovery of the increase by maximizing the recoupment of the R&D of the F-14 from Iran. The Secretary of Defense's sentiment then was that "we are going to recover as much of the R&D and we are going to make Iran pay through the nose for the F-14s, just as they are making us pay through the nose for oil." Therefore, in calculations of the per unit R&D, the Department of Defense arbitrarily decreased the denominator . . . from 430 . . . to 100. That caused an approximate increase of $2.5 million in the per unit price of the F-14 or an approximate increase of $200 million in the total purchase price of 80 F-14s."

19. Ball, *The Past,* p. 456.

20. *Human Rights Practices in Countries Receiving U.S. Security Assistance*, report submitted to the Committee on International Relations, House of Representatives, by the Department of State (Washington: U.S. Government Printing Office, April 25, 1977).

21. *The Status of Human Rights in Selected Countries and the U.S. Response*, prepared by the Foreign Affairs and National Defense Division, Congressional Research Service, Library of Congress (Washington: US Government Printing Office, July 25, 1977), p.20.

22. Ibid., p. 22.

23. Douglas, *Letters,* pp. 287-88.

4

JIMMY CARTER AND THE FALL
OF THE SHAH

When President Jimmy Carter assumed office in 1977, the shah was faced with a new and completely unexpected challenge. He was already having cash-flow problems and he was stretching his resources and his people to the limit. But the Carter phenomenon was something he could not ignore.

President Carter represented his administration as one that would take a fresh approach to foreign and domestic policy. From the beginning he portrayed himself as an outsider, one who would look at things in an unconventional way. He would reverse the policy of blind anti-communism and American support for repressive dictatorships. He planned to reform government behavior with a strong ethics package. He believed passionately in both peace and human rights and was convinced that active promotion of human rights at home and abroad was in our long range interest.

He saw clearly some of our past mistakes and one of his first acts was to pardon those who left the U.S. for Canada to avoid the draft during the Vietnam conflict. But there was an element in his public speeches that suggested the old theme of power and virtue in a somewhat different context. Carter offered his personal virtue as the assurance that no one need fear power in his hands.[1]

Despite his administrative experience as Governor of Georgia, he seemed unaware of the ambiguities inherent in policy decisions. He promised he would never lie or mislead anyone and he was puzzled at the very suggestion that he might be making a promise he could not keep.[2] His belief in the universal nature of goodness and the relevance of American values to the world as a whole was a continuation of a general theme of American presidents.

The new man, then, was not really new, in the sense that he brought a radical change from policies of the past. The change he promised was really a return to past virtues and ideals from which he believed the previous administration had strayed. He said as much in his inaugural address: "I have no new dream to set forth today, but rather urge a fresh faith in the old dream."[3]

A keystone of President Carter's policy was his commitment to human rights and his decision to make his human rights policy a central feature of his administration. It is one thing if a president applies human rights to his domestic policy, which he can control. But Jimmy Carter seemed unwilling to face the possibility that he could not apply it to foreign policy as well.[4] It is painful to see a good man go astray because of his zeal for goodness. But that is what happened to Jimmy Carter.

Perhaps the real problem with Carter's human rights policy is that it became a "policy." A concern for human rights is a fine thing in an individual, but once it becomes policy, it is no longer a pious wish, but an order. It is passed down through the various levels of the State Department and subject to a variety of interpretations. It cannot remain an expression of good will. It must be implemented, that is, enforced. Human rights policy directives are written by undersecretaries and other minor officials. People are disciplined because they fail to look into the human rights aspects of some minor regulation. Our friends abroad cannot always be sure they are complying with our policy. Our enemies, on the other hand, do not care.

The worst thing about such a policy, once it becomes official, is that it encourages hypocrisy. Congress or the administration is asked to certify that such-and-such a nation is living up to the human rights directives of the administration or that they are making progress in the direction of improved human rights. In such circumstances it may be better to have been a tyrant because one has so much room for improvement. Any leader can show an effort to comply with this new policy, simply by proposing some minor changes in the laws of his country. If someone objects that he is not going far enough, he can always point out that one cannot change overnight. A too rapid change in an authoritarian regime might encourage lawlessness and revolution. If the changes are never enforced, at least he has made the "effort to comply."

PRESIDENT CARTER WORRIES THE SHAH

The shah of Iran was one of the first to become worried about the implications of President Carter's human rights policy. He had never met Jimmy Carter and had had no opportunity for a private chat to sound him out about how much Carter knew about Iran. Even if he knew nothing, there was no guarantee that his ignorance would continue. Former prisoners were reporting on the shah's torture chambers to Amnesty International. The International Commission of Jurists had dissected his legal system and reported on it at length. The International Red Cross was demanding to have a look at his prisons and talk to his prisoners. Carter would have to be blind and deaf not to find him out. In any event, what could the shah do to make Iran pass inspection? He was dying of cancer and rushing to build a powerful state (as he understood power) to hand down to his son. Steadily, step by step, his policy had grown more repressive, more authoritarian.

A major blow against his credibility was struck by Reza Baraheni, a writer and professor of English who was imprisoned and tortured by SAVAK in 1973 for 102 days. Amnesty International and PEN, a writer's organization, aroused public opinion by a letter campaign to the shah and public officials in his government. The widespread publicity given to this campaign embarrassed the shah's administration enough to secure Baraheni's release and exile to the United States. There, he wrote *The Crowned Cannibals*, published in 1977, at the beginning of the Carter administration. It was a detailed account of the administration of the shah and a chilling description of the various methods of torture used upon himself and others in SAVAK's prisons.

Who, now, would believe the shah if he announced a new human rights policy? Not his people, who had experienced his heavy hand since 1953. Certainly not SAVAK, which would carry on as usual, arresting and torturing, on the assumption that his new "policy" was another bit of subterfuge. His only hope was to fake it.

Some time in March 1977, the shah began to contact his critics. To the Commission of Jurists he let it be known that he needed a bit of advice on how to improve the human rights situation in Iran. The Red Cross was invited to send teams of investigators into his prisons. He assured them that even the "interrogation centers" would not be off limits.

William J. Butler, representing the jurists, flew to Iran in May to give the shah some specifics. He proposed that trials be taken out of the hands of SAVAK and transferred to a miliary court. The shah rejected that suggestion without further discussion. He was sure he could make SAVAK do the right thing. Dr. Butler followed with a number of other suggestions. The shah listened carefully. He assured Dr. Butler he could make substantial changes that he would submit to the Majlis (Iranian Parliament).[5]

Neither party mentioned that torture was already outlawed in Iran. After all, it does take time to make real changes in human rights. The shah was not the only person in Iran to hear about the new Carter policy on human rights. Many intellectuals and business leaders were encouraged to believe that there would be major changes in American foreign policy. Various groups came out of hiding. Medhi Bazargan organized a committee for the defense of human rights and liberties. Karim Sanjabi revived the old National Front. Pamphlets and underground news sheets circulated about the new American policy and what might be done to take advantage of it. Writers called for freedom of speech and the abolition of censorship. In August, when the Ayatollah Khomeini called his people into the streets of Teheran again, many intellectuals and business leaders joined the religious rebels for reasons of their own. Thus, without a word of criticism of the shah, Jimmy Carter, simply by announcing his human rights policy, had stirred up a storm of activity in the government and in the people of Iran.

President Carter approved the shah's request for AWACs aircraft (a form of aerial radar surveillance) over the strong objections of Congress. In the public debate over this program both Congress and the State Department raised the issue of the abuse of human rights in Iran. The Carter administration was clearly embarrassed when the press questioned the sincerity of Jimmy Carter's commitment to human rights. David Dimbleby of the BBC put it this way:

Mr. Dimbleby: I think people may be a bit puzzled now about quite where this is leading and wonder also why you have concentrated on Russia and human rights there, where ·you are not actually able to do very much, and haven't apparently done anything, for instance, in Iran, a country which you have very close ties with and where you could presumably influence what, in fact, went on.

The President: . . . Our policy is very clear. It doesn't relate just to the Soviet Union. I've always made it clear that it doesn't. . . . It is an undeviating commitment that I intend to maintain until the last day that I'm in office.

Mr. Dimbleby: But has anything been done, for instance, about human rights in Iran since you came to office?

The President: We feel that it has. But that's something for the Iranian government to announce and decide.

Mr. Dimbleby: But privately you are putting pressure on them.

The President: Both privately and publicly. I think there are few leaders in the world who don't realize . . .

Mr. Dimbleby:. . . May not other countries say . . . America doesn't mean it?

The President:. . . My own best approach has been to treat these countries' violations in a negotiating way so that I can talk to a president or to the leader of a country and say this is a very serious problem between us, we don't want to put public pressure on you which would make it embarrassing for you to release political prisoners, for instance.

Mr. Dimbleby: But you did with Russia, very public.[6]

There was more than diplomacy behind the president's reluctance to criticize the shah. Human rights was, for Jimmy Carter, not merely a policy that was in America's long-range interest. It was a matter of good and evil. He found it difficult to acknowledge that the United States would support a tyranny for any reason. On the other hand, Iran was important to us, not only for the oil, but for our strategic military interests in the region. There was another reason Mr. Carter needed the shah. He had a desire to play a personal role in securing a peace treaty in the Middle East and he wanted to brief the shah on his plans and ask for his support during the planned visit of the monarch to the United States in the fall of 1977. For all these reasons he could not attack the human rights policies of the shah in the same way he had those of the Soviet Union.

However, he had made an "undeviating commitment" to human rights and he had said he would never lie to the American people. Did he remember how we had put the shah on his throne? Did he know of the CIA role in training SAVAK, the sudden arrests without a warrant, the torture chambers? Jimmy Carter was a master of detail. He was not the kind of president who got his information from briefings. Those who briefed him generally discovered that he knew more than they did about the subject. Nor did he skim lightly over the surface of a problem, leaving the details to others. He studied carefully the history and government of every nation with which he might have diplomatic relations. I think we have to assume that he knew everything. There was only one way out. He had to convince himself that the shah was, indeed, making rapid progress toward democracy. It was this step of self deception that was crucial to the policy that followed.

THE SHAH SEDUCES THE PRESIDENT

Iranian students were determined not to let the president remain unaware of what was happening in Iran. When the shah visited Washington in November 1977, they organized a protest group, determined to march on the White House. The shah was expecting trouble and sent his own supporters. In addition to his Iranian troops that were being trained in the U.S., Armenian and Assyrian civic organizations recruited members to be flown to Washington, each participant receiving a hundred-dollar bill.[7] By the time of the shah's arrival in Washington on November 15 he had mustered some 1,500 supporters, but the anti-shah demonstrators numbered 4,000.   As they surged toward the welcoming ceremony, mounted police and tear gas were required to hold them back. Mr. Carter later reported that the cries of demonstrators could be heard in the distance and his eyes were filled with tears from the irritating gas.[8]

The election of Jimmy Carter had been a painful surprise to the shah. Despite his effort to contact human rights organizations in the U.S. and show them how hard he was trying, he wondered if he could convince the president. He had always managed to get along better with Republican presidents and he was afraid Jimmy Carter could be another Kennedy.[9]   However, he was determined to charm the new president and impress him with the progress of Iran under his rule.

Carter, for his part, was aware of the shah's apprehension. He needed the shah and he wanted to put him at ease. He assured him that he was aware of the strategic importance of Iran and that he planned no significant change in the Nixon-Kissinger policy of weapons procurement. He found the shah a "likable fellow" who was "surprisingly modest in demeanor." The shah quoted statistics to show improvement in employment, education, housing, transportation, and health care in Iran. He was responsive to Mr. Carter's request for some recognition of the Sadat trip to Jerusalem and he gave public support to this peace mission.[10] As to human rights, he made it obvious in his conversation that he believed in suppressing dissent and he was scornful of Western leaders who did not do the same. We do not have the full details of his conversation with the president, but other accounts suggest he had an Orwellian gift for changing the meaning of words. In an interview for *Kayhan*, the shah described Iran as a democracy in the true sense of the word, where a strong police force was the guarantor of civil liberty and where women were not robbed and stabbed in the streets in the broad daylight as they were in many Western nations.[11] When the president asked him if there was anything he could do to improve human rights in Iran, he pleaded the dangers of communism. Besides, he added, the complaints about repression in his country originated among troublemakers and lawbreakers. Naturally such people would be opposed to strict laws that prevented them from molesting law- abiding citizens. It was clear to President Carter, at the end of their conversation, that the shah was immovable. He would not alter his policies.[12] But despite the shah's rigidity on human rights, he evidently charmed the president and his wife, Rosalyn.

When Mrs. Carter was asked with whom she would like to spend New Year's Eve, she replied, "Above all others I think with the shah and the Empress Farah." Despite the fact that the shah had visited Washington in November, Carter arranged to see him again in Iran that December, as part of a nine-day trip to several other nations. The visit provided another opportunity for Jimmy Carter to reaffirm his support for the shah, this time before the Iranian people. In his toast of the evening Carter said,

Iran, because of the great leadership of the Shah, is an island of stability in one of the more troubled areas of the world. This is a great tribute to you, Your Majesty, and to your leadership and to the respect and the admiration and love which your people give to you.

As I drove through the beautiful streets of Tehran today with the Shah, we saw literally thousands of Iranian citizens standing beside the street with a friendly attitude expressing their welcome to me.[13]

To some who witnessed this display of friendship it seemed that Jimmy Carter was bringing the shah an endorsement of his human rights policies in Iran. Fereydoun Hoveyda wondered how a man as well informed as the president of the United States could be so wrong. He knew that the friendly people the president passed in his limousine, had been rounded up by SAVAK and pressed into service. Tenants were ejected so that police could occupy all the apartments along the route the president would travel and the motorway leading from Mehrabad Airfield to the imperial palace had been closed to the public for two days, just to make sure there would be no trouble.[14] The president, who wanted to believe the shah, had little motivation to question what he saw.

It is an unfortunate truth that a president has no private life. If one is president of the United States, one does not simply ask one's wife where she would like to be on New Year's Eve. If Mrs. Carter had said she would like to drop in on an old friend who ran a country store in Georgia, that would have been fine. But a president has too wide a selection of friends to throw the door open like that. As they say in protest marches, "The whole world is watching." There were people in Iran who were looking for any sign, any hint as to how the president felt about his human rights policy. Was he really sincere? Did he want to encourage the people of Iran to take a real stand on human rights?

There were human rights groups forming all over Iran, particularly in Tehran. They were watching every statement, every gesture of the American president. They wondered if he had heard of them. Did he wish them well? Did he even know they were out there? From the day Jimmy Carter announced his human rights policy, and before he had actually done anything, the tests of that policy began. The Pahlavi government was also testing the policy by arresting some of these leaders.[15]

This was before the Carter trip. What must they have thought after his praise of the shah? Whether he intended it or not, President Carter was sending a message to the underground democratic groups and dissident intellectuals of Iran. He was saying that no one in a leadership role in the U.S. government saw them or heard them, much less supported them.

But there was one person who was not at all discouraged by Carter's praise for the shah. The Ayatollah Khomeini had been preaching that the shah did not belong to his people. He was an agent of the United States. He was an infidel, in league with the "Great Satan." Like the shah, the Ayatollah had nothing but contempt for the democratic political leaders. For years he had been saying that there was only one legitimate form of opposition to the shah. That was Islam, represented by the religious leaders who supported the overthrow of the shah and the abolition of all his immoral Western reforms. The Ayatollah welcomed President Carter's statement. It was another blow against those foolish pro-Western intellectuals who chattered about the United States as a bastion of democracy and a source of support for human rights.

A REVOLUTION OUT OF NOWHERE

Despite the nice things Jimmy Carter said about the shah, he noticed that, in the months after his return to the United States, things seemed to get worse in Iran. Street riots were on the increase. Pictures of a strange religious leader were carried in these marches. The incredible persistence of the protestors and the use of troops to fire on demonstrators disturbed him. By mid-1978 the revolution was national in scope and even his professional advisors and diplomats in the State Department were beginning to wonder openly if the shah could last the year. How did it all happen so fast? Where were all the experts who should have warned him of such an impending calamity?

There was, indeed, an "intelligence failure" in regard to Iran, for many reasons. For one thing, the CIA had put the shah on his throne. Of course, CIA military operations are supposed to be kept separate from the business of intelligence gathering, but both come under the same Director of Central Intelligence (DCI). Only a few days before the shah's visit to Washington the president had received a favorable intelligence report on the monarch's position of strength and some of the improvements he had made in judicial and social programs.

Actually, the problem goes beyond the gathering of intelligence. To a large extent, the CIA can only tell the administration what it is willing to hear. During the Kennedy administration there were still many contacts with dissident groups in Iran. But in the Nixon administration CIA procedure had been shaped by an attitude that the shah was the instrument of American policy. Mindful of his distrust of any American contacts with elements of the political or religious opposition, the CIA had pulled away from efforts to assess the attitude of the urban masses and the business and intellectual community toward the shah. Not everyone in the CIA was content with this approach. Caveats were raised by a number of individual analysts, and in August 1978 a senior CIA analyst complained that "we knew much more about the views [of key Iranians toward the monarch] 15 or 20 years ago."[16] But alarms of this kind were generally ignored by CIA leadership.

The problem was not simply a CIA failure, but a broad failure of U.S. policy that began at the top and extended through the entire administration. The United States, already closely identified with the shah in 1953, became ever more careful of offending him as they raised him to a regional power. Further, opposition groups in Iran had learned to identify the U.S. with the shah. They had become increasingly suspicious of any attempts to contact them, as they feared the shah's secret agents. Finally, the CIA simply backed away from making even clandestine contacts with the opposition. If they looked for a possible change in attitude from the new president, Carter's New Year's Eve visit to the shah and his public endorsement of the monarch seemed to ratify and continue previous policy.

Nevertheless, important information was available in other parts of the government hierarchy if one knew where to look. Congressional committees had already begun to investigate the deteriorating situation in Iran. In October, Professor Thomas Ricks reported to a House committee that, since the CIA coup in 1953, the American government was involved in almost every phase of the Iranian administration, that the military and CIA played an active and dominating role in all aspects of the Iranian mass media, and that the uprisings and killings of thousands of people were as much a reaction to this increased American role as to the human and civil rights violations of the Pahlavi regime. Professor Richard Cottam told the same committee that many dissident groups were looking for an indication of our real human ritghts policy and that all our actions in regard to Iran were signals as to the sincerity of our statements.

With no response from the American president, where did the democratic opposition turn? The numerous groups had always lacked unity. The division of his opponents was an important aspect of the shah's technique for maintaining power. But, as SAVAK began to disrupt the organizing efforts of the National Front and the Writers Association of Iran without significant protest from the United States, many business and professional people began to realize that a united opposition was their only hope. Khomeini was rapidly becoming the single figure, the absolute leader of the opposition. Unlike the political opposition, which was discouraged by censorship, intimidation, and beatings, the followers of the ayatollah sought martyrdom with a religious frenzy. One had only to see a group of them, spattered with blood and whipping themselves with chains as they marched in the streets of Iran, to recognize the role of suffering in the Shiite religion. While still in exile, the ayatollah could send his voice anywhere in Iran. He was already well known through his leadership of religious protests against the shah. On November 3, 1977, his son died mysteriously, and it was rumored to be the work of SAVAK. This further enhanced his stature. It was shortly after that, in January 1978, that the shah learned of the cassette tapes that the ayatollah had smuggled into Tehran, preaching the overthrow of the government as a religious duty. In his anger he ordered an anonymous article published in the local press accusing the ayatollah of homosexual tendencies and slandering his family. It was, according to Hoveyda, "the spark which would touch off the powder keg."[17]

Throughout the riots of 1978, American journalists visited Iran to report on the growing opposition to the shah. In July Max McCarthy observed that the U.S. role in the 1953 coup was still well remembered and mentioned with resentment. Nevertheless, even at that late date, there were people who admired American democratic tradition, struggling to hold a middle ground between the Communist (Tudeh) party and the religious right.[18] There were beatings and bombings in the homes of members of human rights groups. People were reluctant to sign petitions, make public statements, or even give their name to a reporter for fear they would be identified by SAVAK. Only in a massive crowd could they retain some feeling of anonymity—and the ayatollah knew how to put together the biggest crowds. Slowly the middle ground began to give way. Many sought cover in the religious right. There was even the hope of some safety from the beatings and shootings in these religious masses, for the ayatollah called on the soldiers to be loyal to Islam and to refuse to fire on religious demonstrations.

In August 1978, another major riot occurred in Esfahan. Hundreds of youths with cans of gasoline surged into the town center, burning police vehicles, banks, and cinemas. The army opened fire and more than a hundred people were killed. The shah imposed a state of siege, but the people defied his curfew. Strikes, protests, and demonstrations occurred all over the country. Religious leaders had long opposed the importation of pornographic movies from the West. On August 19, the Rex cinema in Abadan was burned, killing 377 people. The government blamed religious fanatics, but the people, ignoring the charge, continued to direct their criticism at the government.

The shah had left for his annual vacation to the Caspian Sea, but he was forced to return by the intensity of the disturbance. Fearful of the mounting criticism from the press and the unchecked demonstrations, he dismissed his prime minister and appointed Jaafar Sharif-Emami to form a new cabinet. Emami was known for his religious devotion and his strong ties with the Shiite leaders. He promised release of political prisoners, free elections and an end to government corruption. He also closed night clubs and gambling casinos, changed the calendar from imperial to Islamic, abolished the post of women's affairs, and forbade public drinking and pornography.

The democratic liberals had always been a diverse group. Some favored modernization and industrialization. They believed the shah could be led slowly to Western-style progress and finally democratic reforms. The appointment of Emami showed that the shah's reforms were so much window-dressing. All of it consisted of hospitals, schools, cinemas, and departments for this or that freedom, which could be quickly abolished. There was never any real encouragement of political opposition, no real move to share any of his power. Now, he allowed two decades of modernization to be reversed because of religious pressure. It was clear from this move who the shah was trying to appease. But at the same time he was desperately calling out for endorsement and support from all his friends, unmindful of the fact that the endorsement of some would be a proof of his treason to others.

JIMMY CARTER IS PREOCCUPIED

Jimmy Carter was quite busy. In his memoirs covering this period he tells us that he was at work on peace in the Middle East. It was constantly on his agenda and on his mind. He referred to Jerusalem as the "land of the Bible," where, years before as Governor of Georgia, he had visited "holy places" at the invitation of Prime Minister Golda Meir of Israel. Now he had a unique opportunity to play a role in bringing peace to that region. It was, for him, not only a great diplomatic effort, but a moral and religious quest as well. After President Sadat's dramatic flight to Jerusalem, Carter prayed publicly for peace at the First Baptist Church in Washington. He was deeply involved in the interchange between Prime Minister Begin and Sadat.

On September 5, 1978, he welcomed Sadat and Begin to Camp David, where a joint statement was issued the following day asking people of all faiths to pray for peace and justice. He was so completely preoccupied with his momentous task that he asked Vice-President Mondale to take charge of things in Washington. In his own comments of that period it is clear that he felt like a man going into battle, facing one of the great political risks of his career.[19] He was indeed facing one of the great political risks of his career, but it was not where he thought it was. On Sunday, September 10, the sixth day of negotiations, he was having difficulty sleeping and was struggling to work out an American proposal that would break the deadlock between Sadat and Begin. At some time during that day Ardeshir Zahedi, the shah's ambassador to Washington, called Zbigniew Brzezinski, Carter's national security advisor, outlining the deteriorating situation in Iran and making an urgent request for a show of support by the president. President Carter called the shah that same, day assuring him of his confidence and his willingness to provide a public statement to that effect.[20]

On September 7, after the government of Iran had banned all demonstrations, about half a million people marched on the Parliament building carrying pictures of Khomeini and calling for his return from exile. On September 8, after the declaration of martial law, students were told to leave the vicinity of Jaleh Square, where they were gathered peacefully to protest. Instead of leaving they sat down and bared their chests to the soldiers. Thousands were shot. Mobs filled the streets, stoning banks and government buildings. In the face of all this, the government announced President Carter's phone call supporting the shah. To the rioters in Iran, it was as though the devil himself had stepped forward to claim the shah as one of his own.

Even a month later President Carter still did not know, and apparently no one would or could tell him, how bad things really were in Iran. In a news conference on October 10 he was still insisting that the shah was in trouble because people were opposed to his moves to establish democracy and his progressive attitude toward social problems.[21] Several people were alarmed by the president's apparent ignorance of conditions in Iran. A State Department official who had just returned from Iran in October listened to Carter's news conference. He had himself witnessed the revolution that was sweeping the country and wondered why no one had explained the situation to the president. He complained to Haynes Johnson, a journalist on good terms with the Carter administration, that he could not get through to President Carter, but he urged his information on Johnson in the hope that articles in the Washington press would force the government to face reality.[22]

In a question-and-answer session on November 13 with PBS newsman Bill Moyers, the president again spoke of American interest in a strong and stable Iran, but he would not admit that this was in conflict with his human rights policy.

Mr. Moyers: [There are several] contemporary and very live issues. One is Iran. What are the options facing you there?

The President: . . . having a strong and independent Iran in that area is a very stabilizing factor. The shah has been primarily criticized within Iran because he has tried to democratize the country and because he's instituted social reforms in a very rapid fashion.

Mr. Moyers: But he was also criticized, Mr. President, for running a police state—political prisoners—

The President: That's exactly right. I think the Shah has had that criticism, sometimes perhaps justified—I don't know the details of it. But I think there is no doubt that Iran has made great social progress and has moved toward a freer expression of people. . .[23]

Indeed, there was a great deal of free expression going on in Iran at that time, but riots and street demonstrations calling for "Death to the Shah" were not exactly what the president had in mind. Despite his growing doubts, he was getting favorable reports on the shah's strength from the CIA. His White House advisor on national security, Zbigniew Brzezinski, favored American support for a more aggressive policy in which the shah would use maximum military force to crack down on all dissident groups. Brzezinski's primary contact in Iran was Adreshir Zahedi, son of the general the shah had used in the 1953 military coup and currently the Iranian ambassador to Washington. A former son-in-law of the shah, Zahedi was close to the royal family and his own position depended on keeping the shah in power.[24] Zahedi still had close ties with Henry Kissinger and met with him during the mounting crisis. Despite the avowed human rights policy of the Carter administration, the old guard, both in Washington and Iran, was still influential.

A LAST DITCH EFFORT

In November, Secretary of the Treasury Michael Blumenthal met with the shah and was alarmed by his distraction, depression, and indecisiveness. The shah seemed bewildered by the growing power of the revolution and the open calls for his death by his people. He had become the victim of his own propaganda and he could not understand why his people "suddenly" turned against him.[25] Later, still unable to believe that he had fooled himself (through the efforts of SAVAK) about the love of the people for him, he concluded that this strange transformation was really a CIA plot. Like his people, he was utterly convinced that nothing happens in Iran without the approval of the CIA.[26]

Blumenthal suggested to Carter that he needed an independent assessment of the Iranian situation by an outside source, someone who was not already deeply involved in the current administration and had no stake in current policy. He recommended George Ball, a former undersecretary of state, for the job, and Carter agreed. Ball, a man of much experience on the Washington scene, proved to be a salty and outspoken observer. It was clear that there was a major force organizing the opposition to the shah and orchestrating the demonstrations. Some people were still saying it must be the Communists. To Ball it was apparent that the shah no longer had the credibility to form a new government. The regime of the shah, he said in his report to the president, was on the verge of collapse and the U.S., in its reliance on the Nixon Doctrine, was responsible for the situation. The U.S. had encouraged the shah's grandiose schemes to the point that we were completely dependent upon him. Even at this late date Ball recommended a reversal of our policy. He called for the convening of a "Council of Notables" in Iran, which would have the mandate to form a new government that no one could dismiss. Chosen from a broad spectrum of Iranian life, this council would include leading members of all influential groups in Iran except the Communists (Tudeh Party). The shah could retain his position of commander in chief and his title, but the council would make the administrative decisions. It was Ball's hope that this policy change could give support to the pro-Western democratic elements in Iran. At that point no one knew to what extent the democratic leaders had already decided to make their peace with the ayatollah.

Meanwhile, Jimmy Carter was making a public demonstration of his refusal to admit that there was anything seriously wrong with the shah's stand on human rights. At a White House breakfast with journalists, he remarked that the shah was trying to bring about democratic reform and, yes, there had been some human rights violations in Iran, "But I hasten to add that we have those kinds of violations in our own country as well."[27] Did the president really mean there was no substantial difference between human rights policies in Iran and the U.S.? The alternative was to say that he was supporting the shah for strategic reasons—that we needed Iranian oil, regardless of the shah's human rights policy. Apparently that just sounded too immoral for him to stomach.

On December 9, alerted to George Ball's preliminary appraisal on Iran and the general uncertainty in Washington regarding the growing revolutionary movement, the president expressed some doubt about the ability of the shah to survive. It was a casual remark. Nevertheless it made headlines. The State Department issued a hasty "clarification," but the Iranians regarded this as a direct signal of nonsupport for the shah. On December 12, Carter again tried to erase this impression:

I think the predictions of doom and disaster that came from some sources have certainly not been realized at all. The shah has our support and he also has our confidence. . . . The difficult situation there has been exacerbated by uncontrolled statements made from foreign nations that encourage bloodbaths and violence. This is something that really is deplorable and, I would hope, would cease after the holy season passes.

I think its good to point out that the Iranian people for 2,500 years, perhaps as long as almost any nation on earth, have had the ability for stable self-government. There have been changes in government, yes, sometimes violence, but they have a history of ability to govern themselves.[28]

There is a paraphrase of Rudyard Kipling's famous poem, *If*, which goes something like this, "If you can keep your head when all about you are losing theirs—maybe you don't understand the situation." There was no doubt the president was keeping his head, but he was virtually alone in his assumed attitude of calm control.

When George Ball finally delivered his report on December 14, he found the old guard arrayed against him. Zbigniew Brzezinski, who wanted massive military support for the shah, had already spearheaded the opposition to a "Council of Notables" in a meeting of the Special Coordinating Committee on December 13. He was supported by Ambassador Sullivan's report from Iran. After two full years of support for the shah, President Carter had many reservations about telling his old friend that he had to step down. The fact that the Ball report did not have the unanimous support of the Special Coordinating Committee and that Brzezinski strongly recommended against the proposal helped confirm Carter's decision not to accept the Ball proposal. Ball understood how things were going. Not one to wait around trying to push a lost cause, he left Washington that evening.

Jimmy Carter continued his support for the shah. Loyalty to a friend may be commendable in a private citizen, but the president is responsible for maintaining the image of his office. He should not commit political hara-kiri on the steps of the White House for the sake of personal friendship. At this point there was almost nothing left to save in Iran. After a year of turmoil and three months of street demonstrations and strikes, many businesses and banks were closed, the flight of capital was a major problem, and the economy had slowed to a halt. The shah had lost all thought of lawful procedure. He had turned loose his soldiers on the people, insisting that they give orders that the shah be respected and to shoot anyone who disobeyed. Soldiers were stopping motorists and forcing them to place a picture of the shah on their windshields, shooting them if they refused. When a car approached bearing a picture of Khomeini, the windshield was smashed. The tradition of martyrdom was bringing everyone into the streets regardless of the shootings. Prominent figures in Iran were calling for the shah's abdication.

COULD THE SHAH HAVE BEEN SAVED?

The shah left Iran in January of the following year, little more than a month after Jimmy Carter's December 12 speech of full faith and confidence. Throughout the Carter administration there was conflict between the State Department and Zbigniew Brzezinski, the president's chief advisor on national security matters. Brzezinski wanted to urge the shah to "get tough." In his own account of these years, Brzezinski complains about the push toward democratization sponsored by the State Department:

This is not to say that Iran was lost by the State Department, for the record does show that the Shah had enough encouragement from Carter and me to have taken—had he wanted to and had he had the will to do so—the tougher line. But he might have been pressed harder to do what he did not do consistently and effectively—to assert his power and afterward to initiate the needed reforms."[29]

When the shah used promises of reform as a method to bring out the rebels so they could be arrested, he lost the trust of the people. When he put together the kind of state police apparatus represented by SAVAK, he created a monster he could not dismantle without turning it against himself. "Needed reforms" were not possible in such a regime.

By the time the Carter administration took office, the opposition to the shah had been building for years. It was already beyond the point when "getting tough" could save the shah. Even dedicated soldiers reach a point when they lose their stomach for killing, particularly with the tradition of martyrdom that characterized Iran. The shah had no base of political support. He had crushed the democratic opposition and these were the only people who could have worked with him. Discouraged by the shah's absolutism and the failure of the Carter administration to offer them open support, the democratic opposition had joined the religious demonstrators in the streets in the mistaken belief that they could overthrow the shah and sort things out later. George Ball's suggestions were good ones, but they probably came too late.

Toward the end of 1979, Jeane Kirkpatrick, one of the leading theoreticians of the Reagan political team and later President Reagan's UN Ambassador, published an article in *Commentary*, in which she criticized Jimmy Carter's human rights policy. She said he had failed to look after the real interests of the United States and that he had collaborated in the replacement of "moderate" autocrats who were friendly to American interests—in both Nicaragua and Iran.[30]

By no stretch of the imagination could the shah and Somoza be called "moderate." They were both ruthless dictators who used state-sponsored murder and torture to keep their people in line. Previous American administrations, in their support of these dictators, had stirred up the feelings of their people against "American imperialism." They had created a growing reservoir of hatred toward the United States. Support for the regimes of the shah and Somoza was clearly contrary to the American interest. Keeping them in power would have involved an increasingly costly commitment of American military force. And this increasing commitment of force against the people of Iran and Nicaragua would have further increased the hatred of the people.

President Carter assumed office quite late in the careers of both the shah and Somoza, but he could have allied himself with the democratic elements in Iran and in Nicaragua. He had promised an end to blind anti-communism, but he failed to fulfill the expectations he generated. Fortunately, the U.S. State Department had been working on the situation in Iran for a number of years. If anyone could be accused of "undermining" the shah, Somoza and, later, Marcos in the Philippines, it would be the State Department. The support of American administrations for all three dictators had allied us, in the eyes of many people in these countries, with torture and repression. The State Department has people with specialized knowledge of the major nations in the world. They can provide some consistency in our policy, despite the whims of a new president. Unfortunately, since the creation of the National Security Council, the State Department has less influence on foreign policy than it had prior to 1947.

No matter what Jimmy Carter's faults may have been, it would be difficult to accuse him of collaborating in the replacement of the shah. He supported the shah until the last moment, beyond all indications that the monarch was a lost cause. His policy represents perhaps the best example of the American struggle with the twin motives of power and virtue. Carter believed it was in the interest of the United States to support existing American power in the Middle East. Being the kind of person he was, he could not do it unless he could believe he was also supporting human rights. Therefore, he struggled desperately with the facts, twisting reality to suit his need for personal virtue. Despite the numerous confrontations with reporters, he continued to maintain that the shah was trying to bring democracy to Iran. That was the cause of his troubles. Jimmy Carter did what he did, regardless of criticism, but it would have been much easier on him if he had *not* invested his own sense of personal goodness in the shah and his supposed democratic policies. He needed to acknowledge, to himself if to no one else, his real reasons for supporting the shah. This would have made it possible for him to let go when there was nothing left to save.

THE ELUSIVE PROBLEM OF AMERICAN INTEREST

U.S. policy toward Iran during this period highlights the problem of American interest. Our first goal was to make ourselves useful to a primitive nation that needed financial and military assistance. At the time of our early missions we were a large and economically powerful nation, but not a major world power. It was felt that it would be in our long range interest to inspire the respect and gratitude of Iran and its people. But following World War II, both our status and our sense of responsibility changed. We felt we had to defend the "free" world against communism and the Soviet Union appeared to be our primary opponent. Not only the military might but the ideology of communism threatened our leaders. It appeared to the Eisenhower administration (and to John Foster Dulles, the architect of our policy in Iran in 1953) that it was in the American interest to replace Mossadegh with the more malleable shah. Dulles overlooked the fact that the regime of the shah had a very narrow power base, and that the shah had usurped a fledgling democracy which, erratic and unpredictable as it was, had the support of the Iranian people. Perhaps his fear that Iran might "go Communist" was a central factor in Dulles's decision to engineer the overthrow of Mossadegh. Despite the fact that the shah was a frightened young man, lacking in self- confidence, Dulles felt he could surround his new ruler with CIA advisors and American military support to keep him in power, like the monarchs of old, who ruled despite the opinion of their people. He forgot that he was living in the twentieth century, when the few remaining monarchs had wisely relinquished direct rule in order to retain a semblance of their status. They had placed democratically elected legislatures between themselves and the people, thus broadening their power base.

President Kennedy was aware that the shah stood alone, dependent on military force to protect him from the growing anger of his people. He felt the shah could not remain in power because of his top-heavy administration. The only other political force in Iran was the nationalist-democratic element, many of whom belonged to the National Front, the old Mossadegh organization. While he was concerned by the many conflicting elements in this group, Kennedy was also aware that many of its members were pro-Western and favored the shah's program of modernization. They were ambivalent about the role of the United

States; they despised the CIA and SAVAK, but were sympathetic to American democracy. Kennedy hoped to pressure the shah into forming a constitutional government with a broad power base among the Iranian people. Unfortunately his plans were cut short by the bullets of an assassin.

A leader who doubts himself and who fears the anger of his people needs more and more weapons to defend himself from a political uprising. The shah continued to ask for more weapons from the United States. As one administration after another capitulated to his demands, he sought greater and more powerful tools of destruction. He was no longer content to dominate Iran; he wanted to be the head of a regional power. Megalomania is only another symptom of low self esteem. Powerful weapons made him feel powerful. Toward the end of his administration he went on regular buying binges and the Nixon administration proved itself eager to feed his hunger.

By the time of the Carter administration there was no longer a possibility of a rapprochement between the shah and the nationalist-democratic movement. The arrest and torture of members of the political opposition had become endemic. Iranian students in the United States, their faces covered by masks to avoid detection by SAVAK (which also had its representatives in the U.S.) were marching and protesting, telling the world about SAVAK's enemas of boiling water and electricity applied to the genitals. If the shah had offered amnesty to this student group, his word would not be trusted. It was assumed that any show of conciliation was merely an attempt by the shah to bring them out in the open so they could be identified. The shah had already tried this tactic with some success. It is difficult to say what Carter could have done at this point. Perhaps the suggestions of George Ball might have worked if he had been called in at the beginning of the Carter administration. But Carter would have had to take a strong stand against the absolute monarchy of the shah and insist on the installation of a democratic parliament with a powerful foreign minister. He would have had to condemn SAVAK in the strongest terms and insist upon disbanding it. Only if this were done would the democratic forces have had a chance against the growing power of the fundamentalist Moslem movement of the Ayatollah Khomeini. As it was the ayatollah was so strong at the point Carter came to office, and so uncompromising, that Carter probably would have been held responsible for the fall of the shah no matter what he did. It occurred on his watch.

NOTES

1. B. Glad, *Jimmy Carter in Search of the Great White House* (New York: Norton, 1980), p. 354.

2. Ibid., p.355.

3. J. Carter, Inaugural address, January 20, 1977. *Public Papers of the Presidents of the United States*, Vol. I, 1977 (Washington: U.S. Government Printing Office, 1977), p. 12.

4. J. Carter, Interview with the President and Mrs. Carter. Question and answer session with Barbara Walters of ABC. December 14, 1978. *Public Papers of the Presidents of the United States*, Vol. II, 1978, (Washington: U.S. Government Printing Office, 1978), p. 2256.

5. *Human Rights in Iran*, Hearing Before the Subcommittee on International Organizations of the Committee of International Relations, House of Representatives, October 26, 1977, (Washington: U.S. Government Printing Office, 1977).

6. J. Carter, European Broadcast Journalists Question and Answer Session, May 2, 1977. *Presidential Papers*, Vol.I, 1977, (Washington: U.S. Government Printing Office, 1977), p. 1725.

7. M. M. J. Fischer, *Iran: From Religious Dispute to Revolution*, (Cambridge: Harvard University Press, 1980), p. 193.

8. J. Carter, *Keeping Faith*, (New York: Bantam, 1982), p. 380.

9. G. Sick, *All Fall Down: America's Tragic Encounter with Iran*, (New York: Random House, 1985), p. 22.

10. Carter, *Keeping Faith*, pp. 436-37.

11. F. Hoveyda, *The Fall of the Shah* (New York: Wyndham, 1979), pp. 26-27

12. Carter, *Keeping Faith*, pp. 436-37.

13. J. Carter, Toasts of the President and Shah, December 31, 1977, *Presidential Papers*, Vol. II, (Washington: U.S. Government Printing Office, 1977), pp. 2220-2222.

14. Hoveyda, *The Fall of the Shah*, pp. 15-16.

15. *Human Rights in Iran*, hearing, pp. 8-16.

16. *Iran: Evaluation of U.S. Intelligence Performance Prior to November, 1978*, Staff Report, Subcommittee on Evaluation, Permanent Select Committee on Intelligence, House of Representatives, January, 1979, (Washington: U.S. Govt Printing Office, 1979), p. 3.

17. Hoveyda, *The Fall of the Shah*, p. 23.

18. M. McCarthy, "Iran's Rising Opposition." *Washington Post,* July 9, 1978, p.1. See also *Country Reports on Human Rights Practices*, Report submitted to the Committee on International Relations, U.S. Senate, by the Department of State, February 3, 1978, (Washington: U.S. Govt. Printing Office, 1979).

19. Carter, *Keeping Faith,* pp. 273, 312-325.

20. Hoveyda, *The Fall of the Shah,* p.53.

21. The President's News Conference of October 10, 1978, *Presidential Papers,* Vol. II, 1978, p. 2210.

22. H. Johnson, *In the Absence of Power: Governing America,* (New York: Viking, 1980), pp. 272-73.

23. Interview with the President, Question and Answer Session with Bill Moyers of PBS, November 13, 1978, *Presidential Papers,* Vol. II, 1978, pp. 2108-2109.

24. Ball, *The Past Has Another Pattern,* (New York: Norton, 1982, p. 458.

25. H. Jordan, *Crisis: The Last Years of the Carter Presidency*, (New York: Norton, 1982), p. 94. The shah was later to tell Hamilton Jordan of this period, that it seemed one month the people crowded into the streets to cheer him and two months later they were screaming for his death. He could not understand what brought about the change.

26. Sick, *All Fall Down,* pp. 96-97

27. Interview with the President, Remarks and a Question and Answer Session at Breakfast with Members of the White House Correspondents Association, December 7, 1978, *Public Papers of the Presidents of the United States*, 1978, Vol II, p. 2172.

28. The President's News Conference of December 12, 1978, *Presidential Papers,* Vol. II, 1978, p. 2226.

29. Z. Brzezinski, *Power and Principle,* (New York: Fairer, Straps and Garrets, 1983), p. 356.

30. J. Kirkpatrick, "Dictatorships and Double Standards." *Commentary,* vol. 68, no. 5, November, 1979, pp. 34-45.

5

NICARAGUA: THE RISE OF SOMOZA

There are many parallels between United States policy in Iran and Nicaragua. There was the same support for a dictatorial regime that had declared itself "pro-American," the same buildup of US military support for the dictator who was stealing from his people and lining his own pockets, the belated recognition of the terrible vulnerability of our puppet and the disappointment and anger when the new government seemed to turn against us. It seems we are always surprised and hurt to find that others do not appreciate us, which is, of course, a sure indication that we do not recognize our own aggression.

After half a century of American-sponsored repression in Nicaragua, President Ronald Reagan, speaking before a joint session of Congress on April 27, 1982, remarked that, despite our generosity and good faith, the government of Nicaragua had treated us as an enemy.[1] There were, indeed, a few short periods of U.S. generosity and good faith both before and after the Somoza regime in Nicaragua. But the outbursts of good will were preceded by a long period of intervention and domination, the history of which is essential to an understanding of the attitude of Nicaraguans toward American intervention.

The initial attitude of the United States toward all of Latin America was one of support for independence. Following Napoleon's 1810 invasion of Spain, many Hispanic American colonies rebelled and established themselves as independent republics. The United States, having recently arisen from colonial status, sought to protect the independence of these new republics against the repressive power of the Holy Alliance in Europe—an alliance that had already put down revolutions in Naples and Spain. In his message to Congress on December 2, 1823 (which later became known as the Monroe Doctrine) President Monroe stated that we had not and would not interfere with the existing colonies of any European power, but we would vigorously support the right of those states that had declared their independence, and would oppose the efforts of any European power to oppress them.[2]

The Latin American states, far from perceiving this doctrine as a declaration of U.S. hegemony, were favorably impressed by the president's statement and asked for our aid in their defense in the years that followed. At that time we were a young republic ourselves. We were not really capable of opposing the European powers in Latin America and we could not always supply the aid requested by our friends.

Nicaragua attracted U.S. interest because it offered the prospect of a canal linking the two oceans. After the discovery of gold in California in 1852, Cornelius Vanderbilt founded the Accessory Transit Company, transporting passengers from the East across Nicaragua to the Pacific Ocean. Nicaragua was not a peaceful country at the time. Each of the two major political parties, Liberal and Conservative, had its own army. Both parties were ruled by oligarchies, political leaders who exploited family alliances to develop their power. Elections were a mere sham and the parties gained power by military force. Two rival cities, Leon, the Liberal capital, and Granada, the Conservative stronghold, struggled for control of the countryside. When the Liberal commander, Francisco Castellan, suffered a military defeat, he sought the help of William Walker, a soldier of fortune from Tennessee. Walker raised a force of sixty-six men, received an offer of financial support from Cornelius Vanderbilt, and invaded Nicaragua in support of the Liberals.

Each participant in the Walker invasion had his own private goal. Castellan sought a military victory for his party. Cornelius Vanderbilt wanted the country pacified for smooth transportation, and Walker had a plan to turn all of Central America into a new slave territory. Meanwhile, the U.S. and British governments sent in their own men to influence the course of the conflict, working mostly undercover. Walker soon dropped his pretext of support for the Liberal party and had himself declared president of Nicaragua on June 10, 1858. His government was immediately recognized by the United States. English was declared the official language and slavery was introduced. But now the other Central American states became concerned by Walker's ambition for conquest. They formed an alliance with the British to oppose him. In 1861 Walker was captured by a British naval captain, turned over to the Honduran government, and shot on September 12.

THE POLICEMAN OF THE HEMISPHERE

Despite the fact that Walker and Vanderbilt were both private citizens and Walker came to Nicaragua at the request of a local political leader, the alacrity with which the U.S. recognized his government and the support he received from U.S. ships in the region gave a distinct North American flavor to his invasion. His government is still remembered today as the first U.S. occupation of Nicaragua.[3]

The years that followed Walker's brief rule were marked by hostility to U.S. influence. In 1893, the Liberal General Jose Santos Zelaya came to power.

Zelaya was the first to see the Monroe Doctrine as an instrument of American imperialism. He openly invited the intervention of European powers and Japan through concessions to their governments. He intervened in the affairs of other Central American republics and sought to mold them into a single nation. While many of his ambitions and his dictatorial methods were similar to those of Walker, he was a man of Hispanic origin and a native of the region. It is not surprising, therefore, that his memory is more closely associated with Bismarckism than foreign imperialism. The pressure by nations outside the Central American region had strengthened the sense of Hispanic unity and a greater tolerance for internal as opposed to external intervention.

The Big Stick policy of President Theodore Roosevelt served to intensify the opposition to outsiders, and Roosevelt's interpretation of the Monroe Doctrine strengthened the impression that it was an instrument of American hegemony. In 1904 Roosevelt stated, in his annual message to Congress,

Chronic wrongdoing or an impotence which results in a general loosening of the ties of civilized society may, in America as elsewhere, ultimately require intervention by some civilized nation, and in the Western Hemisphere the adherence of the United States to the Monroe Doctrine may force the United States, however reluctantly, in flagrant cases of such wrongdoing or impotence, to the exercise of an international police power.[4]

Thus, the Monroe Doctrine, which was originally a statement of mutual respect and an offer to support independence, if requested, was reinterpreted by Roosevelt as a responsibility of the more "civilized" United States toward the more "primitive" Latin American nations. There was also a suggestion in Roosevelt's statement that the Monroe Doctrine, through its long period of acceptance, had become a kind of international law to which the United States would be forced to adhere, "however reluctantly." One is reminded of the speech of President Nixon in which he declared that the United States did not seek power; it was thrust upon us.

In 1912, at the request of the Conservative Adolpho Diaz, President Taft sent a force of 2,700 Marines to Nicaragua to put down revolution and to make sure the country paid its international debts. The finances of Nicaragua were placed under the control of the Seligman Company and the banking firm of Brown Brothers. The bankers were backed up by the Marines. There was bitter congressional criticism of the president's action. Some warned that we would become bogged down in a foreign war from which we could not disentangle ourselves. It was, in many respects, our first Vietnam.

While the Marines were able to control Managua, the capital, revolution continued in the countryside and additional U.S. troops were required to put down the rebellion. A withdrawal of U.S. forces in 1925 proved premature. In the conflict that followed, the Mexican government began arming Juan Sacaso, the Liberal leader who had fled the country. Fearing "Mexican bolshevism," President Coolidge sent in the Marines again to support the U.S. favorite, Adolpho Diaz. Once again the president was faced with formidable opposition from Congress. Diaz was seen as a Wall Street lackey, who might pull us deeper in the mess in Nicaragua. In February 1927, the Coolidge policy came under fire from the Senate, which grilled the chief of the Latin American Division of the State Department, Stokley W. Morgan, in a secret session.[5] Coolidge had taken the position that the U.S. was neutral, but under intensive cross examination Morgan was forced to admit the U.S. supported Diaz.

It was a crucial point in American policy. A National Citizen's Committee for Relations with Latin America was already in formation, including among its members several senators, educators, and journalists. The group, headed by John F. Moors of Boston, was vigorously opposed to intervention anywhere in Latin America and regarded the Coolidge policy as "a violation of every sound American tradition."[6]

Coolidge used the standard U.S. pretext for intervention, calling on Diaz to tell him whether he could protect the lives of U.S. citizens in Nicaragua. Diaz informed him he could not. The Senate continued to oppose the Coolidge policy and many leading public figures also objected. Finally, on April 26, 1927, Coolidge turned on his critics, accusing them of a lack of patriotism. In a major policy statement, he defined the U.S. role as that of a policeman for the hemisphere. With the critical American press in mind, he chose the twentieth anniversary dinner of the United Press Association for his speech.

"We are not making war on Nicaragua," he assured the gathering, "any more than a policeman on the street is making war on passers-by." Speaking of our "moral responsibility toward governments this side of the Panama Canal," he affirmed our right to "discourage revolutions and encourage peaceful elections." While others had pursued a course of military aggrandizement, this was not in the spirit of the American people. Nicaragua, he said, was once more peaceful and orderly under the protection of our forces. Then he turned to the press, scolding them for being injurious to our trade. They constantly misrepresented our policy and made foreign nations suspicious of us. We needed more trust in the world, not suspicion. "Whenever any section of our press turns on America and American institutions," it will be destined to defeat and failure. "No American can profit by selling his own country for foreign favor. . . . An American press, which has all the privileges which it enjoys under our institutions . . . ought to be first of all thoroughly American."[7] In its limitation of our moral responsibility to republics "this side of the Panama Canal," it was a statement that was to be compared frequently with the Monroe Doctrine, although in many respects it was the antithesis of that document. Instead of supporting independence and calling for non-intervention, it was a statement of our right to intervene in Central America as a policeman.

The *New York Times* was mildly positive on the speech, but the European press was openly critical and there were protests by several opposition groups outside the U.S. The National Citizen's Committee for Relations with Latin America took the position that imperialism, such as that proposed by Coolidge, would only alienate the Latin American states, and that a firm policy of nonintervention was in our long range interest. Senator Wheeler, in a Cleveland speech, said Coolidge was waging his own private war in Nicaragua in defiance of the U.S. constitution, and that he had reduced Nicaragua from a sovereign state to a Wall Street protectorate.

Coolidge continued his efforts for a forced peace, using not only American military power, but American dollars to bring about a new government and a reorganized Nicaraguan military force under U.S. control. The Liberal General Moncada received a handsome stipend from the United States as did several of his top officers. Many accepted influential positions in the new government. In the famous "peace of Tipitapa," soldiers of both the Liberal and Conservative forces turned over their rifles at $10 each (a considerable sum in Nicaragua), the national army was dissolved, and a new force, the National Guard, was organized and trained by U.S. Marine officers. While it appeared to be a successful pacification, this intervention finally gave rise to the Sandanista movement.

THE FIRST SANDINISTA

The Liberal General, Augusto Sandino, turned down the American offer of a sinecure. On July 1, 1927, he issued a manifesto denouncing the agreement with the United States and called for an ongoing struggle against U.S. occupation. He fled to the hills with 400 of his followers, saying he would not stop fighting until the last U.S. Marine left Nicaragua. While U.S. officials referred to him as a "Nicaraguan bandit," he gained increasing international support in Central America, in Europe, and from the antiimperialist elements within the United States. Carlton Beals, a U.S. reporter, visited Sandino several times and did much to enhance his image within the United States.

Sandino's methods resembled the broad, indiscriminate anti-Americanism that was to characterize later terrorist groups. He would strike suddenly, frequently killing many civilians, both Nicaraguan and U.S. citizens. Several of his victims were tortured and mutilated. His chief targets were U.S. businesses and his major pronouncements were in opposition to US exploitation of Nicaragua. While he had considerable popular support, he had little money for food, weapons, and medicine. Sandino was not the first revolutionary leader to discover that one cannot oppose U.S. intervention without support from somewhere. In 1927 the Soviet Union was the only world power with an interest in opposing the United States by giving support to Communist movements anywhere in the world. It appears that Sandino was not an ideological Communist until he brought his army into the mountains. His Communist connection was, at first, merely opportunistic. As he began to address Communist rallies, his support within the United States declined.

In 1932, in a U.S. supervised election, Sacasa was elected president of Nicaragua. The United States made plans to turn over the National Guard to Nicaraguan officers and Sacasa appointed Anastasio Somoza Garcia, a Liberal general, as *jefe director* (commander) of the Guard. Somoza was educated in the United States and cultivated U.S. approval, having acted as a translator for Secretary of State Henry Stimson. His wife was the niece of Sacasa. The oligarchic structure of Central America, plus U.S. support, were crucial factors in his advancement.

Sandino had pledged that he would cease fighting when the last U.S. Marine left Nicaragua. President Hoover made a commitment to end the occupation, and Franklin Roosevelt, in his inaugural address on March 4, 1933, declared his Good Neighbor Policy in world affairs. It was only a sentence at the time but, as a result of Latin American response and his own growing awareness of the importance of Pan-American relations, it came to represent a policy of nonintervention and respect for Latin American independence. This evidently brought Sandino out of the hills, and he arrived in Managua to a hero's welcome in 1933.

SOMOZA HAS A PLAN

Sacasa, although nominally president of Nicaragua, was unsure of his own power and, impressed by the welcome given to Sandino, sought an alliance with him against Somoza and his National Guard. Somoza saw Sandino's popularity and his international recognition as a serious threat to his own power and determined to assassinate him. As Sandino had long been a declared enemy of the U.S. occupation, Somoza assumed that U.S. officials would be delighted by his plan. But when he approached U.S. Ambassador Arthur Bliss Lane with a proposal that he might "lock up" Sandino, his offer was flatly rejected. After some argument he finally gave his word of honor that he would do nothing without consulting Lane. However, he later assured his lieutenants he had U.S. support for the assassination.[8]

On February 21, 1934, National Guard troops, acting on the orders of Somoza, abducted Sandino and his chief aides as they were leaving a farewell dinner at the National Palace. Sandino and several of his lieutenants were executed in a nearby field. But the Sandanista movement was not dead. Sandino had many survivors in his lieutenants and in his men who remained loyal to his memory. Just two months after his assassination (April 14, 1934) Colonel Ferreti, a young Sandanista, published charges in the Costa Rican press that the killing of Sandino was prearranged by Lane and Moncada. On June 26, Lane denounced the rumor in a State Department press release.[9] Lane's actions at that time, his letters and his efforts to release the only witness to the events, support his contention that he denied approval to Somoza. After the death of his only potential ally, Sacasa surrounded his own headquarters with the Presidential Guard, a rival but smaller military force. Ambassador Lane was concerned by this development. He distrusted Somoza because of his duplicity in the Sandino incident and he feared that if the general assumed power he would establish a military dictatorship. He felt that the National Guard should be reorganized in such a way that it would be under the direct control of the president and that the U.S. should sponsor such a proposal.

But the situation in Washington had changed. Cordell Hull, the new secretary of state, was cool to his proposal. The ambassador tried another approach. Knowing the constitution of Nicaragua made Somoza ineligible for the presidency, because of his relationship through marriage to the president and his position as head of the National Guard, Lane pushed for a strong official statement that the U.S. would support the constitution of Nicaragua and would deny recognition to a revolutionary government. He warned the State Department that the U.S. role in organizing the National Guard was known throughout Latin America and the Mexican charge d'affairs in Managua was already stressing that responsibility in his public speeches. Lane insisted that if Washington failed to stop Somoza's bid for power the U.S. would take the blame for the dictatorship that followed.[10]

Again his proposal was rejected. The climate in Washington had altered so completely that even nonrecognition of a new government was considered a negative form of intervention. The State Department was leaning over backward in order to avoid the former charge of U.S. imperialism. Without acknowledging this change, which was not yet publicly announced, Secretary Hull told Lane that he could not provide the requested statement, nor could the U.S. do anything about the balance of military power in Nicaragua. While Lane supported the policy of nonintervention it seemed to him that the United States, after years of military occupation, had saddled Nicaragua with a fascist entity (the National Guard). The result was an instrument that could destroy the constitution if left to operate unchecked. Under these circumstances, nonintervention seemed to him a form of irresponsibility.[11] By leaving the Guard to guarantee and supervise "free" elections, we had left the fox to guard the hen house.

The Sacasa government made matters worse by a clumsy attempt to assassinate Somoza and by an ill-conceived plan to suppress the Guard through a military alliance with the forces of El Salvador and Honduras. In February 1936, rioting erupted in Nicaragua. Sacasa ordered Somoza to use his troops to restore order, even if he had to fire on the crowds. Somoza refused. As the disturbance mounted, Sacasa finally resigned and, after a brief interim presidency, the constitution was altered to permit Somoza to become a presidential candidate. Somoza won an overwhelming majority in the December elections, which were "supervised" by his guard.

SOMOZA COURTS U.S. APPROVAL

From the beginning of his rise to power Somoza was not well regarded by the U.S. press. He was criticized for his dictatorial methods, and his "slick" and "clever" manipulations, and he was soon under investigation by Congress for profiteering in U.S. arms sales to the National Guard. However, the Roosevelt Good Neighbor policy was based on acceptance of the government in power, and

Somoza's government was recognized in 1937. Somoza declared that Roosevelt was his hero and began a program to charm the American president. In August 1937 he announced his Nicaraguan New Deal, outlining public works projects similar to those underway in the United States. In 1939 he began making plans for a U.S. visit. At that time the United States was concerned by the rise of Hitler and the Axis powers. Roosevelt was also fearful that Spain's Fascist dictator, Franco, would exercise an undue influence on the Spanish-speaking nations of Latin America. As the date approached for Somoza's visit, Roosevelt determined to make it a show of U.S. military power that would impress the Nicaraguan dictator and other Latin American leaders, discouraging them from an alliance with Franco.

Somoza was quite willing to be impressed. He spoke excellent English. His two sons, Anastasio, Jr. and Luis, were in training at the LaSalle Military Academy on Long Island. He participated in all the events planned for him and invented a few of his own, attending a baseball game, and visiting fairs and public functions everywhere. He had courted Roosevelt's approval for a long time, but now the courtship was coming from Washington. He was given a royal reception and personally greeted by Roosevelt, and a special military parade was organized in his honor. He returned home with words of praise from the American president and several promises of financial support for his projects in Nicaragua. In 1941 he issued a statement of support for the Roosevelt-Churchill Pact and declared war on the Axis powers in 1942. This provided a basis for calling a national emergency and banning all opposition political parties. Thus, the man who had once been called a Nicaraguan fascist was welcomed into the great democratic crusade against fascism.

For a while, Somoza enjoyed a period of acceptance if not popularity in the United States. After the war he was one of the wealthiest men in Central America and rumors of his graft and corruption began to surface again. It was said in Nicaragua that he made a profit of more than $80,000 on a piece of land he exchanged with the United States and that he could not have negotiated the deal without U.S. collusion.[12] He was becoming an increasing embarrassment, and his efforts to put forth his candidacy for another term of office, despite the constitutional prohibition, aroused protest in Nicaragua and Costa Rica (where many of his opponents had fled). Congress put pressure on the Truman administration to express official opposition and the *New York Times* carried an account to the effect that the February 1947 elections were already stolen.[13] The U.S. withdrew its ambassador and Somoza, always sensitive to U.S. opinion, withdrew his candidacy and offered his hand-picked successor, Leonardo Arguello, who won easily with the backing of the National Guard. But Arguello refused to follow orders. He proposed several changes, including the reduction of the power of the National Guard and holding regular elections. He gathered around him a number of long-time democratic opponents of Somoza, such as the highly respected Arturo J. Cruz, Sr. When Somoza activated his Guard to crush the new government, Cruz was jailed for his active support of Arguello. Cruz began to play an increasingly important role in the opposition to Somoza. In 1954 he was involved in an attempted coup against Somoza and was jailed again.

AN HEREDITARY PRESIDENCY

Before his death from a heart attack, Anastasio Somoza (called Tacho by his intimates) had already begun to convert his dictatorship into a hereditary institution. Luis Somoza, his eldest son, was groomed to take his father's place, and he was designated by Congress to succeed him in the presidency.   His second son, Anastasio Somoza Debayle, (or Tachito) was commanding the National Guard at the time of his father's death. The transition was relatively smooth.

In the early 1960s, with the election of President Kennedy, many opponents of Somoza began to hope for the end of American support of the hated dictator. Arturo Cruz, Jr. (son of the highly respected democratic advisor who was jailed by Somoza) reports that the picture of Kennedy began to appear in a favored place on top of the radio in Nicaraguan homes. He was handsome and Catholic, and he seemed to indicate that he would not support Somoza. Not only in his inaugural address when he spoke of paying any price to support freedom everywhere, but in his gestures, which were watched closely by the Nicaraguan people, he seemed to be offering a signal to them that the U.S. support of the Somozas had come to an end. Kennedy's trip to Central America was featured in all the local newsreels, where he was seen to embrace all the Central American presidents, but when it came to Luis Somoza, he only shook hands. "An embrace for democrats, a handshake for dictators," became the watchword of all the anti-Somocistas.[14]

Kennedy had some brilliant plans for Latin America in his Alliance for Progress. His travels in the region had taught him there was a growing movement toward revolution that was inevitable. His goal was to channel it in a democratic direction and he sought to identify and support the more democratic leaders of that movement. However, Arthur Schlesinger Jr., who worked closely with Kennedy, points out that there were many in the military and the state department who opposed this view.   Prominent generals and admirals had allowed themselves to develop close personal ties with their Latin American counterparts and they pressed for a blind support of anti-communist regimes regardless of their principles.   Within the state department there were many experienced officials who believed we should try to keep a lid on revolution and help our 'tested friends' who voted with us in the United Nations, clear the way for lucrative contracts for American corporations and provide land for our military bases.

Kennedy felt that the so-called realism of the right would be more likely to stimulate anti-Americanism in our hemisphere. He believed that revolutionary change was inevitable and that a policy of support for social change was the only true realism for the United States.[15]

This is what he believed. But we cannot avoid placing these noble thoughts against the live action of the Bay of Pigs. Despite his avowed opposition to blind anti-communism, Kennedy was unduly influenced by the prior invasion plans of the Eisenhower administration. He was impressed by the alleged expertise of Allen Dulles, head of the CIA. Senator William Fulbright tried to warn Kennedy of the consequences of the proposed invasion of Cuba—even if successful—for his Alliance for Progress and for the image he sought to create of a president who supported revolutionary change. The warning went unheeded.

In some respects Kennedy put the disaster behind him, making changes in the Department of State, in the CIA, and in his own decision process to make sure a similar mistake would not happen again. Perhaps, if he had lived longer, his policy in Latin America would have recovered from the blow dealt it by the Bay of Pigs. But after his death the Alliance for Progress foundered in neglect, despite the efforts of his brother, Robert, to keep it alive.

It is ironic that Luis Somoza, whom Kennedy would not embrace publicly, was embraced quietly by the CIA when he provided a launch site for the Bay of Pigs invasion at Puerto Cabezas on the east coast of Nicaragua.

NEVER ENOUGH MONEY

Fidel Castro's stature increased throughout Latin America after he repelled the invaders at the Bay of Pigs. He interacted more closely with the many divergent opposition groups in Nicaragua to help organize them into a single revolutionary force, the *Frente Sandanista de Liberacion Nacional* or FSLN. By taking the name of Sandino, this organization clearly established its stand, not only against Somoza but against the intervention policy of the United States. In the year that followed, the FSLN avoided major armed conflict with the National Guard. Instead, it concentrated on gaining international support and recruiting membership from local peasants and student groups. Conspicuous Marxist-Leninist rhetoric was avoided.

Meanwhile, Luis Somoza attempted to establish the legitimacy of his government against growing criticism from liberal elements within the United States and from the Organization of American States (OAS), which now proposed to supervise the 1963 elections in Nicaragua. Luis Somoza rejected this supervision as an affront to Nicaraguan sovereignty, but he reiterated his earlier statement that he would not stand for reelection and no member of his family would be allowed to succeed him. Nevertheless, elections were controlled by fraud and intimidation by the National Guard and a hand-picked Somoza candidate, Rene Schick, was elected.

In April 1967, Luis Somoza died of a heart attack, as had his father before him. He was only forty-four. Anastasio Somoza (Tachito) advanced his own candidacy. This galvanized the major opposition parties into a march on Managua in which they called for the National Guard to revolt. The Guard fired on the marchers and over forty people were killed. Others were arrested, including Pedro Joaquin Chamorro, a former classmate of Somoza and now the prize-winning publisher of the internationally known opposition newspaper, *La Prensa.* The arrest of Chamorro aroused widespread opposition in the United States and throughout the hemisphere.

Tachito was declared the victor in the February elections, which were, as usual, "supervised" by the National Guard. He had 70 percent of the vote. In his inauguration speech in May he called on the OAS to take collective action against guerrilla warfare in the hemisphere, which he said was inspired and supported by Fidel Castro. In August the Sandanistas (FSLN) attacked small villages in the mountains north of Managua in the first major clash with the National Guard. But internal feuding between the three major factions within the FSLN prevented them from organizing an effective assault. The Guard quickly controlled the situation.

Tachito lacked the political skills of his father and brother. He began to rely increasingly on corruption, fraud, and the brutal suppression of all opposition. Despite the rapid decline of his reputation, he managed to improve his relationship with the United States through strong anti-Communist pronouncements and a vigorous support of U.S. policy in the region. His National Guard troops participated in the U.S. invasion of the Dominican Republic in 1965.

Tachito never had enough money. His greed, always excessive, was further stimulated by the visit of Howard Hughes to Nicaragua in the early 1970s. Hughes rented the top two floors of the Intercontinental Hotel, where he did business primarily through intermediaries. He was already a recluse and Tachito did not get a chance to see him, but he witnessed the sweep of Hughes power and his wealth. Tachito was rich in commodities, but Hughes was rich in American dollars and he did business with the world in joint transactions from his headquarters in Nicaragua. Somoza's blatant theft and diversion of funds, as well as the corruption he tolerated in the National Guard, impoverished many Nicaraguan citizens.

In 1972 the bishops of Nicaragua issued a joint pastoral letter critical of economic and social conditions. They boycotted the ceremony transferring Somoza's power to a ruling junta—a mere formality as he still retained full control. Living conditions were desperate for much of Nicaragua's population. The country had the third-highest rate of illiteracy in the western hemisphere. Over half the nation's children were malnourished. Gastroenteritis was a major cause of death. Nicaragua had Central America's highest rate of alcoholism and the world's highest murder rate.[16]

On December 23, 1972, the worst earthquake in the history of Nicaragua struck Managua. It destroyed 75 per cent of the housing and 90 per cent of the city's commercial facilities. The National Guard proved unable to handle the situation. Many left to care for their own families. Others looted the homes and wide open shops of the crumbling city. The city was without food, water, and electricity, and fires burned everywhere. A major international relief effort was undertaken, including aid of $25 million from the United States. Somoza had himself appointed head of the Emergency Reconstruction Committee which managed international aid and relief flowing into the country. He appropriated much of the money and channeled the rest through his privately owned companies.

After the collapse of the National Guard, U.S. troops arrived in Managua to keep order and Somoza took full advantage of their presence to have himself photographed with the Americans. Much of the food and medical supplies sent by foreign governments were stolen by the Guard and sold on the black market. Warehouses were looted and shops were built on the spot to sell the goods. Over half the population could not rebuild unless they had the funds to buy supplies on the black market.

Somoza's cement, asbestos, roofing, and demolition companies were heavily involved in reconstruction. The price of cement rose steadily for the next two years. Following the earthquake Somoza made many enemies among the bourgeoisie in Managua. These were former members of the oligarchy who had been doing fairly well in the business world until Tachito moved in to seize control of all the major construction and land contracts. His real estate firm bought up much of the land and sold it later at vastly appreciated prices. The former members of the oligarchy could not get building contracts unless they purchased their land from Somoza or bribed his company officers.   Pedro Joaquin Chamorro reported on the widespread corruption in *La Presna*.

In May, 1974 censorship was imposed on the press, to halt the growing influence of Chamorro, who had organized a democratic opposition group, UDEL. When Tachito had the constitution altered to allow him to run for president in September, the public outcry was intense, even within his own Liberal party.

On September 27, 1974, the FSLN, in a spectacular commando raid, seized several leading politicians and business leaders at the home of a prominent Somoza supporter who was entertaining the American ambassador.   The government was forced to negotiate for their release and on December 30, in a complete capitulation, fourteen political prisoners were released and a ransom of a million dollars was paid to the FSLN. As a further condition of the release of the hostages, the government was required to publish, in *La Presna,* the charges of corruption against the Guard and the Somoza regime. The government was thoroughly humiliated.

Somoza retaliated by declaring martial law, a state of siege, and imposing even more draconian censorship on the press. Mass arrests and executions followed. UDEL, the Catholic church, and labor unions continued to spread the word of government terrorism. By the end of the 1970s most of the major industries in Nicaragua were controlled by Somoza, his friends, or his returned Guard officers. The shift in political power from the oligarchy to the National Guard was now complete. Many of the former ruling families joined the UDEL. This party was actually composed of a number of opposition groups from the far left communist party (PCN) to the middle class. It began to gain increasing status in the United States due to the influence of its illustrious leader, Pedro Joaquin Chamorro. In 1976, a Jesuit priest appeared before the U.S. Congress to denounce Somoza's abuse of human rights and to accuse the U.S. of supplying troops and planes to help him crush the guerilla movement. Somoza's support in the U.S. began to erode rapidly.

NOTES

1. R. Reagan, "Let Me Set The Record Straight on Nicaragua," in P. Rosset and J. Vandermeer, *The Nicaraguan Reader*, (New York: Grove, 1983), p. 32.

2. D. Perkins "The Monroe Doctrine" in D. J. Boorstin, *An American Primer*, (Chicago: University of Chicago Press, 1966), pp.255-262.

3. H. Weber, "The Nicaraguan Background," in P. Rosset, and J. Vandermeer, *The Nicaraguan Reader*, (New York: Grove, 1983), p. 312.

4. "New World Policy Seen in Speech," *New York Times*, April 26, 1904, pp. 1, 10.

5. "Coolidge Policy Under Hot Fire of Senate Criticism," *New York Times*, March 10, 1927, p. 23.

6. "Oppose Nicaragua Policy," *New York Times*, April 1, 1927, p. 23.

7. "Full Text of President Coolidge's Speech," *New York Times*, April 26, 1927, p. 10.

8. V. Petrov, *A Study in Diplomacy*, (Chicago: Henry Regnery, 1971), p. 32.

9. U.S. State Department Press Release, January-June 1934 (June 26, p. 432).

10. Petrov, *A Study in Diplomacy*, pp. 43-51

11. Petrov, *A Study in Diplomacy*, pp. 68-69.

12. "Somoza said to net $80,000 on U.S. Deal," *New York Times*, August 26, 1946, p. 10.

13. Ibid.

14. A. J. Cruz, Jr., *Memoirs of a Counterrevolutionary*, (New York: Doubleday, 1989), p.46.

15. A. M. Schlesinger, Jr., *A Thousand Days: John F. Kennedy in the White House,* (Boston: Houghton Mifflin, 1965), pp. 197-201.

16. J. D. Rudolph, ed., *Nicaragua: A Country Study,* (Washington: U.S. Government Printing Office), 1982, p.37.

6

SOMOZA AND THE CARTER PRESIDENCY

In 1977, with the election of Jimmy Carter, Congress began a policy of withholding arms sales and aid to a country until it was "certified" as meeting certain human rights standards. Tachito Somoza felt uneasy with this new president, but aside from mouthing a few phrases about democracy and human rights in his public speeches, he showed no sign of a change in policy. In July 1977 he suffered a heart attack, as had his brother and father before him. He flew at once to the U.S. for medical treatment and, during his recovery, he interviewed several members of Congress regarding what he might have to do to get further aid. At the conclusion of his visit the U.S. made an agreement for further military aid to be supplied only if Congress could continue to approve his human rights policy. At that time Somoza's regime was in a condition similar to that of the shah. Arrest and imprisonment without warrants, torture, government censorship, police threats and intimidation to opposing political groups were common features of life in Nicaragua. It seemed that, in order to be certified in the field of human rights it was only necessary for a dictator to inquire of Congress as to what changes he might make and to offer a few minor changes in the laws, on paper, with the promise that more reforms would be forthcoming.

It was also in 1977 that Fidel Castro, who had limited himself to sheltering and training Sandanista leaders, now took a more active role. He began working with the three feuding factions of the FSLN and helped them organize into a single military force. The flow of weapons from Cuba to the Sandanista forces increased rapidly during this period.

Humberto Ortega Saavedra, leader of the strongest of the three Sandanista factions, met with a group of writers, educators, politicians, business men, and religious leaders. Calling themselves Los Doce (The Twelve), this group made plans to seek international support for an alternative government based on democratic principles. At this point Somoza's reputation had reached a new low in international circles.   In November *La Prensa* published the Los Doce manifesto. The group began to serve as a council of notables, commenting on the political situation, calling for Somoza's resignation, and offering to form a new government.   It was the first moderate group to include the FSLN as a participant.

At a very late point in the regime of the shah, George Ball had proposed that the United States support a similar council of notables for Iran. This was now our chance to seek support from the moderate democrats in Nicaragua. Time was running out on the Somoza regime and he was about to engage in an act of desperation. But of course this was not obvious to most Americans. The CIA should have understood what was happening, but, once again, they were in bed with the Somoza regime. So President Carter was left with the impression that Somoza, if not exactly a popular leader, still had widespread support in Nicaragua.

On January 10, 1978, Pedro Joaquin Chamorro, the editor of *La Prensa* and the major democratic opponent to Somoza, was assassinated. The Somoza government "investigated," but nothing conclusive was discovered. The day after the murder, 30,000 people took to the streets and on January 12, at the burial of Chamorro, more demonstrations erupted. A general strike was called and a boycott of the February elections was announced. The leaders of the strike called for Somoza to resign. When Somoza suspended the strike, the FSLN launched a series of attacks. Venezuela and Panama denounced the Somoza government. The Carter administration, still unwilling to oppose Somoza directly, took the step of suspending military assistance.

In February, Somoza made a major speech announcing that he would not run for reelection when his term expired in 1981 and he promised to relinquish his title of commander in chief of the military forces at that time. However, after years of suffering through his engineered elections and his hand-picked successors, the public showed no support for his proposal. Los Doce, which had gained in public and international influence, issued a new statement in March, setting forth the conditions for a new government and calling for the participation of the FSLN in any negotiations.

Somoza announced several improvements to comply with the Carter human rights policy, including an offer to allow an investigation in Nicaragua by the Inter-American Commission on Human Rights of the OAF (Organization of American States). President Carter sent Somoza a personal letter on June 30, encouraging him in these new steps. When the Carter response was leaked to the press, many moderate Nicaraguans, who had hoped Carter would take a strong stand against Somoza, began to give their support to the FSLN.

Carter was faced with the flaw of any human rights policy—once it becomes a formal policy. Somoza had a great advantage over his opponents. He was so far in the hole that any step looked like an "effort to comply." And once he had made that token effort, it was more difficult to side with his opposition because, after all, he had showed that he was trying to change.   To attack him because he had not gone far enough seemed unreasonable. On the other hand the people of Nicaragua had, by now, plenty of familiarity with the graft and corruption of Somoza and his National Guard. No government which retained either of these abominations was acceptable to them. For the democratic groups to make a compromise with Somoza, at this point, would simply give him more opportunity for fraud and deceit. Los Doce, UDEL, FSLN, the Nicaraguan Democratic Movement, and several small human rights groups formed a broad popular front of opposition: *Frente Amplio de Oposición* (FAO). As a result of its presence in this group, the Sandanistas were a force to be considered in any dealing with Somoza.

THE PRESIDENT HANGS ONTO HOPE

In July 1978, the FSLN fired rockets from the Hotel Intercontinental on the National Guard headquarters and in August, Eden Pastora Gomez, disguising his men as members of the National Guard, raided the national palace. Congress was in session and Pastora, a popular, charismatic leader known as Comandante Zero, took over 1,000 hostages including government officials and Somoza's cousin. The guerrillas again demanded ransom and the release of political prisoners. Officials of both Costa Rica and Panama and the archbishop were involved in the negotiations. Again the guerrillas were successful, but this time the publicity was even more impressive. Photographers and television cameras from the world press recorded the triumphant journey of the released FSLN prisoners to the local airport accompanied by the ambassadors from Venezuela and Panama and cheered by thousands of spectators. Camandante Zero became an international figure and the image of the Somoza regime was dealt a fatal blow from which it would never recover.

Following the debacle at the national palace, factionalism became evident within the National Guard. There were rumors of a coup against Somoza because he had yielded to FSLN demands. Thirty Guard officers were relieved from duty and others were arrested on conspiracy charges. In a series of attacks in September, the FSLN took control of one major city after another. The Guard recaptured some of the cities at great cost, bombing and strafing residential areas. The population, many of whom were homeless and without food, and others who were tortured by the Guard as FSLN sympathizers, began to flee to Honduras and Costa Rica.

Criticism of the Somoza regime increased in the U.S. Congress and State Department. Somoza, who had always used his anti-Communist credentials effectively to gain U.S. support, now began to accuse the Carter administration officials of being Marxist. From a military and psychological standpoint it appeared that Somoza had lost control. He had defeated the insurrection in September at the cost of a bloodbath that alienated much of the population and made refugees of the rest.

The FAO announced the formation of a provisional government in September and the OAF created a team to mediate between Somoza and the FAO. Negotiations dragged on for a time until Somoza finally agreed to a plebiscite. But Somoza wanted the National Guard officers to work closely with any new government. This was unacceptable to the FAO which felt that no one who had learned corruption, bribery, and intimidation of voters in the Guard could ever become a part of any legitimate democratic government.

In October 1978, Jimmy Carter was in a serious quandary. He wanted Somoza to leave office, but he was afraid of a takeover by the FSLN. He sent a special envoy, William Bowdler, to negotiate a diplomatic settlement. Bowdler met with Los Doce, but not the FSLN. He could see that Somoza had to go, but he was overly polite, in part because Somoza insisted on taping their conversation. As a result, Somoza retained his position.

In November the Inter-American Commission on Human Rights issued the report of its investigation, condemning the Nicaraguan government for wanton murder of civilians, torture, political repression, and other crimes. With Somoza insisting on being a part of any new government, it seemed that armed conflict was inevitable. Mr Carter, who had been praying that the negotiations would bring peace, was deeply disturbed at the prospect of further fighting and killing. He hoped desperately that he could bring the two sides together. On December 7, 1978, at a White House breakfast with reporters he remarked, "He [Somoza] has agreed to a plebiscite under certain restraints. My understanding the last few hours is that his opponents have now tentatively agreed at least to those plebiscite terms."[1]

On December 12, he was still optimistic. "In Nicaragua, I think, instead of violent and massive bloodshed, we now have the parties negotiating directly with one another for the first time in terms of a plebiscite."[2] At this point the two parties were so far apart that it seemed violence was inevitable. The stench of Somoza had to be cleared out of Nicaragua. There was no serious possibility of a compromise.

Finally, toward the end of December, after talking with both sides, U.S. members of the mediating commission told Somoza the bitter truth, that only his departure could bring peace to Nicaragua. Somoza refused, and the U.S. representatives reported back to Washington. There was no way to get him out except to withdraw all U.S. support. The U.S. military mission was withdrawn from the country and all remaining members of the U.S. National Guard were sent back to the United States. Several aid projects were cancelled.

On January 10, 1979, there was a massive demonstration in Managua on the anniversary of the assassination of Pedro Joaquin Chamorro. Violence erupted again and several hundred people were killed. To what extent Jimmy Carter influenced the proposal that followed, we do not know, but it was certainly consistent with his style to hang on desperately to any hope of peace. The U.S. delegation proposed to a meeting of the OAF that Somoza resign and a caretaker government be appointed. This government would be based on all shades of political opinion, including the old Somocistas and the National Guard, which would remain as the primary military force in the country. The new president was to be picked by the Somoza-dominated National Assembly. The FAO was outraged. They said that the National Guard had become a hated symbol of oppression, despised by most Nicaraguans. They immediately rejected the proposal as did the OAF.

We will never know if the U.S. leadership could have salvaged the situation if we had thrown our full support behind one of the moderate anti-Somoza groups working with the Sandinistas. It would have been a risky move as we would have had to tolerate the dominance of the FSLN in any new government. Even Los Doce, which was ostensibly a broadbased political opposition group, had moved further to the left since its inception and it was now largely controlled by Humberto Ortega and the Tercerista faction of the FSLN. In any event, Los Doce regarded the final U.S. proposal as evidence that the United States was negotiating in bad faith. They began a tour of Latin America in an effort to generate support for the FSLN. The Sandinistas had concluded that only another military force could oppose the National Guard and they were determined to become the new national army of Nicaragua.

In early 1979 Mr. Carter was still holding out some hope that he could make peace in Nicaragua by some compromise that would be acceptable to both sides. Meanwhile, one nation after another in Latin America was breaking diplomatic relations with Somoza's government and throwing full support to the Sandinistas. After the spectacular victory of Commandante Zero (Eden Pastora) in 1978, the international status of Somoza and his National Guard had taken a steep drop. Venezuela and Panama became FSLN supporters shortly after that incident. After the news came to Mexico that thousands of Nicaraguan citizens had followed Eden Pastora to the airport, cheering him all the way, as they watched their ambassador board the plane with Pastora and the released FSLN prisoners, relations between Mexico and Nicaragua began to decline. On May 20, 1979, Mexico recalled its ambassador and severed diplomatic relations with Nicaragua.

On June 16, 1979, the FSLN announced the formation of a provisional government headed by a unified command. It consisted of Daniel Ortega of the FSLN, Sergio Ramirez of Los Doce, Dr. Moises Hasan Morales of the FPN (the political arm of the FSLN) and two moderates, Alfonso Robelo, a wealthy industrialist, and Violetta Chamorro, widow of the publisher of *La Prensa*.

On June 17, Ecuador recalled its ambassador. The Andean Pact nations issued a declaration of full belligerent rights to the FSLN. Finally, on June 20, newsman Bill Stewart of ABC was shot by a national guard trooper in full view of the news cameras. The film of his murder, showing that he was shot while lying on the ground by a guardsman standing over him, was smuggled out of Nicaragua and shown on network television in the United States at the very time Somoza was trying to blame his death on the FSLN. Under strong public pressure, the Carter administration finally called for an end to the Somoza regime.

THE ROLE OF COSTA RICA

Somoza continued to hang onto power. Crucial to his military position was the attitude of Costa Rica. While the Costa Rican Civil Guard was not a significant military force, a vigorous effort by Costa Rica could have denied the FSLN sanctuary in the jungles along the border of the two countries. Since 1856, when Costa Rica invaded Nicaragua to put down the forces of William Walker and was forced to withdraw under fire, each nation had called on world opinion to witness border violations of its neighbor. In 1948 Nicaragua supported the efforts of former Costa Rican President Calderon Guardia to regain his position by armed invasion, and only OAF intervention prevented a fullscale war.

In 1977, claiming hot pursuit of the FSLN, the Nicaraguan air force strafed three Costa Rican gunboats inside the national territory. The incident was witnessed by a group of journalists and received wide media coverage inside Costa Rica. Before they began to gain international recognition, Los Doce was granted asylum inside Costa Rica and finally returned in July 1978, having been allowed to return by Somoza, who was seeking to improve his human rights image in the U.S.

Citizens of Costa Rica were not completely comfortable with the FSLN. Many feared a Communist Nicaragua and in September 1978 the government of Costa Rica offered to mediate between the FSLN and the Somoza government, but the offer was immediately withdrawn after another incident of hot pursuit by Nicaragua. Nevertheless, a force of 200-300 FSLN troops was denied passage from Panama to Nicaragua, as it was felt that this would be a violation of Costa Rican neutrality. On December 26, 1978, Somoza threatened to invade Costa Rica if the FSLN were not cleared out of the border area.

Meanwhile, in the fall of 1978, a series of opinion polls were conducted in Costa Rica. While opinion was divided regarding the Communist orientation of the Sandinistas, most people (87.1 per cent) felt the Sandinistas were fighting for a just cause. Even among those people who believed the Sandinistas were linked to Communists, 54.6 per cent approved Costa Rican support. Among the poorer people of the country, 97 per cent said Costa Rica should help the Sandinistas, whereas only 58.8 per cent of the wealthy people felt that way.[3] The polls may have been influenced by the decision of President Carazo of Costa Rica to call on the OAF for protection from a potential Nicaraguan invasion (by the Somoza government) and to launch an open campaign to persuade other Latin American nations to break diplomatic relations with the Somoza government.

In May 1979, despite the fact that international opinion was turning against him everywhere, Somoza called for an emergency meeting of the OAF to protest Carazo's actions. Finally, in June 1979, the FSLN was allowed to set up a government in exile in San Jose, the capital of Costa Rica. This was followed by immediate diplomatic recognition by several other governments of the region. Costa Rica dropped all pretense of efforts to clean out the FSLN troops in the border areas and offered sanctuary openly to the Sandanistas. The Nicaraguan National Guard was now spread too thin to put down uprisings and repel FSLN raids across the border at the same time.

Carter still was not ready to recognize the new provisional government for Nicaragua. Representatives of the Carter administration let it be known that the provisional government must accept more conservatives into the ruling political body. In exchange, Carter offered to call on Somoza to resign and he made postwar economic aid contingent on FSLN compliance. The FSLN, sensing that victory was at hand, refused, and Somoza fled to Miami on July 17, 1979. The government collapsed. National Guard troops fled across the border and the FSLN, as the only significant military power in Nicaragua, became the primary source of law and order in the country.

JIMMY CARTER REACHES FOR PEACE

Contrary to the charge that President Carter actively collaborated in the replacement of a moderate autocrat in Nicaragua,[4] he held on much too long to his relationship with a blatant dictatorial regime in that country. In both Iran and Nicaragua the Carter administration supported dying regimes far beyond the point where they had lost all credibility and respect in the world at large. Jimmy Carter, the presidential candidate who, in his well-run political campaign, had championed a new approach to world affairs and an end to the blind anti-communism of previous administrations, proved to be rather conservative when he assumed office. He did not try to contact democratic elements during the reign of Somoza or the shah. On the other hand, he did place limits on American intervention. He did not call in the Marines to keep a defunct dictator in power—as had several previous American presidents.

While the Marxist FSLN was clearly the most popular political force in Nicaragua, Jimmy Carter opposed its leadership from the beginning of the new government. There were, of course, many other choices available besides Somoza and the FSLN. Eden Pastora, the famous Camandante Zero, was a national hero and very dissatisfied with his position in the new government. He had been named vice-minister of defense and national chief of the People's Militia, but this proved to be a position without any real power. Alfonso Robelo and Violetta Chamorro, widow of the famous editor of La Prensa, were also discontented with their role on the five-person junta of the new government. They were all ideological moderates. In 1978, before the fall of the Somoza government, President Carter made a tentative move in support of other democratic groups within Nicaragua. He signed a "finding" authorizing the CIA to provide covert support to democratic elements in Nicaragua.[5] However, any movement to support democratic elements in Nicaragua—even as late as 1978—needed the full and open backing of the U.S. Government. At that time Carter was still striving for peace between the FAO and Somoza. It was the same mistake he made with the shah. One cannot commit fully to a new opposition democratic movement if one is still providing support—any support at all—to a hated dictator.

Despite all his doubts, and his covert assistance to opposition groups within Nicaragua, the president made a favorable impression on the Sandanista leadership. On September 24, 1979, Carter met with a group of Nicaraguan leaders on their way to New York to lead the delegation of the government of Nicaragua in the United Nations General Assembly. The delegation included Daniel Ortega, Sergio Ramirez, Alfonso Robelo, Miguel d'Escoto (the minister of foreign affairs for the new government), and Rafael Solis (ambassador designate to the UN). The exchange was a positive one and it appeared to Daniel Ortega that the long history of U.S. intervention in Nicaragua was over. He began a dialogue with President Carter. For once Carter seemed to strike the right note. Without endorsing the Sandanistas, he took the position that the U.S. would like to maintain a peaceful relationship with this new government. The delegation probably knew that he was giving support to other, more democratic groups in Nicaragua, but they were pleased to accept the formal recognition as a first step.

Later, on March 25, 1982, with the Reagan administration supporting the build-up of the contra army in Nicaragua and adjacent nations, Daniel Ortega made a speech to the United Nations in which he accused the United States of waging covert aggression on the Sandanista revolution and he warned that U.S. intervention in Nicaragua was imminent. He described a familiar pattern: training camps in Florida for former National Guardsmen of the Somoza regime, similar camps in the Republic of Honduras receiving arms from the United States, U.S. bases under construction in Honduras, U.S. reconnaissance aircraft violating Nicaraguan air space, and surveillance equipment aboard a U.S. Navy destroyer off the Nicaraguan coast.

Ortega said it was not just these many violations of neutrality that bothered him, but the inconsistency in American policy. He conceded that in the dialogue he had established with President Carter in 1979, he had hoped for an improved relationship between Nicaragua and the United States, but with the election of Ronald Reagan the situation had changed to one of open hostility and outright subversion.

NOTES

1. J. Carter "Remarks at a Question and Answer Session at breakfast with members of the White House Correspondent Association," December 7, 1978. *Public Papers of the Presidents of the United States,* vol. 2, 1978, (Washington: U.S. Govt Printing Office), p. 2165.

2. J. Carter, "President's News Conference," December 12, 1978. *Presidential Papers,* Vol. II, 1978, p. 2172.

3. T. W. Walker, *Nicaragua in Revolution,* (New York, Praeger, 1982), pp. 336-340.

4. J. Kirkpatrick, "Dictatorships and Double Standards." *Commentary,* vol. 68, no. 5, November, 1979, pp. 34-45.

5. J. Brecher, with J. Walcott, D. Martin, and B. Nissen, "A Secret War for Nicaragua," *Newsweek,* November 8, 1982, pp. 42-53.

7

RONALD REAGAN AND
THE CONTRAS

When the Sandanista government first took over Nicaragua after the fall of Somoza, there was an ecstatic feeling of hope among the people. While still in exile, the Sandanistas announced plans for freedom of speech and open elections. After victory, the new government impressed the world by abolishing the death penalty and undertaking a program to improve literacy. They had over 2,000 former Guardsmen in prison. All were tried for war crimes, about a third were set free and the rest received prison sentences of various degrees of severity.

The primary failure of the Carter administration in Nicaragua (as it was in Iran) was to wait too long to withdraw its support from a regime that was already in disgrace and was tottering on the brink of destruction. When President Carter met with the Sandinista leadership on September 24, 1979, there was a feeling on both sides that the long intervention of the United States in the affairs of Nicaragua had finally come to an end. However, just as things began to look peaceful for the Sandinistas, the Republican candidate in the United States, Ronald Reagan, was announcing he would cut U.S. aid and support the opponents of the government of Nicaragua.

The Marxist principles of the Sandinistas were nothing more than the end result of the initial decision of Sandino to drive the Americans out of Nicaragua and to overthrow Somoza. If any leader in Central America wants to oppose an American-supported regime there is nowhere he can go for weapons and financial support except to the Communists. The Sandinistas had received extensive aid from Cuba and the Soviet Union. Cuban doctors, nurses, teachers, and military officers were influential in all their civilian and military institutions. Regardless of their policies, candidate Reagan saw the very existence of a Marxist government in Nicaragua as a threat to the security of the United States.

RONALD REAGAN INTERVENES

After he assumed office in 1981, President Reagan was determined to take a completely different approach to foreign policy. He appointed Jeane Kirkpatrick as his permanent representative to the United Nations. She was the professor who had attracted his attention by her article in *Commentary* on "Dictatorships and Double Standards," in which she explained how the Carter administration had lost Iran and Nicaragua by its failure to give whole-hearted support to the shah and Somoza.

As the new president gathered his forces it soon became apparent that there was to be a major shift in U.S. policy. It began with a reshaping of our attitudes toward past events, particularly our "Vietnam syndrome," as it was described by the president and his new secretary of state, Alexander Haig.

President Carter had regarded our war in Vietnam as a major error in U.S. policy. He used it frequently in his news conferences as a reason why we should not try to intervene in other revolutionary situations such as Iran and Nicaragua. President Reagan insisted that Vietnam was a "noble war." We had not lost it. We had simply been denied a victory. On February 24, 1981, at a Medal of Honor ceremony, he remarked that American fighting men came home from Vietnam "without a victory, not because they'd been defeated, but because they'd been denied permission to win." He spoke eloquently of our compassionate army, as President Johnson had done before him. He was touched by the "incurable humanitarianism of our troops, erecting schools, giving toys to orphanages."[1] Our war crimes and our casual cruelty, such as My Lai, interrogation by torture, the burning of villages, the body count, forced relocation—all were to be erased from our memory of the Vietnam war.

With the arrival of Ronald Reagan the U.S. effort to influence events in Central America took on the outlines of a full scale war between Nicaragua and the United States. But it was more than that. It became, almost from the beginning, an effort to change reality with words. Ronald Reagan was a former movie actor and he knew how a beautiful story can paint a convincing picture of reality. On the other hand, he was faced with a group of reporters who had matured a good deal during the Watergate years. They were determined not to swallow press releases and backgrounders from the White House. The story in this chapter is, in large measure, a record of this conflict between the president and the national media for the control of the American view of reality—at least as it concerns Nicaragua.

President Reagan was moved by concern for the people of Nicaragua, who were suffering from what he called a "totalitarian Marxist regime." But forceful intervention by the United States was prohibited by the Neutrality Act, which forbade Americans to make war against a country with which the United States is at peace. So he shifted his focus to the role of interdicting the arms that he claimed Nicaragua was supplying to the guerrillas in El Salvador. No one doubted that arms were being supplied to the guerrillas in El Salvador by the government of Nicaragua. The issue became the size of the effort mounted to stop this shipment of arms. In the U.S., major budget requests were prepared to support an expansion of tactical forces, an increased role for U.S. advisors, and increased funding for the CIA.   The president knew he could not mount a major effort without changing the perception of Congress and the American people in regard to what was going on in Nicaragua. It was an enormous task, but he approached it with great enthusiasm and selfconfidence.

By February 19, 1981, a "textbook case of a Communist plot" had been developed in a White Paper presented by the Reagan administration to foreign embassies in Washington.[2] The problem presented was the insurgency in El Salvador, but the memo described the role of Nicaragua as a key link in supplying Soviet and Cuban arms to the guerrillas in El Salvador. The president could not legally intervene to topple the Nicaraguan government.   He began to set the stage to intervene on behalf of a friendly state (El Salvador) that had asked our help.   To proceed with his policy, Reagan had to build a case against both Nicaragua and Cuba (the original source of the Soviet arms).

The memo was allegedly based on documentary evidence of massive arms shipments from Nicaragua to the rebel forces in El Salvador. Secretary of State Alexander Haig sent Lawrence Eagleburger to Western Europe to explain the significance of this memo to the European powers. The documents on which the memo was based were said to have been captured from guerrilla forces in El Salvador in November and January.

This was not the first time such charges had been made, but the February offensive by the Reagan administration, in its historical scope, in the distribution of the charges, and in the summary of the supposed documentary evidence, made it clear that the administration was launching a case in international diplomatic channels and in the media, prior to a major move in Central America.

The European capitals were cool to the U.S. mission. They did not question the authenticity of the sixteen pounds of documents Eagleburger brought with him, but many of them pointed out that communism was not the only problem in Third World nations. Three days after the U.S. delegation arrived in Mexico to present the evidence against Nicaragua and Cuba, President Jose Lopez Portillo announced that Cuba was the Latin American country "most dear" to Mexico. Mexican officials indicated they felt the speech was a direct rebuff to Reagan's efforts to condemn Cuba for its role in smuggling arms to Marxist guerrillas. The documentary evidence was presented by General Vernon Walters, formerly deputy director of the CIA, but General Walters was refused an audience with President Lopez Portillo.[3]

In an article in *The Nation,* dated March 28, 1981, James Petras began to take apart the evidence in the U.S. White Paper, pointing out that it was lacking in substance.[4] In June, Robert Kaiser cast further doubts on the White Paper with an article in the *Washington Post.*[5] It was clear that the American press, which had often accepted government evidence in the past, was not buying the case for intervention in Nicaragua.

There was some concern that we might be on the thin edge of the wedge toward another Vietnam. When Walter Cronkite raised this question with the president on March 23, 1981, Reagan pointed out we were not just fighting in Nicaragua. He stressed the problem of combating hemispheric terrorism sponsored by the Communist block nations, including Russia, Cuba, the PLO, Qadhafi in Libya, and so forth. It was a regional problem, yes, but it had worldwide implications for the security of the United States. The moral standard of the Communists was "without God." It was an issue as simple as right and wrong.[6]

The Sandanistas were not unaware of the Reagan military buildup and they were shaken by what appeared to be an orchestrated campaign against the Nicaraguan government. They postponed elections, claiming that, with a hostile U.S. president organizing a military force to threaten the stability of their government and funneling money to their opponents, with the country on the verge of economic disaster, and with severe problems of illiteracy, they could not afford the further disruption of a political campaign.

GOOD CONTRAS AND BAD CONTRAS

On December 1, 1981, President Reagan signed his own "finding" authorizing CIA assistance for a contra force in Nicaragua. The group was called the Nicaraguan Democratic Force (*Fuerza Democratia Nicaragöuense)* or FDN. This title was not used in press releases by the Reagan administration, which preferred the general term "contras." The FDN was a group commanded by former members of the hated National Guard of the Somoza regime, based in Honduras near the northern border of Nicaragua. Since there was more than one group fighting the Sandanistas, it did not serve the purposes of the administration to identify themselves with any one group.

The president let it be known that the contras were people from Nicaragua, former Sandanistas, who were disappointed with the failed promises of the Sandanista regime and who were determined to fight for free elections and a democratic government.   Actually, there were members of the Sandanista government who were disappointed with the failed promises of the regime. But these were not the people who made up the contra group trained and supported by the United States.   Eden Pastora, a Sandanista and one of the heros of the fight against Somoza, left his post in the Sandanista government in mid-1981. In early 1982 he was running his own group of contras out of Costa Rica. He claimed complete independence from the Reagan administration's contras in the north. Pastora's group consisted of some of his loyal troops who fought at his side in the battles against the Somoza regime.

It was not until John Brecher's story in *Newsweek,*"A Secret War for Nicaragua," broke on November 8, 1982, that the American public began to learn something about the composition of the contras. While there had been many reports of secret operations along the Nicaragua-Honduran border the *Newsweek* story described "extensive details of a campaign that has escalated far beyond Washington's original intentions. Administration sources told *Newsweek* that there are now almost fifty CIA personnel serving in Honduras— certainly the longest manifest in Central America."[7] Evidently the administration had tried to destabilize the Sandanista government using Miskitu Indians and some anti-Sandanistas from within Nicaragua, under the direction of U.S. Ambassador (to Honduras) Negroponte. But the Indians were slow to adapt to military discipline and the other forces proved insufficient for the job. Said *Newsweek*,

When the covert policy was first developed, direct US dealings with exiled Somocistas were officially ruled out. . . . But Negroponte, under pressure from Haig and (assistant secretary of state) Enders, to produce some successes against the Sandanistas, turned to the only promising group available—the Somocistas. . . . Sources in both Washington and Honduras say the ambassador has been careful to deal with the Somocistas through intermediaries to preserve his deniability.[8]

The Reagan administration, acutely aware of the importance of image in any operation that was likely to attract the attention of the press, understood that they could not appoint a leader of the contras who was in any way connected to the hated Somocistas. They tried to cultivate Eden Pastora because of his great popularity, his reputation as Commander Zero, the hero of the revolution, and his large following within Nicaragua. When Pastora announced his own organization, ARDE (the Democratic Revolutionary Alliance) he called himself a "true Sandanista" and vowed to live simply, not like his former friends who had taken over mansions in Nicaragua and were driving their Mercedes Benzs to their government offices. With him were Arturo J. Cruz, Sr. who had resigned as ambassador to the United States, Alfredo Cezar Aguirre, who resigned from his post as president of the Central Bank and Alfonso Robelo, a former member of the five-man ruling directorate in the Sandanista government. In his criticism of the current government (the censorship of the press, antidemocratic trends, and Soviet-Cuban influence) Pastora's stand sounded similar to Reagan's. But when he was approached he said he would not work with the CIA or with any former members of the hated National Guard. In retaliation Ambassador Negroponte prevented Pastora from working and organizing a force in Honduras.

"As a result," said Brecher in the *Newsweek* article, "despite Washington's intentions, Negroponte has alienated the only group likely to attract widespread support inside Nicaragua."[9] So there it was. There were good contras and bad contras and, as usual, we were supporting the bad guys.

REPACKAGING THE CONTRAS

The *Newsweek* article had the makings of a public relations disaster. For a man who made a point of painting his enemy as evil, the article was a serious blow to the president's credibility. In his news conference he was plagued by questions about his covert efforts to topple a recognized government as well as the reputation of his chosen contras as bloody and corrupt brutes. Somehow he had to turn this thing around and make *his* contras the good guys.

The first step was an effort to "repackage" the FDN leadership. The military command was superseded by a political leadership of Nicaraguans who had taken a public position against Somoza. The new FDN leadership was unveiled at a press conference on December 7, 1982, just a month after the *Newsweek* article. Francisco Cardinal, the former FDN leader, was hustled out of town for the occasion and a new FDN leader, Nicaraguan businessman Adolfo Calero, was presented to the press.[10] While Calero had a history of opposition to Somoza, he was a former manager of the Coca Cola franchise in Managua, a man not likely to present a credible image to the peasants and working people of Nicaragua.

The CIA had worked for months to organize the press conference. They asked Edgar Chamorro, a scion of the famous family that had been influential in conservative democratic circles in Nicaragua, to handle public relations for the new leadership. Chamorro reports his role in the conference as follows.

The CIA saw me as a useful tool not only because of my respectability in Nicaragua, but also because my experience with public relations would come in very handy for the work of the *contras*. . . . Our first project in the campaign was for the new Directorate to have a press conference. I was a bit uncomfortable with this idea, because as a newly formed group, we obviously did not have much to announce. But the press conference was the first priority of our advisors; their whole purpose in appointing a new Directorate was to improve the image of the *contras*. They did not want us to *function* as a Directorate as much as they wanted us to give the *image* of a Directorate and to be visible. The background and profession of each of the members was important, but not so much for what that person could contribute as a leader as for the appearance of balance and broad support.

The American advisors trained the Directorate well for our first public appearance. . . . They asked us the questions they anticipated would be raised in the press conference and when we answered "incorrectly," or with information they did not want revealed, they instructed us to change our answers. One advisor said to me, "Let's say a reporter asks you, 'Mr. Chamorro, do you receive money from the U.S. government,' what will you say?" My initial response was to say, "Yes, we have received some money—" But I was told to say no, to say that we had received money from many concerned individuals, from people who supported our work, but who would remain anonymous because they had a right to their privacy. . . we were instructed to say that we had not met with anyone else, and it was particularly important that we deny having met with any U.S. government officials.

We rehearsed our responses to very direct and specific questions with forthright and firm answers. Indeed, at the press conference the morning of December 7, 1982, at the Hilton Convention Center in Fort Lauderdale, Florida, the reporters did ask, very directly, precisely the questions that we had been told they would ask. I, as the spokesman for the Directorate, answered just as directly with responses that were often, in fact, quite untrue.[11]

The press conference was only the first step in repackaging the contras. The CIA set up a communications office in Tegucigalpa, Honduras, directed by Edgar Chamorro, whom they provided with a budget of $35,000 a month. The money was used to pay foreign journalists to write favorable articles on the contras. Said Chamorro, "Each journalist had to be approved by the CIA before being put on our payroll. My staff and I took them out to lunch and followed their work, developing an employer-employee relationship with many of them."[12]

But Chamorro was not happy. He believed passionately that the mission of the contras should be to overthrow the Sandanista government and he resented the insistence, on the part of the CIA, that he must not speak of this goal in front of reporters as it was against the law in the United States. He felt constrained, unable to speak openly of his pride in the true mission of the contras. Instead, he had to take orders from the Americans. It was their war and he was only an employee. The contra leadership was constantly being instructed in tactics and criticized for their failure to win over the Nicaraguan people. Dewey Claridge, the CIA chief of Latin American Operations, tried to explain to them how to build up a guerrilla army in the "classic" model.

He pointed to Eden Pastora who, he said, had a better style of warfare, one closer to guerrilla war. Pastora was better at going after, and getting, the support of the people than the FDN was, and Claridge thought the FDN could imitate Pastora's "style" to gain popular support. The military people of the FDN had been trained as National Guard soldiers whose duty it was to maintain order by repressing the population. . . . Claridge seemed to think that "getting popular support" was as easy as changing the style, but not the substance of the FDN.[13]

Unable to change the public image of their contras, the CIA began to realize they needed more name recognition. Again they approached Eden Pastora and offered certain inducements to get him to unite his group with the FDN. But Pastora was unmoved. Fully aware of the attitude of the Nicaraguan people toward the old National Guard and the CIA, he would have nothing to do with the repackaged FDN. The Reagan administration was equally adamant. The FDN, it was admitted, did have a few former National Guardsmen in its ranks, but these men constituted a minority. Most of the FDN were younger men, recruited after the revolution, who had never been in the Guard. It was a mistake to brand them all Somocistas.

PASTORA WORKS ON PUBLIC RELATIONS

Pastora held a press conference in which he outlined his reasons for refusing to join the northern contras. He pointed out to reporters that the contra force in Honduras (the FDN), regardless of its composition, was commanded by officers who had gained their experience under the repressive Somoza regime. The new "recruits," half of them still in their teens, some kidnapped from peasant villages and forced into service, were trained by the veteran Somocistas in the same brutal methods and terror tactics that had characterized the old National Guard. If the people of Nicaragua were inclined to forget such things, they were quickly reminded by a contra raid in which crops were burned, village leaders abducted and tortured, women raped, and children murdered.

The leaders of Pastora's ARDE took an opposite approach, particularly in the initial stages of their campaign. Pastora avoided military action, relying instead on his mystique and his popularity with the Nicaraguan people. His agents sought to make friends with the peasants and to organize an opposition from within Nicaragua.

The Reagan administration found it difficult to deal with these two opposing contra forces. The forces in Honduras were simply too numerous and too important to be abandoned in favor of the more respectable ARDE. If Pastora would not work with them, perhaps others in his organization could be won over. Fernando (El Negro) Chamorro, who had gained fame by firing a rocket at Somoza's bunker, was induced to break away from the ARDE and join the FDN. In April, Alfonzo Robelo was contacted by the CIA, but he made a public statement reaffirming his alliance with Pastora and announcing that ARDE would soon engage in military action against the Sandanista government.

The big problem for Ronald Reagan was that Pastora was a charismatic leader and a master of public relations. He may have been a better actor as well. He traveled to Europe and charmed the Spanish and German officials. His pose as the true revolutionary went over very well when he talked at a dinner party in New York put on by *New York Magazine* for reporters. He also spoke at Columbia University, Johns Hopkins, and several organizations interested in American foreign policy. Even when he went back to the jungle, reporters sought him out. He was adept at arranging photo opportunities. Whenever he had a military victory a network television crew seemed to turn up and he obligingly restaged the action so he and his men could make the evening news.[14] He persisted in his denial that he worked for the CIA. In a sense this is probably true. Although Pastora did accept money from the CIA, he would not follow orders, particularly in regard to a union with the northern contras (the FDN). Agents sent to control him regularly complained that he was unmanageable. He contradicted them and insisted on remaining independent.

There was more than one reason Pastora would not join the contras of the north. True, he could not tolerate the presence of former National Guardsmen in a leadership role, but he was also vain and ambitious. He wanted to be the star performer in any theater. It was rumored that, after the fall of Somoza, he had hopes of becoming President of Nicaragua, but he was outmaneuvered by the Sandanista army and his forces reached Managua too late to take part in the initial seizure of power. When the Sandanistas took over the government they gave him a mansion and a position of leadership, but he refused to fill the swimming pool and left several of the rooms unfurnished. His image was a man of the people who was not interested in wealth and luxury.

THE PRESIDENT LOSES CREDIBILITY

President Reagan was finding it difficult to refuse to discuss his not-so-secret war in Nicaragua on the grounds that CIA operations were classified. Reporters badgered him at his press conferences to provide details of what was going on. There were frequent articles describing the contras as holdovers from the hated Somoza regime and citing the ARDE, headed by Eden Pastora, as the true revolutionaries. Editorials in the press openly discussed CIA activities and questioned the legality of U.S. involvement. The president was asked how he could defend such a policy.

With the defection of Fernando Chamorro to the FDN, the Reagan administration had one "true" revolutionary on board. With this in mind, and perhaps anticipating further defections, he faced reporters at a question and answer session on March 29, 1983. He was asked,

Q: Mr. President . . . You've consistently refused to discuss reports of covert U.S. aid to anti-government forces in Nicaragua. In recent days a number of our allies have indicated at the UN that they believe the United States is working to overthrow the Nicaraguan government. . . . Aren't you in danger of losing credibility in the same way the U.S. government did with its secret war in Cambodia?

The President: Well I think this is something . . . intelligence matters . . . I'm not going to discuss them now . . . Now what we're seeing in Nicaragua is the fact that it was a revolution by a coalition of groups that were all opposed to the dictatorial Somoza rule. And, as happens so often in that kind of coalition, when the revolution was over, one faction . . . simply took control and ousted the other revolutionary partners . . . And what we're seeing now are the other revolutionary actions—totally ousted from any participation in the government—now fighting back on that.[15]

The president described the antigovernment forces as though they consisted of nothing but the small band in Costa Rica led by Eden Pastora. With the exception of the recent defection of Fernando Chomorro to the FDN, Pastora's was the only group made up of former members of the Sandanista government who had been ousted (actually, resigned) from power. Reagan said nothing about the other contras, the FDN, who were receiving the lion's share of U.S. support.

As Nicaragua came under attack by the contras, there was an urgent need to increase the size of the Sandanista fighting forces. They stationed some troops in the jungle to protect the small villages. They arrested opposition political leaders and censored the press. They described the massive buildup of U.S. forces in Honduras and they warned that the U.S. was about to invade their country. Some congressmen claimed that President Reagan unified the Sandanista government and he provided them with a justification for their repressive measures. The Sandanistas complained that the pressure from the Reagan administration prevented them from reaching an agreement with business leaders because these leaders, and many elements of the press as well, were funded by the CIA. They were paid by the CIA to maintain an attitude of defiance toward any efforts by the government to reach an agreement. If they did respond to government efforts at mediation, they would lose their CIA support.

The issue of the legality of the president's actions remained. Reporters persisted in their efforts to get him to confirm or deny U.S. efforts to overthrow the government of Nicaragua and to identify the individual people in the contra group supported by the U.S. government. The president continued to insist that U.S. funds for the contras were not being used to overthrow the government of Nicaragua, but only to interdict the weapons for the guerrillas in El Salvador. However, there were American film crews and reporters roaming the jungles of northern Nicaragua, talking with participants in the conflict. A writer from Skylight Pictures bumped into "Commander Mack" (Jose Benito Bravo Centeno), who had served in Somoza's National Guard from 1956 to 1979 and worked as a bodyguard for Somoza's son. Mack assured the reporter that he was not working to solve the problems of El Salvador, but to overthrow the government of Nicaragua. With great pride he described his training in the United States in this "sacred war" against a "godless communist enemy."[16]

A *Wall Street Journal* report indicated that a CIA internal planning memo, prepared in 1982, set a goal for the fall of Managua, the Nicaraguan capital, by Christmas 1983, with the hope of dividing the country in two and establishing a contra shadow government.[17] This certainly sounds like an attempt to overthrow the government. If it failed, it was not for lack of intent but lack of ability.

In a *New York Times* article on April 1, 1983, Tom Wicker pressed the issue. Citing the Boland Amendment, which prohibited support for paramilitary forces, he pointed out that the U.S. was trying to maintain that it was attacking Nicaragua but not really attempting to overthrow the government. "That's like saying you're hitting a man with a hammer, but not trying to kill him; and its the kind of sleazy, hair-splitting, 'deniability' that debases language and credibility alike."[18] Pointing to the numerous supporters of the Somoza regime among the Reagan contras and the presence of a former Guard officer on the FDN directorate, he asked how the Reagan administration could defend the support and training of former members of the brutal and corrupt Somoza government.

On April 14, the president was asked by reporters if the U.S. was "supplying any of the dissidents along the Honduras border. "Anything we're doing in the area," he said, was simply to interdict the supply of weapons from Nicaragua to the guerrillas in El Salvador. By implication he excluded any effort to topple the Nicaraguan government. But the questions became more insistent. A reporter asked if our government was doing anything to overthrow the Nicaraguan government. "No," said Mr. Reagan, "because that would be violating the law."[19]

Congress was raising questions about the funding for the contra forces in the north (the FDN). An international group of writers charged the president with waging an inhuman war against Nicaragua. Several members of the House

Intelligence Committee threatened to cut off CIA funding for the war on the grounds that it represented an illegal effort to overthrow the government of Nicaragua. Some congressmen had toured Central America and were reporting on their findings. The committee was split along party lines, but by meeting with representatives of the Nicaraguan government in Managua, the Democrats were giving wide credence and publicity to the charge that the contras in the north were led by former officers of the old Somoza National Guard.

Nicaragua obtained a seat on the UN Security Council in January 1983 and in March Daniel Ortega, coordinator of the Nicaraguan junta accused the US of launching an undeclared war on his country. At the request of Nicaragua an international advisory group was formed to try to bring peace to the region. Consisting of representatives from Colombia, Mexico, Panama, and Venezuela, it was called the contadora group. Support for Nicaragua increased in Europe. Loans were arranged with West Germany and France. A successful literacy campaign was improving the international stature of Nicaragua.

Stung by the public accusations and the growing opposition of Congress the president called a joint session of Congress for April 27, 1983, at which he made a major address to resolve what he called a crisis. We had been generous with aid to Nicaragua, he said, but the government was treating us like an enemy. It had rejected our peace efforts and broken its promises. It had insulted and mocked the Pope, censored the bishops, and seized control of the media. "The opponents of the Sandanistas," he said, "are not diehard supporters of the previous Somoza regime. In fact, many are anti-Somoza heros and fought beside the Sandanistas to bring down the Somoza government."[20] Again, the existence of a contra force in the north (the major military force opposing Nicaragua) was ignored. One could easily get the impression that the only people fighting the Sandanistas were the "heros of the revolution" who had been ousted from power by a dictatorship.

On May 3, 1983, after the house voted to stop funding covert operations against Nicaragua, concern about the public view of the contras increased in the Reagan administration. It seemed they could get nowhere as long as Reagan's contras were perceived as a bunch of marauding butchers. There is some suggestion in his conversation with reporters on that day that he was already planning to make an end run around Congress and felt he would need public support more than ever. For the first time he admitted to reporters that there was a group of contras in the north, who were fighting the government of Nicaragua. He thought he had covered all this in his address to Congress, he said, but perhaps not. The location of the group was not specified. It consisted of "forces" that were "under what you might say is a sort of a group." It was governed by a "kind of committee" of seven leaders and "most of them" were former anti-Somoza people.

Q: Mr. President, can I follow up on something you said earlier? Did I understand you
    to say that, if you were forced to stop aid to Nicaraguan guerrillas, that you would
    try to funnel it through other countries?

The President: No, I was saying . . . the committee said we would have to go
    overt and then, in going overt, you can only give money to another government. And
    if you did that, then you would be depending on—well, maybe those other
    governments in Central America would give the money to the freedom fighters in
    Nicaragua.

Q: Can I just—all of a sudden now we're aiding freedom fighters. I thought we
    were just interdicting supplies into other countries.

The President: I just used the word, I guess "freedom fighters," because the fact that we
    know that the thing that brought these people together is the desire, as I said, for the
    same revolutionary principles that they once fought and have been betrayed in.[21]

The president seemed to be saying *our* contras were the former Sandanistas.
They were our freedom fighters. While the president spoke publicly as though
all the heros of the revolution were already part of our contra forces, he was
struggling furiously behind the scenes to bring Eden Pastora into his camp. His
position was desperate and he needed a man with Pastora's stature to brighten up
the image of his rather tarnished contras. But Pastora, the primary figure in any
unification, was adamant about not working with Somocistas. The CIA began
contacting the ARDE leadership once again, trying to pry one or more of them
loose from the organization.

THE BOMBING AT LA PENCA

After the ARDE failed to take and hold San Juan del Norte, a town in the
south of Nicaragua, the CIA made another major effort to unite the two contra
groups. Robelo and Cruz, Sr. were agreeable, but Pastora demanded that before
he would join the northern contras (FDN) they must purge their ranks of all
Somocistas.[22] This, of course, would have decimated the northern contras.

After much negotiating back and forth, the other leading members of ARDE
voted to form an alliance with the contras in the north. Pastora was furious. He
announced that he would call a news conference in which he would let the world
know about the northern contras, the efforts of the CIA to disrupt his leadership,
the destructive effect of CIA meddling in Central America and what he felt was
a U.S. partiality to former followers of the deposed dictator, Somoza.

This was a risky step, a direct refutation of the explanation of the contra war
as offered by the Reagan administration for the past year.   It was an open
attempt to upstage Ronald Reagan, which no actor can tolerate for long. Pastora
was evidently aware that his life might be threatened. He would not hold his
conference in a major city, but chose a remote location where his own men could
have complete control of security.   The reporters wishing to attend were
assembled at a San Jose hotel in the late afternoon and driven to the San Juan
River where they boarded motor launches.   They travelled two hours on a

downstream trip to the village of La Penca, just over the Nicaraguan border. There they were led up a steep muddy hill to a two-story frame house. Pastora was on the second floor at the head of a table. The reporters gathered around him and exchanged greetings as Pastora made a few preliminary statements. At this point a tremendous explosion, which seemed to come from the center of the journalists, shook the room. Screams were heard as three reporters were killed and twenty injured.[23] Eden Pastora, gravely wounded, was hauled aboard a motor launch by his men and barely escaped with his life.

The news conference was held in rebel territory in an area closely guarded by Pastora's men. It was obvious that the bomb must have been smuggled in by someone among the group of reporters at the conference. In the investigation that followed it appeared that a man using a Danish passport of Per Anker Hansen and posing as a Danish journalist had planted the bomb. The passport had been reported missing by Hansen for over a year. Pastora blamed the CIA for the attempt on his life. U.S. officials began promoting the idea that the Sandanistas were responsible. Ambassador Curtin Winsor, Jr. was quoted as saying, "There's nobody else I can think of who would have the motive. The CIA doesn't do this kind of thing."[24]

Clearly the assassination attempt had been well planned. The impostor of Hansen had traveled with Peter Torbiornason, a Swedish journalist and television producer who had been working on a documentary on Central America. They met in early May at the Hotel Gran Via in San Jose, Costa Rica. Torbiornason's assistant was Luis Fernando Prado of Bolivia, who mentioned that the supposed Danish journalist spoke little Danish and later gave an interview in flawless, unaccented Spanish. He departed on a flight for Miami the day after the bombing.[25]

Several reporters were killed and others injured in the bombing. One of the injured was Tony Avirgan, the husband of Martha Honey, also a reporter working in the area. Martha was waiting for Tony outside the emergency entrance of the San Carlos Hospital when she noticed a man who appeared unhurt sitting in a wheel chair near the entrance. The nurses told her he was Per Anker Hansen, a Danish journalist. Near dawn, when Tony arrived, wounded from the bombing, she noticed the wheel chair was empty. A few days later she read the report that identified the man carrying the passport of Hansen as the bomber. Honey and Avirgan also had a friend, Roberto Cruz, who was very badly injured in the bombing. They determined to track down the people responsible for this crime.

After an extensive investigation, involving over 150 interviews in Central America, they uncovered a terrorist group operating in Costa Rica, which had planned the Pastora assassination and other crimes. They prepared a book, *La Penca Report,* describing all the parties to the crime and demonstrating that the CIA was behind the operation. They named John Hull, a wealthy rancher in Costa Rica, as the CIA contact for the assassination attempt.

Hull sued them for libel, perhaps thinking they could not get the witnesses to prove their case. Just to make sure, one important witness, Steven Carr, was picked up two days before the trial by a U.S. embassy car. After the trial he called from a jail in Naples, Florida to apologize. But Honey and Avirgan put together a remarkable group of witnesses including John Mattes, a federal public defender in Miami, who had investigated a number of illegal contra activities, Jack Terrell, a mercenary who had fought with the contras and worked with both the northern and southern groups; and Pastora himself, whose testimony proved to be of less value than some of the other witnesses, but his presence had a certain psychological value. Terrell testified at the trial as follows:

There were two meetings in the US. The first was in Houston, Texas, and Adolfo Calero asked me to leave with Mr. Hull. On this opportunity Mr. Calero gave me the instructions that the motive for which I had to meet was that the US wanted to show a united front in Costa Rica. That the two groups which I talked about had to meet on John Hull's farm to train. He told me that Mr. Hull was the CIA connection with the FDN in Costa Rica. He told me that he was going to call Mr. Hull first and advise him that we had to meet. . . . we talked about the assassination of Eden Pastora. When it was finished it was also stated that we would meet again in Miami, Florida. . . . Adolfo Calero was angry with statements made by Pastora. He said that Pastora had said that the FDN were homicidal, Somocista sons of bitches. He stated in the presence of these people that Pastora had to go.[26]

After his testimony, Oliver North recommended in a memorandum that Terrell be formally accused. He was later indicted for violating the Neutrality Act (see note 25).

Amac Galil, a Libyan terrorist, was identified as the false journalist, and several other associates of Hull were implicated. Hull lost the case, appealed the verdict to the Costa Rican Supreme Court, and lost again.[27] In support of Hull's suit, his attorney, Alberto Baldi, pointed out that if Hull had really been guilty of the crimes alleged by Honey and Avirgan, the Republic of Costa Rica would have charged him and brought him to court. This would indeed be the next step, but it would come much later. Hull might have initiated the interest of the public prosecutor through his lawsuit. Certainly Avirgan and Honey, in their defense of the charge against them, developed much of the evidence that was later used to support the charges against Hull.

Eden Pastora was finally taken out of action, not by assassination, but by financial and political pressure, a slow process that finally eroded his support and, at last, his will to fight. A new umbrella organization was formed called the Nicaraguan Opposition Unity (UNO), including leaders from both the ARDE and FDN. But the Reagan administration had won a pyrrhic victory. Throughout the campaign against him, Pastora traveled to the United States and Europe, searching for financial support, contacting European leaders, naming the former Guard officers in the FDN, and describing the scenes of rape and murder in the peasant villages they had attacked. He buttonholed U.S. congressmen, complaining loudly of the pressure tactics used by the CIA to try to get him to unite with the FDN. When he had finished, the reputation of the contras was more bloody and their notoriety more publicized than when the campaign against Pastora began.

OUR FREEDOM FIGHTERS

The opposition of Congress to the president's policy intensified in April 1984, after it was revealed that the CIA had directed the mining of Nicaraguan ports. The incident aroused widespread international sympathy for Nicaragua. The British government protested, and the French offered the Nicaraguans help in clearing their port of mines. The House Foreign Affairs Committee approved, by a vote of 32 to 3, a resolution opposing the use of government funds for mining Nicaraguan harbors. Nicaragua announced its intention to appeal to the International Court of Justice in the Hague, and the U.S. sent a hasty declaration to that body that it would not accept its authority on Central American affairs for a two-year period. Nevertheless, the court voted 14 to 1 to reject the contention of the United States that it had no jurisdiction, and on May 10 issued preliminary orders asking the U.S. to refrain from taking any action on Nicaraguan ports. Robert Owen, a member of the American Society for International Law, said that the U.S., in rejecting World Court jurisdiction, had created the impression that we are trying to turn the rule of law into a one-way street.[28]

This was followed by the resignation of Senator Daniel Moynihan from the Senate Select Committee on Intelligence in protest of CIA involvement in the mining, a resignation that was finally withdrawn after an apology from CIA Director, Bill Casey. In a *New York Times* poll in April 1984, only one American in three supported the president's policies in Central America and nearly half feared U.S. involvement in a war in that region. In June the Senate, in a vote of 88 to 1, approved the deletion of aid to the Nicaraguan contras in a spending bill.[29]

But the president, emboldened by his success in winning over everyone in ARDE except Pastora himself, had begun to tout a new, improved image of the contras. Seizing on his former casual remark that they were "freedom fighters," he now used the name with more boldness and added that they were "the moral equivalent of our founding fathers." He meant, of course, the contras in the north, whose leadership had been dressed up by the addition of Alfonso Robelo and Arturo Cruz, Sr. As for himself, Reagan insisted, in a proclamation for Captive Nations Week, that he wanted peace, not war:

We're a peaceful people. We occupy no countries. We seek no confrontation with any nation. As I've said repeatedly, there's nothing we want more, nothing we're trying harder to achieve than to bring about a more peaceful world.[30]

The Soviets, he said, were acting against the will of the people of Afghanistan, but we were supporting the right of the people of Central America to decide their own fate. As he stated,

and today, I'm appealing to those who refuse to help the freedom fighters in Nicaragua, refuse to assist their courageous struggle for democracy, for freedom of the press, for freedom of assembly and worship in their homeland.[31]

The president, having rid himself of Eden Pastora and having absorbed much of the leadership and the manpower of ARDE, now felt he had firm grounds for calling his contras the "true" revolutionaries. Gone was the reserve and vagueness about his freedom fighters. In an interview with Forest Sawyer, he said the contras were courageously struggling for democracy in Nicaragua. Furthermore, they were revolutionaries, not counterrevolutionaries. What we were doing is supporting their "honest desire" to have the revolution that was promised them.[32]

THE ELECTIONS

The Sandinista government countered with the announcement of free elections scheduled for November 4, 1984. They proposed to allow twelve weeks for the opposition parties to wage their electoral campaigns. One might have expected that Reagan would be delighted. Was this not what the contras were fighting for? Instead, the administration announced that it doubted the Sandanista government could or would conduct free elections.

Most of the contra leaders lived in Miami, but Arturo J. Cruz, Sr. (the former ambassador) made plans to return from the U.S. to Nicaragua to explore the possibility of running for president. In July he was nominated by a coalition of union leaders and business groups. But the Reagan administration began to worry that he might give credence to the Sandanista-sponsored elections if he accepted the nomination. Cruz held back, demanding further concessions from the government, including their willingness to negotiate with the contras, before he would agree to become a candidate. Finally the government placed a deadline on all political parties to register for the coming election. When the deadline passed in August, Cruz, and the three parties that supported him, were denied legal status for the coming elections.

Cruz made a tour of Europe and Latin America to drum up support for his position, but candidates from six other opposition parties were running in the election and his stand evoked little enthusiasm in Latin America. President Betancur of Colombia, an old friend, told him he would urge Nicaragua to reopen registration, but Cruz would have to reduce his demands. This he did, putting forth four conditions to which the Sandanistas readily agreed. But he also asked that elections be postponed until January, a demand the government refused on the grounds he could have registered earlier as a candidate.[33]

The real issue behind much of this maneuvering was the legitimacy of Cruz's candidacy. Was he a real candidate or a tool of the Reagan administration, sent to Nicaragua to discredit the elections? His associate, Mario Rappaccioli, did not help matters when he told a group of reporters that Cruz had no intention of running in the November elections.[34] The situation was further complicated when a U.S. congressional delegation visited Managua and set up a meeting at the U.S. embassy with representatives of the Coordinatora group, a coalition of three right-wing parties that supported Cruz.[35]

Evidently the Cruz candidacy was not the only aspect of the election subject to U.S. influence. Marv Corrales, from the youth section of the Democratic Conservative party in Nicaragua, in a letter published in *The Nation*, maintained that the political secretary of the U.S. Embassy in Managua offered several high-ranking members of his party a bribe if they could get the Democratic Conservative party to pull out of the elections. The offer was $300,000 to the party and $50,000 to each of them. "Three of those went along with the deal, but the party treasurer did not and he quietly reported the maneuver to the candidate, Guido." The result was a demonstration at a party meeting calling for full participation in the elections.[36]

In November, Daniel Ortega, candidate of the governing Sandanista National Liberation Front (FSLN) won an overwhelming majority of the votes. The November election was clearly flawed, by limitations on the candidate's ability to campaign and by unnecessary censorship of the press, which was in no way related to the war effort. Nevertheless, the election gained the full support of Willie Brandt in Germany and other European and Latin American countries. In an OpEd article in the *New York Times*, Raymond Bonner compared the human rights record of El Salvador (the government of which was supported by the U.S.) and Nicaragua, pointing out that, while there was repression in Nicaragua, there were no death squads or murders of religious leaders, as there was in El Salvador. He raised the question of the administration's peculiar choice of friends and enemies.[37]

The *New York Times* editorial maintained the election results were a product of the rules blocking full participation, but John B. Oakes, a former senior editor for the *Times,* who returned from Central America in November, said the most fraudulent thing about the elections was the part played by the Reagan administration in pressuring opposition politicians to withdraw from the elections in order to discredit the Sandanistas.[38]

THE CIA IN TROUBLE

Throughout the long struggle in Nicaragua the Reagan administration had managed a certain deniability in regard to the terrorist acts of the contras. There was no doubt about the acts themselves, but to what extent were assassination of village leaders and the falsification of documents the result of training by the CIA? One would think the National Guard already had sufficient experience in these tactics without further explicit instructions. But in late 1984 an Associated Press release reported that the CIA had produced a manual instructing the Nicaraguan contras in the art of assassination and document fabrication, advising the contras to "neutralize" government officials by the "selective use of violence."[39]

The CIA manual covered a wide range of techniques, including helping the peasants with the harvest and medical aid, and providing food for the community. But the advocacy of blackmail, mob violence, and assassination provided the first real connection between the terrorist activities of the contras and the CIA instruction. The manual recommended assembling the population of a village to witness an execution. If a citizen attempted to leave town, he was to be shot and the people told he was an enemy. False witnesses were to be used to supply evidence against uncooperative individuals. Mob riots could be provoked and shock troops, armed with lethal weapons, could march behind the innocent and gullible participants. Professional criminals could arrange the death of fellow-rebels, who would then become martyrs to the cause.

A spokesman for the White House denied that the Reagan administration had advocated or condoned political assassination, and two inquiries were launched to discover who was responsible. After a brief investigation it was discovered that the manual was only a first draft and had never been used in the field. The final draft allegedly contained none of the objectionable material. But Edgar Chamorro, a director of the FDN, told reporters this was not true. There was only one draft, assembled by a CIA man last October with help from the FDN. It had been used in the field for over six months. Classified Defense Department documents revealed that the guerrillas had been involved in assassinations as early as 1982.[40] The investigation also revealed the bloody acts of the contras in more detail. In a *Washington Post* exclusive, Brian Barger reported that intelligence sources had corroborated accounts of contra atrocities from the rebel leaders themselves.[41]

All of this was particularly embarrassing to President Reagan. He had taken the stand that only the Communists lie, cheat, steal, and murder. Could he acknowledge that the manual prepared for his beloved contras did, indeed, advocate assassination, the manufacture of false evidence and the mass murder of innocent civilians? At a question-and-answer session for reporters on November 3, 1984, he was asked,

Q: Why are you suppressing the CIA manual findings until the election?
The President: We're not. We turned them over to the—the oversight—the commission—the oversight commission of all intelligence. And Casey's been very forthcoming in his statements about it. And I think you're going to find that it was all a great big scare, and that there was nothing in the manual that had anything to do with assassinations or anything of that kind.
Q: Well, it told them how to proceed on assassinations.
The President: No . . .
Q: But sir, it said, "neutralize," and can't that be construed as meaning assassination.

The President: I suppose you could construe it in any number of—several ways. But in the context in which it was recommended, actually, that was not the choice, the original choice of the word. The real word was "remove," meaning remove from office. If you come into a village or town, remove from office representatives of the Sandanista government. When they translated it into Spanish, they translated it "neutralize" instead of "remove." But the meaning still remains the same.

Q: Well, how could you go about doing that without violence or force?

The President: No, you just say to the fellow that's sitting there in the office, "You're not in the office anymore." (General laughter).[42]

Recalling the Nixon coverup of the Watergate affair, the *New York Times* referred to the president's response as a deliberate effort to prevent the investigation into CIA accountability. The president's contempt for the law, said the editorial, would be an impeachable offense in another time.[43] This was a full two years before the Iran-Contra scandal became known to the public.

THE PRESIDENT SURVIVES

Aware that his contras had been caught in many human rights abuses, Ronald Reagan sought to paint the Sandanista government with the same brush. In many of his speeches he accused the Sandanistas of totalitarian destruction of free speech, religious persecution, genocide against the Miskito Indians, drug running, and political murder. The Drug Enforcement Administration could not substantiate Reagan's charges of drug smuggling. As to the charge of religious persecution, the Catholic Church, the major religion in Nicaragua, as well as several protestant denominations and Jewish temples, operated in complete independence from government control. Several political parties were outspoken in their criticism of the government, and none were barred from participation in the election.

Americas Watch, a politically independent international organization that had established a reputation for accuracy in reporting human rights abuses in the Western Hemisphere, made the following complaints against the Reagan administration in their 1985 report:

The Americas Watch does not take a position on the U.S. geopolitical strategy in Central America. But where human rights are concerned we find the administration's approach to Nicaragua deceptive and harmful. . . . Such a concerted campaign to use human rights in justifying military action is without precedent in U.S.-Latin American relations, and its effect is an unprecedented debasement of the human rights cause. This debasement of human rights contradicts President Reagan's professed commitment to such rights. Far from being the 'moral center' of U.S. foreign policy toward Nicaragua, the human rights issue has been utilized in the service of a foreign policy that seeks to advance other interests. Whether or not those interests are legitimate is not the province of the Americas Watch; what is of concern to us is the attempt to proclaim a false symmetry between promoting those interests and promoting human rights. . . .

    The misuse of human rights data has become pervasive in officials' statements to the
press, in White House handouts on Nicaragua, in the annual *Country Report* on
Nicaraguan human rights prepared by the State Department, and most notably, in the
president's own remarks. . . . In Nicaragua there is no systematic practice of forced
disappearances, extrajudicial killings or torture—as has been the case with the 'friendly'
armed forces of El Salvador. While prior censorship has been imposed by emergency
legislation, debate on major social and political questions is robust, outspoken, and often
strident. The November 1984 elections, though deficient, were a democratic advance over
the past five decades of Nicaraguan history. . . . The Nicaraguan government must be
held to account for the abuses which continue to take place, like restrictions on press
freedom and due process. But unless those abuses are fairly described, the debate on
Nicaragua ceases to have meaning.[44]

    Nevertheless Ronald Reagan survived his opponents. Although they deprived
him of funds, he found money elsewhere. Through his manner, his style, his
charisma—call it what you will—he managed to ride out the criticism from an
angry Congress, press, and civil rights organizations. On November 6, 1984,
after four years of his Nicaragua policy, he was reelected by the biggest landslide
in our history. It is a remarkable testimony to the power of the Reagan
personality. In spite of the fact that three-quarters of the people opposed his
policy in Nicaragua, Reagan was still a popular president. No one, and no
group of congressmen, was strong enough to oppose him. He even managed a
few pro-contra demonstrations in front of the White House.
    President Reagan, like many national leaders before him, sought both power
and virtue. But did he really believe he was genuinely virtuous, or was it all
a publicity stunt? How is it possible to lie to Congress and the press, and break
the law, while maintaining an inner belief in one's virtue? The answer is that,
difficult as it is to believe, neither Ronald Reagan nor those close to him
believed that he had lied to anyone. Before he held a press conference on Iran-
Contra, the president called in the leaders of both parties and told them we had
supplied arms to Iran but it was only a small amount and we had not swapped
arms for hostages. Over a year later, Donald Regan (the president's press
secretary) described this meeting in his memoirs. He said, "Some of those men
were skeptical—you could see it in their faces, hear it in their voices. But they
had no choice but to accept what the President told them. Ronald Reagan had
never lied to them (or in my experience, to anyone). And there is no question
in my mind that he believed he was telling the truth."[45]
    It was said the president was misinformed when he held the press conference.
Perhaps he was, but he was present at the initial meetings when the first contacts
with Iran were discussed. He was told that Israel would supply the weapons and
he gave his assurance that Israel could purchase replacements from the U.S.[46]
But he managed to believe he was not trading arms for hostages. This is the key
to understanding the psychology of Ronald Reagan. He had an almost incredible
capacity to believe those things he wanted to be true. When he said that his
contras were the true Sandinistas and that they were a valiant band fighting for

freedom, the fact that only a minority of people believed him did not alter his opinion. In fact, it may have been his own personal conviction that he was on the side of justice, that carried the day for him. When President Nixon said, "I am not a crook," people laughed. President Reagan made no such protestations of his honesty, but most of the people who elected him felt that, if he was saying something that wasn't true, it was only because he believed that it *was* true. In the selection of a leader in America, sincerity (or the appearance of sincerity) is more important than the facts. If he lies to himself, the president may then tell others what he believes to be the truth. To the American people, bad faith is OK if one means well.[47]

EPILOGUE

On January 6, 1990, over five years after the La Penca bombing of Eden Pastora's news conference, the public prosecutor in San Jose, Costa Rica, finished his judicial investigation of the incident. The preliminary report named John Hull, a CIA operative, and Filipe Vidal as the planners of the bombing. The report linked Hull, Vidal, and Manual Noriega in a conspiracy that involved cocaine runs through northern Costa Rica to raise funds for the contra operation. As possible motives for the bombing the prosecutor indicated Pastora's refusal to cooperate with the U.S. by joining forces with the northern contras, his refusal to work with anti-Castro Cubans or to accept the help of arms from pilots who were also involved in cocaine trafficking under Noriega.[48]

In February 1990, on the prosecutor's recommendation that Hull be charged with first-degree murder in the bombing, Hull jumped bail and fled to the United States. An attempt was made to extradite him, without success. Lindsey Gruson reported in the *New York Times*, that Hull had ties with the Reagan White House and that he, along with Vidal, was sought by the Costa Rican government. The man who posed as Per Anker Hansen and actually placed the bomb was identified as Amac Galil, a Libyan, but his and Vidal's whereabouts were unknown.

In the prosecutors report it was also revealed that the CIA had placed its operatives deep within the intelligence directorate of the Costa Rican Public Security Ministry. The CIA group was allegedly used to plant false leads to sidetrack the investigation of the bombing of La Penca.[49]

To what extent was Ronald Reagan responsible for the attempted assassination of Eden Pastora? Certainly Pastora was a burr under his saddle and it would have been convenient to have him out of the way, particularly when he threatened to expose the Reagan administration in his press conference. But, as in the case of Iran-Contra, Ronald Reagan did not have to say a word. He was surrounded by a group of underlings, eager to anticipate what he might want. The Director of the CIA, Bill Casey, was in close contact with Oliver North and the leadership of the National Security Council. No one wanted to embarrass the president by asking his permission to engage in illegal activities. All he had to do was set the tone for what was to follow. It would be ridiculous to search for assassination orders. The CIA knew what to do.

NOTES

1. R. Reagan, Remarks on Presenting the Medal of Honor to Master Sergeant Ray P. Benavidez, February 24, 1981, *Public Papers of the Presidents of the United States,* vol. 1, (Washington: U.S. Govt. Printing Office, 1981), pp. 155-158.

2. J. de Onis, "U.S. Says Salvador is Textbook Case of Communist Plot,"   *New York Times,* February 20, 1981, p. 1.

3. A. Riding, "Mexico Stresses Ties with Cuba in an Apparent Rebuff to Reagan," *New York Times*, 21, 1981, p. 1.

4. J. Petras, "Blots on the White Paper: The Reinvention of the Red Menace," reprinted as chapter 36 in *El Salvador: Central America in the New Cold War,* ed. by M.E. Gettleman, P. Lacefield, L. Menashe, D. Mermelstein, and R. Radosh, (New York: Grove Press, 1981), p. 179.

5. R. G. Kaiser, "Further Blots on the White Paper: Doubts About Evidence and Conclusions," Reprinted as chapter 37 in *El Salvdor,* p. 192.

6. R. Reagan, "Excerpts from an Interview with Walter Cronkite of CBS News," March 3, 1981, *Presidential Papers*, vol. 1, 1981, pp.191-202.

7. J. Brecher, with J. Walcott, D. Martin, and B. Nissen, "A Secret War for Nicaragua," *Newsweek*, November 8, 1982, pp. 42-53.

8. Ibid., p. 46.

9. Ibid., p. 48.

10. D. Ignatius, and D. Rogers, "Aiding the Contras: Why the Covert War in Nicaragua Evolved and Hasn't Succeeded," *Wall Street Journal*, March 5, 1985, p.1.

11. E. Chamorro, *Packaging the Contras: A Case of CIA Disinformation*, (New York: Institute for Media Analysis, 1987), Monograph Series Number 2, pp. 10-11.

12. Ibid., pp. 45-46.

13. Ibid., p. 48.
Chamorro was in chronic difficulty with his CIA handlers. He told reporters that the goal of the contras was to overthrow the government of Nicaragua and he admitted that National Guard officers ran the FDN. After several arguments and threats from the CIA leadership, his resignation from the contras was requested and he left the organization

November 21, 1984. *Packaging the Contras* was written as an attempt to analyze his own ethical dilemma in doing some of the work he had done for an organization which he felt was antithetical to the best interests of his country.

14. A. J. Cruz, Jr., *Memoirs of a Counterrevolutionary*, (New York: Doubleday, 1989), pp. 155-56.

15. R. Reagan, "Question and Answer Session with Reporters on Domestic and Foreign Policy Issues." March 29, 1983, *Presidential Papers*, 1983, vol. 1, p. 467.

16. J. B. B. Centeno, "We're not Doing this to Solve the Problems of El Salvador." A chapter in the *Nicaraguan Reader*, pp. 236-238.

17. Ignatius and Rogers, "Aiding the Contras," p.1.

18. T. Wicker, "Shame in Nicaragua." a chapter in Rosset and Vandermeer, *The Nicaraguan Reader*, p. 229-241. Reprinted from a *New York Times* article of April 1, 1983.

19. R. Reagan, "Remarks at a Question and Answer session with Reporters on Domestic and Foreign Policy Issues," April 14, 1983, *Presidential Papers* 1983, vol. I, pp. 539-540.

20. R. Reagan, Address Before a Joint Session of Congress on Central America April 27, 1973, *Presidential Papers*, vol. 1, pp. 539-540.

21. R. Reagan, Question and Answer Session with Reporters on Domestic and Foreign Policy Issues, May 4, 1983, *Presidential Papers*, Washington: US Government Printing Office, 1983, vol. 1, pp. 637-38.

22. "Contras Split Over US Demands for Unity," *New York Times*, May 24, 1984, p. 13.

23. R. G. Miller, "A Survivor's Story: Blinding Explosion Among Journalists." *New York Times*, June 1, 1984, p. 4.

24. R. J. Meislin, "Attack on Pastora. Much Intrigue But Few Facts." *New York Times*, June 14, 1984, p. 4.

25. Ibid.

26. T. Avirgan, and M. Honey, eds., *La Penca: On Trial in Costa Rica*, printed in Costa Rica, (San Pedro: Montes de Oca, 1988), pp. 84-86.

"After Terrel [sic] testified first before the national authorities [in Costa Rica] and later before the U. S. Senate Commission, Oliver North described him in a memorandum, as a misinformer harmful to the interests of the United States and suggests [sic] that he be formally accused. Terrel, after his statements, was accused in Florida and faces charges of violation of the U. S. neutrality laws for his help to the contras." From a document *Public Prosecutor's Investigation on 'La Penca' Case,* San Jose, Costa Rica 26 December 1988. Translated from the Spanish by John B. Anderson, certified court reporter. This document references the report of the Kerry Committee for its information.

"Mr. Terrell had been charged with violating the Neutrality Act for helping mount paramilitary operations against Nicaragua. Of the hundreds of Americans involved in such activity, only he and several underlings were indicted--but only after he became a key source of disclosures about Mr. North's secret network, talking freely to Congress and the press about his experiences on missions in Costa Rica and Honduras," (From *The National Law Journal,* Monday, March 24, 1990, vol. 12, no. 29, p.1,).

27. Ibid.

28. *New York Times,* April 15, 1984, p. 12.

29. *New York Times,* June 26, 1984, p. 1.

30. R. Reagan, "Remarks on Signing Proclamation 5223, July 16, 1984," *Presidential Papers,* 1984, Vol. 2, p. 1031.

31. Ibid.

32. R. Reagan, "Interview with Forest Sawyer of WAGA-TV in Atlanta, Georgia." *Presidential Papers,* 1984, vol. 2, p. 1104.

33. M. Cook, "The Reluctant Candidate," *The Nation,* October 13, 1984, p. 347.

34. Ibid.

35. Ibid.

36. A. Cockburn, "Beat the Devil." *The Nation,* March 15, 1984, p. 294

37. R. Bonner, "The Elections in Nicaragua." *New York Times,* September 14, 1984, p. 31.

38. J. B. Oakes, " Fraud in Nicaragua," *New York Times,* November 15, 1984, p. 31.

39. *New York Times,* October 15, 1984, p. 7.

40. J. Brinely, "Nicaraguan Rebel Disputes US Aide," *New York Times,* October 20, 1984, p. 1.

41. B. Barger, "CIA manual Aimed at Contra Abuses." *Washington Post,* October 31, 1984, p.1

42. R. Reagan, "Question and Answer Session with Reporters in Winterset, Iowa, November 3, 1984." *Presidential Papers,* 1984, Vol. 2, p. 1763.

43. Editorial, *New York Times,* November 13, 1984, p. 30.

44. "Human Rights in Nicaragua: Reagan Rhetoric and Reality," *Americas Watch Report,* July, 1985, pp. 2-4.

45. D. T. Regan, *For the Record,* (New York: Harcourt, Brace and Javonavich, 1988), p. 31.

46. R. C. McFarlane, *Special Trust,* (New York: Cadell and Davies, 1994), p. 34.

47. While it is clear that Ronald Reagan replaced real memories of events with others which were the way he would have liked things to be, it is not clear to what extent this was an early symptom of Alzheimer's disease, which was diagnosed after he left office. Forgetting and confabulation of memories is a symptom of this illness.

48. J. McPhaul, "Costa Rican Prosecutor Links Two Americans to Fatal Bombing." *The Miami Herald,* January 6, 1990, p.1.

49. L. Gruson, "Costa Rica is Asking US to Extradite Rancher Tied to 84 Bombing that Killed 4" *New York Times,* International Edition, March 1, 1990.
When they failed to extradite Hull, Honey and Avrrigan enlisted the aid of the Christic Institute to try Hull in the United States. The institute brought suit against Hull in federal court alleging criminal conspiracy. Secord and Hakim were also defendants. In June 1988, Judge James Lawrence King blocked the suit by granting motions for summary judgement filed by the defendants. He fined the institute one million dollars on the grounds that their lawsuit was frivolous. It was the goal of the institute to expose the workings of the Enterprise operated by Secord and build public support "for an open and lawful government that truly reflects democratic values and respects the principles embodied in our Constitution." (From a letter to WHB from Sarah Nelson, Executive Director, Christic Institute.)

8

MONEY MONEY MONEY

Part of the system of checks and balances built into our constitution is the role of Congress in authorizing funds for the implementation of presidential policy. If the president orders a policy or a military operation that seems not in the best interest of the United States, Congress can restrain the executive by refusing to fund ventures that it considers unwise. Further, Congress can pass laws that control the executive branch, particularly in regard to the disposition of federal funds.

In early 1983 it was apparent that Congress was not willing to give President Reagan the whole-hearted financial support he felt he needed for the contra operation. At that time he began planning an end run around his congressional critics. He would get his own money, regardless of whether Congress appropriated it. In June of that year President Reagan authorized Operation Elephant Herd, a system for sending military equipment from the Pentagon to the CIA. In December of that year, when Congress blocked contra aid beyond $24 million, the Pentagon declared any equipment requested by the CIA to be surplus, with no dollar value.[1] This was only one of a host of secret sources of funds to be tapped for contra aid. It represented a deliberate attempt by the president to get around the control of executive authority provided by the constitution.

An important figure in raising this extra money was a Marine Lieutenant Colonel named Oliver North who worked as a White House staff member of the National Security Council (NSC). North was not only completely devoted to the policy of President Reagan, he seemed to have an inner conviction that he knew what the President wanted. Arturo Cruz, Jr., who worked with him, felt he "sometimes implied he was like a son to President Reagan, that he and the President shared a special relationship."[2] Reporters who called him at ten in the evening found him in his office still at work and willing to talk. The many accounts of his behavior preserved in memos, schedules, and hearings show him as the eager beaver, always pushing the limits to find money for the President's contras. North never waited to be told what to do. He would suggest an action to his superiors. He was an eloquent and persuasive speaker who sometimes, in his enthusiasm for the mission, exaggerated the possible benefits to be gained from one of his proposals. He was persistent. If he was turned down on an idea he would reword it or organize it in a different way to get it approved. At least one of his supervisors (John Poindexter) found it difficult to say no to him.

Congress tried to restrain the administration with the first Boland Amendment which forbade the use of government funds to support an invasion of Nicaragua. But Congress was handicapped because it could not prove that an invasion was underway and it could not be sure how the arms were supplied and by whom. In October 1984 Congress passed a second Boland Amendment. It was as if, by making the language more specific, the legislators hoped to provide a legal block that the administration could not ignore. Congress cut off all U.S. funds for the contras for 1985. Section 8066(a) of the appropriations act provided that "no funds available to the Central Intelligence Agency, the Department of Defense or any other agency or entity of the United States involved in intelligence activities may be obligated or expended for the purpose of supporting directly or indirectly, military or paramilitary operations in Nicaragua by any nation, group, organization, movement or individual."[This was] . . . a rather sweeping prohibition, indicating quite clearly that Congress wanted to wind down U.S. financial support for the contras.[3] Aid was rejected in April 1985, but in June a trickle of support emerged in the form of a grant for $27 million in humanitarian aid to be used for the purchase of food, clothing, and medicine, but no weapons.

North began immediately to look for other sources of money. As early as September 2, 1984, he sent a memo to Robert McFarlane, the president's national security advisor and head of the NSC staff, to get permission to ask a "private donor" to purchase a badly needed helicopter for FDN use. McFarlane, a careful, cautious man who operated by the book, noted at the bottom of the memo, "I don't think this is legal."[4] Obviously the NSC, as the primary intelligence coordinating agency in the country, would come under the Boland Amendment.

McFarlane was later to discover that North went ahead and raised money for the contras without his approval. His testimony makes it clear that North, who professed his devotion to duty, who believed in following orders, and who regarded McFarlane as his boss, began to take a much more active role in contra funding, supply, and direction of the contra activity than McFarlane had ever authorized.[5] As McFarlane became more suspicious he examined in some detail the memos North had sent to him and discovered unmistakable evidence that North had exceeded his authority. When he confronted him, North explained that the memos did not really say what they seemed to say. McFarlane's account follows.

I looked at him intently. "This is not a judge sitting here, Ollie, or your father confessor. It's me, Bud. Now tell me truthfully, one Marine to another. Have you been doing anything against the law?"

North did not hesitate. He looked me in the eye and told me a boldfaced lie. "Bud," he said, "I never did anything illegal."

And despite my suspicions, because I trusted him, I took him at his word.[6]

North began his career in the White House by following orders, but slowly he began to take more and more actions on his own. How did this come about? One has to read between the lines to get the answer, but the evidence is there, in the testimony of the participants. The impetus to do something for the contras came directly from the president. McFarlane reported that Ronald Reagan asked him to do what he could to keep the contra operation going when Congress threatened to shut it down. "We've got to find a way to keep doing this, Bud. I want you to do whatever you have to do to help these people keep body and soul together. Do everything you can."[7] McFarlane told North about the conversation, but while the conservative McFarlane took the president's words to mean "whatever you have to do within the law," North assumed he meant "anything goes."

Later, North was assigned as liaison to work with Bill Casey, head of the CIA. Casey added force to North's own interpretation of the president's words. McFarlane describes Casey as a man who broke with the usual CIA policy of supplying intelligence information. He provided policy advice as well, whether or not it was requested. Speaking of Casey, McFarlane says, "As early as 1982, and certainly by the spring of 1984, it had become clear to me that Casey, convinced that Ronald Reagan lacked the passion for foreign affairs that would lead him to tackle issues on that front decisively . . . was shielding the president from difficult issues, taking on the responsibility for accomplishing things he believed the president would agree with but would not do himself."[8]

North was already impatient with the restraints McFarlane had placed upon him. He saw McFarlane as stiff, reserved, insecure, and a bit too cautious.[9] When his position as CIA liaison put him in contact with Casey, he responded immediately to the older man's active, interventionist approach. He admired Casey "enormously" and he let him know it. Casey seemed to know what was really happening and he explained things. When McFarlane gave North an order he then could turn to Casey for advice on how it might be carried out. Casey filled him in on the details of covert operations, telling him who he should work with on Nicaragua and who to avoid.[10] His supervisor, Robert McFarlane, came to the conclusion that it was North and Casey "who put together the Hakim-Secord 'off-the-shelf' contra-support operation. Casey was a Cabinet officer, the Director of Central Intelligence and, a right thinker. That was good enough for North—indeed, faced with my disapproval, it was the essential support he needed from a superior."[11] North may have justified his insubordination (if he even saw it as insubordination) on the grounds that he was dealing directly with a higher authority. It was one of those informal arrangements that so often subvert the formal chain of command as it appears on an organization chart.

In any event, North was soon calling people and churning out memos for various donor organizations and others who might be used to raise private funds. There were a number of meetings in 1984 and 1985 with Robert Owen, who functioned as a messenger between North and the contras. There were also several meetings with John Singlaub, a retired general who managed the World Anticommunist League, raising funds for right-wing causes, including those of John Hull (of La Penca fame) and Adolfo Calero, commander of the FDN, the military wing of the contras. While North worked through other nongovernment organizations, there is little doubt that he was the driving force behind the contra supply effort. He contacted fund-raisers, spoke to prospective donors, called on retired General Secord to order a weapons drop at a particular location, alerted Calero that the weapons would arrive, and advised him of any postponements. He was crucial in the contra supply operation, from raising funds to dropping weapons. As an active duty professional career Marine officer, he provided military advice.

Congress was suspicious of Colonel North almost from the beginning and sought assurances from McFarlane. McFarlane, without denying that North was raising money, insisted that he was not breaking the law and that no NSC funds were being used to support military operations in Nicaragua.[12]

From January to March 1986 North received fifteen encryption devices from the National Security Agency, a secret organization much less in the public eye than the CIA, which deals with intelligence gained from electronic and voice intercepts. He passed some of the devices on to men upon whom he was relying to get ammunition and other equipment for the contras. Others went directly to CIA and contra leaders in the field. This enabled him to communicate with all parties in the arms supply business by channels unavailable to Congress or other government agencies. Many messages over these channels were concerned with the confirmation of a weapons drop to the contras.[13]

In addition to the encryption devices, there was PROFS (Professional Office System), a secure E-mail message system in the White House. Messages were displayed on a computer screen and could be deleted when they were no longer needed. It was a means of sending written messages without the necessity of using a secretary for typing a memo. It reduced the amount of classified paper and greatly increased security. It could be used by a number of people simultaneously and made informal chats about classified matters easy to arrange, serving as a substitute for meetings. But, in some respects, it was full of holes. When the messages were deleted, they remained in the computer memory. Later, during the Iran-Contra hearings, messages cleaned out of the computer to avoid disclosure to the committee were retrieved by a clever technician from the White House Communications Agency.

THE SECRET FUNDS REVEALED

The president was pleased by the many sources being developed for private contributions to the contra effort, but he wanted the legitimacy symbolized by congressional support. In March 1986 he asked for another tranche of funds for his "freedom fighters." Talking about the "Malignancy in Managua" he warned Congress that Harlingen, Texas was just two days driving time from the stronghold of Sandinista terrorists (actually it is over 2,000 miles). To oppose the Sandinista threat, he said, we needed the strong contra force costing, only a modest $100 million. Former President Jimmy Carter in a television interview stated that the contras were not a strong force and that President Reagan had misrepresented their effectiveness. But the president had his supporters. Pat Buchanan, the White House Director of Communications, appeared on the CBS Morning News to remind the nation that without Jimmy Carter there would be no Sandinista regime. If Carter had not "pulled the rug out from under" the late dictator, we would still have good old Tachito Somoza in charge of things down in Nicaragua.[14] The Reagan proposal was defeated in Congress 222-210, but was destined to be passed later.

On October 5, 1986, the various schemes for secret and unauthorized weapons funding for the contras began to unravel when Nicaraguan troops shot down a U.S. C-123 cargo plane. One of the crew, a former Marine called Eugene Hasenfus, bailed out and was captured. He admitted to the Sandinistas that he was part of a CIA contra supply operation and that his flight originated in Miami. In addition to the Boland Amendment, this was a violation of the Arms Export Control Act and the Neutrality Act, which makes it illegal for Americans to make war against a country with which the U.S. is at peace.

As Congress began hearings to investigate this incident and verify the CIA involvement, the first news of the Iran-Contra scandal broke. On November 13, 1986, after a revelation in a Beirut newspaper Ronald Reagan addressed the nation, telling us that a "diplomatic initiative" had been underway for eighteen months "to renew our relationship with Iran, to bring an honorable end to the Iran-Iraq war, to eliminate state-sponsored terrorism and attain the safe return of our hostages" in Lebanon. He said it was a U.S. initiative and he denied that other nations were involved. He ended with a denial that there had been any trading of arms to Iran in exchange for the release of hostages in Lebanon held by Iranian militants.[15]

Reagan held another news conference on the November 19 in which he tried to clarify just what had happened, but he dug himself deeper into the hole. Despite questions from reporters, the president maintained that no other countries were involved in the arms transfers and that we had shipped only a small amount of weapons, just enough to fit inside a single cargo plane. It was not until November 25, 1986, that President Reagan appeared at a news conference with Attorney General Edwin Meese. This time the two men admitted that arms had been sold to Iran in an effort to secure the release of American hostages in

Beirut and that profits from the Iranian sales had been used to buy weapons for the contras.

The report of the Tower Commission, which was formed to investigate this scandal, contains a chronology of our contacts with Iran, who said what to whom, and who urged what actions. But the chronology proved to be falsified in several places. The report as a whole is far from complete. Many of the principals declined to testify. The report concluded that Reagan's "model" of management, his delegation of authority, kept him out of touch with Iran-Contra. However, in one way he was at the center of Iran-Contra through his insistence that his staff do what they could to release the hostages. Further, in his strong desire to find money, regardless of the source, to supply the contras, he set both the moral tone and the pathway for others to follow. The Tower board concluded that, because of this flawed decision process, the Iran initiative did not receive a rigorous review and the total decision process did not receive the attention of the president. This may be true, but perhaps the goal of deniability, had a higher priority than good decision-making.

That is what Admiral John Poindexter seemed to imply when he testified before congressional panels on July 15, 1987. Poindexter said he had approved the diversion of funds from Iran to the contras without telling the president what he was doing. His reason? "so that I could insulate him from the decision and provide some future deniability for the President if it ever leaked out."[16] But, while trying to protect the president with one statement, Poindexter implicates him with another:

It seemed that this method of financing was completely consistent with what we had been doing in terms of private parties and third countries. . . . I had at that point worked with the President for about five and a half years . . . so I not only clearly understood his policy but I also thought I understood the way he thought about issues. . . . I also felt that it was, as I said, consistent with the President's policy, and that if I asked him, I felt confident that he would approve it.[17]

Deniability never really works. Regardless of what the president knew or when he knew it, he is accountable to the American people for what happened. The fact that his style of administration isolated him from what was going on, the fact that he was "poorly served" by his advisors, as George Shultz tells us—all of these circumstances may explain, but they do not excuse. Reagan had many advisors, including George Shultz who urged him to have nothing to do with a deal exchanging arms for hostages. But it was Reagan who hired the advisors and chose which advice he would follow. Further, he set the tone for the decision process. Poindexter was probably right when he said he knew how the president thought and that the diversion of funds to the contras was consistent with the president's policy.

Of course, the president protested vigorously that the buck did not stop with Poindexter. He insisted that he was the one who was accountable to the American people and that he would never have made such a decision. "No president should ever be protected from the truth," he said. A beautiful and noble expression. But when one has set an atmosphere of concealing vital information from Congress, of covert sources of funding to get around congressional restrictions, it is not surprising that one's associates, who have participated in these earlier decisions, should react with a similar form of gamesmanship.

BEHIND THE SCENE

There is something fishy and a bit self-serving about the story presented by Admiral Poindexter—that he was sacrificing himself to protect the president's deniability. What really happened? When and why was the decision made not to tell the president what was going on? Or was it really a deliberate decision? Perhaps the roots of his secrecy lie in the personality of John Poindexter himself. He was a very conservative and secret individual. Oliver North found him to be extremely reticent in expressing his thoughts or his feelings.[18]

When the Iran-Contra crisis first broke and it was apparent that there would have to be a presidential news conference, a rehearsal was planned. Poindexter was asked to help the president get ready for the foreign policy questions. At this point, if his deniability story was true, he had a perfect chance to say to the president, "Here's the whole story, Boss. I know I should have told you, but I kept quiet to preserve your deniability." Instead, he continued to keep secret, not only the diversion, but several aspects of the Iran-Contra operation and he cautioned the president against revealing other information to the press.

The president did fine in the domestic part of the rehearsal for the news conference, but he floundered in foreign policy. To Don Regan, his chief of staff, who was watching the rehearsal, it was clear that Poindexter was withholding the whole story from the president. Regan took Poindexter aside and warned him that if the situation continued the news conference would be a disaster. Said Regan, "Poindexter, puffing on his pipe and peering at me through his round glasses, seemed to be genuinely embarrassed. But he was still keeping secrets and I think that his anxiety had an effect on the President's state of mind. Ronald Reagan went before the press on November 19, possessed of the idea that he must not reveal Israel's role in the Iran affair."[19] The news conference did not come off well. The president's credibility was damaged, but his basic popularity with the people remained intact.

However, intelligence committees of both houses of Congress announced that they would hold hearings and Bill Casey would be among those testifying. Casey would die of cancer before he could testify. He knew all about the diversion, but evidently Poindexter still believed that Casey would not talk, so he kept quiet. When Regan set up a meeting with the president and George Schultz, who had heard that there would be several embarrassing revelations in Casey's testimony, Poindexter, who was present, "defended the information he had provided the president and offered no new data."[20] It was only then that

Don Regan suggested to the president that Attorney General Meese be asked to verify all the facts in Casey's proposed testimony.

When Meese questioned North, he discovered the excess charges to Iran and the diversion of funds to the contras, so he approached Poindexter, as North's direct superior. Poindexter put it off to the enthusiasm of Oliver North, implying he knew North was up to something, but he didn't want to inquire too deeply for fear of what might turn up. When the president heard this, he demanded Poindexter's resignation. Later Donald Regan asked Poindexter whether he had approved North's operation and he replied, "I felt sorry for the Contras. I was so damn mad at Tip O'Neil for the way he was dragging the Contras around that I didn't want to know what, if anything was going on. I should have but I didn't." In the course of his conversation he gave Regan the impression that he had felt that "interfering with North would, somehow, have been a form of giving aid and comfort to the enemy."[21] All of this has a very different sound from Poindexter's story to the committee.

Poindexter's response gives the impression that North was operating on his own without formal approval, that he could have stopped North, but he couldn't bring himself to do it. Oliver North, on the other hand, makes it clear that he had explicit approval from Poindexter before he took the first step. In North's testimony to the Iran-Contra committee, he reported that he went to Poindexter's office to submit the proposal for the diversion of funds and got his approval.

Lt.Col.North: I don't recall specifically on this case—but my normal modus operandi on making a proposal such as that would be to go over and sit down with the Admiral and talk to him. And, normally, the Admiral would like to think about it. I mean, the Admiral is not a hip-shooter, as I am accused of being . . .

Mr.Liman: Did he discuss the risks of using the funds for the Contras with you?

Lt.Col.North: Yes.

Mr Liman: What did he say?

Lt.Col.North: "This had better never come out." And I took steps to insure that it didn't, and they failed. . . .

Mr.Liman: At the time that you first briefed him on it, did you discuss how much money would be generated for the contras if the 4000 TOWs were sold?

Lt.Col.North: Oh, I think I did. I think I was probably always too enthusiastic in my projections. In the document that we now have shown the world, I anticipated a residual that was in excess of what was realistic.

Mr.Liman: Did you—do you recall how often—how long after you first told him about this orally he got back to you?

Lt.Col.North: No I don't. I guess it was a matter of weeks—or days or weeks, certainly, because, by February, we did it.[22]

So Poindexter did give his formal approval to the project. But it appears that he did it against his own better judgement. In short, North sold him on the diversion with his eloquence and enthusiasm. In fact, he did such a good job that he made Poindexter feel it would be unpatriotic to turn him down. Poindexter regretted it later. This is why he could not bring himself to tell the president what he had done. The deniability story did not come out when he was being questioned by Meese and Don Regan. It was clearly an afterthought, the sort of thing one puts together to make one's behavior appear logical and deliberate.

How about the president? He was not informed by Poindexter, but is it really true that he knew nothing about the diversion until he was informed by Meese? The president was in close contact with the contra operation. Surely he must have been informed of the flow of funds and the degree of support for the contras. The extra money was coming from somewhere. In his own reflections on Iran-Contra, Oliver North was convinced that the president knew everything. Money from the diverted Iranian funds was used to finance a variety of other projects, many of them highly sensitive. North assumed that memos, which he prepared, describing how these funds were to be used, would have to be passed up to the president.[23]

For his part Ronald Reagan seemed to feel that if the arms were not being sent to the Hizballah—the Iranian terrorists who were holding American hostages—he was not really trading arms for hostages.[24]   Aside from the fact that we did not know for sure that none of the arms were going to the Hizballah, it was clear that the Hizballah was under the control of Iranian leaders. The Iranian leaders were tied directly to the Hizballah, even though they were not willing to accept responsibility for the actions of this terrorist organization. So it is a rather thin excuse to say we did not trade arms for hostages, because we did not know the ultimate recipients of the arms we traded.

SELLING INTERVIEWS WITH THE PRESIDENT

Selling arms for the return of hostages and diverting excess funds from this sale to aid the contras was a scandal, but there is another part of the fund-raising effort that appears even more demeaning.   It is clear that the motivation of President Reagan to get money for his contras was so strong that he sold himself and the prestige of his office to get a few more bucks from wealthy donors.

Throughout this period North was working with fund raisers such as General Singlaub and Carl R. "Spitz" Channell of the National Endowment for the Preservation of Liberty (NEPL), who was in touch with many wealthy right-wing Americans. North funneled the money from these fund raisers, through a Swiss bank account, to weapons procurement agencies such as the Enterprise (covered later in this chapter). North, Bill Casey, and various members of the White House staff were also in touch with foreign leaders who might contribute to the contra effort in exchange for favors. The Sultan of Brunei contributed $10 million and the King of Saudi Arabia agreed to pay $1 million a month. Each foreign potentate had an interview with the president. By the time they saw him, it was not necessary that he ask for money. He only had to say something about the contras and how their cause was in trouble because of a denial of funds by Congress. However, according to Oliver North, the president personally solicited

King Fahd of Saudi Arabia, asking him to double his contribution.[25]   McFarlane later testified that, when "a foreign prince" doubled his contribution after talking with the president, the president expressed satisfaction, but not surprise.

There is another more seedy aspect of such fund-raising. Everyone tried to distance himself from this part of the operation, but there was no doubt that interviews and chats with the president were sold for a few hundred thousand dollars each. Many of the participants denied that they were directly involved in actually pitching some of the donors for money. Only Spitz Channell was not at all embarrassed about asking wealthy people to give lots of money for a worthy cause. Channell and North worked together on the pitch.

Oliver North was invited by Channell to speak before a small gathering of potential contributors to the NEPL, a supposedly tax-exempt fund. North was very articulate. He could present an exciting speech on the heroic efforts of the contras who fought for freedom in Nicaragua. He would add many details from his own experience in the field. He would explain that he knew the president and this was a cause very close to his heart. Without asking anyone for any money, he described the various types of weapons used and the cost of each, from helicopters to assault rifles. Then, in order to distance himself from the act of fund-raising, he would leave the meeting room and Channell would go to work on the potential donors, asking for specific amounts. The two of them worked as a team. It was understood by Channell that North must not be compromised by the mention of money in his presence—although it is difficult to understand how North thought he was avoiding complicity.

On March 26, 1986, William O'Boyle was invited to a presentation by Oliver North on the military and political situation in Nicaragua. After North left the room Channell told O'Boyle that he had heard O'Boyle was willing to make a contribution to the contra effort. For a $300,000 or greater contribution he was told he could have a fifteen-minute, unrecorded, off-the-record meeting with the president. When questioned about the fund-raising process by Senator Paul Sarbanes, O'Boyle accepted the characterization that North and Channell worked as a team.[26]

Sometime in April 1986, Ellen Garwood, a wealthy Texas widow, traveled to Washington, D.C. to a meeting of contributors to Spitz Channell's NEPL and to see the president. Channell met her in a room next to a cocktail lounge at the Hay-Adams Hotel. He told her the contras were facing a crisis in Nicaragua. Then Colonel North arrived to describe the crisis with his usual eloquence. North told Garwood that the contras were out of food, clothing, medicine, and other necessities. They were also out of weapons. North left and Channell talked to her about a contribution. She contributed $1,633,506 in shares of stock and cash by wire transfer. She later also accepted the characterization that Channell and North worked as a team.[27]

On April 29, 1987, Spitz Channell pleaded guilty to tax-fraud conspiracy. Like members of the Reagan administration, he was supplying covert funding, but he was doing it as the head of a private foundation at a time when Congress had voted to bar any nonhumanitarian aid. As a private individual he was much more vulnerable than the president or the NSC. Also, by claiming to have a tax-exempt foundation, he was taking money from the U.S. Treasury, which is the prerogative of Congress. Channell raised over $2 million for a project called "Toys," which was represented as funds for Christmas gifts for the children of the contras. He named Oliver North as a coconspirator, but he might as well have named the president. Both men were involved in raising contributions, but both had distanced themselves from Channell's fund-raising activities by a careful shield of deniability, which was as thin as the shield provided by Poindexter.

Conferences were arranged between the president and his donors, sometimes by Colonel North and sometimes by other members of the White House staff. It is clear that the president knew who the people were and why he was talking to them. He admitted talking to a number of people for "political purposes," without acknowledging that he really understood the purpose of these discussions However, it is clear that he understood the reason for the interview.

Following is a sample of the testimony of Oliver North before the Iran-Contra Committee on this subject:

Lt.Col.North: I want to make it very clear. I did tell people I could not and would not solicit, that I wasn't going to ask them for their money, and I do not recall ever being in the presence of Mr. Channell at any time when he asked someone for money, at anytime. Nor do I ever recall Mr. Channell offering someone a visit to the Oval Office or the President of the United States of America for a price. . .

Mr.Nields: Did you arrange such meetings with the President?

Lt.Col.North: I do not believe that I personally arranged—I may have sent forward scheduled proposals . . . So these meetings did happen in the White House, yes.

Mr.Nields: And some of them were with people who had actually made contributions?

Lt.Col.North: Oh yes, Yes.

Mr.Nields: And the contributions had been obtained in part through your efforts?

Lt.Col.North: People give me a lot of credit. If someone wants to say, "it was a speech by Ollie North that made me want to give money to help the Nicaraguan resistance," I appreciate that.

Mr.Nields: Well I would like to turn to exhibit 10. It's in the first book. It is a PROF message from you to Admiral Poindexter, dated May 16, 1986? . . . I would like you to take a look at the bottom of the second page where it says, "I have no idea what Don Regan does or does not know re my private US operation. But the President obviously knows why he has been meeting with several select people to thank them for their 'support for democracy' in Central America." . . . My first question is, what is quote, "my private US operation"? What does that refer to?

Lt.Col.North: Well I don't know. It must mean my activities, my discussions with people.

Mr.Nields: Private contributors?

Lt.Col.North: Sure, I don't know exactly what I meant at that particular point in time.

Mr.Nields: But you don't call it Spitz Channell's operation, you call it your operation. And when you refer to his meeting with several select people to thank them for their support for democracy, I take it those are people who have made contributions?

Lt.Col.North: I would guess so, yes.

Mr. Nields: And I take it that when you gave speeches to these people, one of the purposes was to get them to make a contribution?

Lt.Col.North: One of the purposes of my talking to people was indeed to encourage that they do whatever they felt moved to do to support the cause of the democratic outcome in Nicaragua.

Mr.Nields: Was the President aware of your US operation to raise funds for the contras from private contributors?

Lt.Col.North: Well I think that that PROF note right there indicates that I believed he was.[28]

A few years later, when the president was writing his memoirs on this subject, a rosy glow suffused his recollections. It was all a spontaneous movement in which "churches and other groups around our country began forming committees with the intention of helping the freedom fighters." They got their information from "things they had read in the papers." So he told the members of his administration, "there has to be a way to help these private citizens who otherwise wouldn't know how to get help to the Contras or buy the supplies they need; there must be ways we can help or counsel them if somebody says we've raised some money and want to help the Contras, somebody ought to be able to tell them what channel to use."[29]   The channel was, of course, Spitz Channell, but Reagan never mentioned his name in his memoirs.

CORRUPTION AMONG THE FREEDOM FIGHTERS

There is something about a scramble for money, even when it is raised for a noble cause, that seems to infect everyone concerned with the operation. In spite of all the money raised for the contras they remained short of supplies. Robert Owen, who was sent by Oliver North to deal with the contras in the field, reported back on the corruption that was taking place among the leaders and the troops. In a memo to North dated April 1, 1985 in which he speaks of being approached by a group of northern contras offering to work in the south and help provide a united front, Owen remarks, "Whatever structure is established for the South, tight control must be kept on the money and resources. In the past it has been too easy to sell goods and too many people have learned how to make a living off the war. Money and equipment must be accounted for, and when there are differences, examples must be made."[30]   Indeed, the guerrillas fighting the Reagan-backed government of El Salvador boasted that they could purchase anything they wanted from the contras, provided they had the money to buy it. It did not matter that the guerrillas were Communists and the contras, allegedly, anti-Communist. The Yankee dollar was the primary ideology.

There were others who believed that there was corruption at the very top of the contra command. Certain members of Congress were so indecent as to try to find out what happened to the money, once it was sent to Adolfo Calero, the head of the contra directorate, and his brother. A memo from Robert Owen to

Oliver North on February 27, 1986, speaks of an intelligence report, stolen from the hotel room of Jack Singlaub, which had some very unfavorable things to say about the Calero brothers, including their bank account numbers in Europe and the Caribbean. Owen recommended a change in policy in which "all funds, be they from outside sources or from USG (US Government) sources, go into a UNO account. No more private FDN accounts."[31] UNO was the overall political organization for the contras, the finances of which were controlled by more respectable political figures such as Alfonso Robelo and Arturo Cruz, Sr.

In a memo from Owen to North dated March 1986 there is a more sweeping condemnation of the contra leadership. "There are few of the so-called leaders who care about the boys in the field. This war has become a business to many of them." If aid were to be renewed by Congress "it would be like pouring money down a sink-hole."[32] Said Leslie Cockburn in her investigation of the trail of missing contra funds:

In August, 1985 the State Department began to dispense $27 million authorized by Congress for the purpose of strictly humanitarian aid to the contra fighting forces. . . . If there were any responsible contra leaders, they fell down on the job. As a subsequent General Accounting Office audit and an investigation by a House subcommittee revealed, no less than $17 million out of the $27 million promptly and simply disappeared. A check through the bank records turned up countless illegal signatures for the receipt of cash. . . . Large sums found their way to a Cayman Island bank called BAC, Banco de America Central.[33]

On March 9, 1987, Arturo Cruz, Sr. resigned from UNO, saying he was fed up with "the whole mentality" of the contras. On March 11 the U.S. House of Representatives voted to approve a six month suspension of financial aid to the contras "until previous payments are properly accounted for."[34]

ASK ABOUT COCAINE!

During the public hearings of the Iran-Contra scandal there was little said about the role of drug money in the purchase of weapons. In fact, it was Oliver North who brought up the subject in order to dismiss it. On Thursday July 9, 1987, during his opening remarks, he said that, as a result of stories in the media, he had been accused of almost every crime imaginable, including "that I condoned drug-trafficking to generate funds for the contras." No one on the committee seemed to want to raise any further questions on this issue, but toward the end of the morning hearings a voice was heard from the audience, off-mike. "What about the cocaine dealing that the U.S. is paying for?" When they had the attention of the hearing, the demonstrators raised a banner inscribed, "ASK ABOUT COCAINE. ASK ABOUT THE KILLING OF NON-COMBATANTS." The chairman called a recess to eject the demonstrators and the hearings continued.

The Senate Foreign Relations Committee later conducted secret hearings on the drug connection. One of the chief witnesses before this committee was Ramon Milian Rodriguez, who laundered money for the cocaine cartel. He described how he and his clients had aided the contras with cash contributions. According to Leslie Cockburn, who later interviewed Rodriguez (whom she designates as "Milian") for CBS, in 1981 he received an invitation to the presidential inauguration "in recognition of the $180,000 in campaign contributions from his clients (the cocaine cartel) that he had channeled to the victorious camp in $1,000 dollar lots."[35]   In an interview in June 1987 he admitted that, at the request of a former CIA operative who was working for the White House contra supply network, he had laundered $10 million from the Colombian cocaine cartel to the contras. Milian repeated his story under oath to the Senate Foreign Relations Subcommittee in July 1987 (the same year North testified in the hearings). "Ten million dollars in cash was disbursed, the accountant told the senators, through an established network of couriers in Miami, Guatemala, Costa Rica and Honduras. The first payments were made, Milian testified, in late 1982 and continued through 1985."[36]   Payments were made at the request of Felix Rodriguez, an old friend and close associate of both Oliver North and George Bush.

In her book, *Out of Control,* Cockburn gives a detailed account of the work of George Morales, a wealthy Colombian drug lord who was an important source of funds for the FDN (the military arm of the contras). She reports substantial evidence that Morales had the protection of the CIA. In another interview with Gary Betzner, one of Morales's pilots, he reports flying weapons into John Hull's ranch in Costa Rica and flying back to Florida with a load of cocaine. According to Betzner, Hull "physically saw the weapons coming in" and "physically saw the bags" of cocaine loaded on the aircraft for the return trip.[37]

While the story of drug money supplied to the contras was an embarrassment to the Reagan administration, the CIA had been involved in financing some of its operations, by cooperating with drug dealers or their representatives, through several previous administrations. In a *Frontline* broadcast on PBS entitled "Guns, Drugs and the CIA," produced by Leslie and Andrew Cockburn and aired in May 1988, the history of CIA drug trafficking as far back as the secret war in Laos was documented by interviews with individuals who had witnessed the movement of heroin on CIA aircraft.

The U.S. was officially neutral in Laos, so we could not use our own troops. Instead, a handful of CIA officers directed 85,000 soldiers drawn from the mountain tribes of the Hmong or Meo people of Laos. These people had been growing opium for years before the CIA arrived. But CIA aircraft greatly facilitated their drug distribution network. Ron Rickenback, an official of the U.S. Agency for International Development from 1962 to 1969 stated,

Rickenback: Early on, I think, what we were doing was in the best interest of
     America. We were, in fact, perhaps involved in some not-so-desirable aspects of the

drug traffic. However, we believed strongly in the beginning that we were there for a just cause. . . These people were willing to take up arms. We needed to stop the red threat . . . and people believed that, in that vein, you made certain trade-offs for a larger good.

Narrator. By the end of 1970 there were 30,000 Americans in Vietnam addicted to heroin. GIs were dying from overdoses at the rate of two per day. . . . A secret Pentagon report put the Defense Department contribution to the war in Laos at $146 million in 1970. But the report also showed the CIA was spending $60 million more than they were getting from Congress.[38]

The habit of expediency grows on an organization. Many of the CIA veterans of the secret war in Laos were called upon once again when experienced men were needed to fly military equipment to the contras for the Reagan administration's secret war in Nicaragua. The Cubans of brigade 2506, after the failed invasion of Castro's Cuba, were maintained by the CIA for a variety of "black operations." The *Frontline* documentary brings us up to date:

Narrator. In 1984 when Congress cut off contra funding, the White House turned to other sources for support. According to documents, Ramon Milian Rodriguez had been laundering foreign payments for the CIA up through 1982, at the same time as he was laundering cash for the cocaine cartel. He says the CIA turned to him again.

Milian Rodriguez: To have people like me in place that can be used, is marvelous for them. The agency, and quite rightly so, has things which they have to do which they can never admit to an oversight committee, all right, and the only way they can fund these things in through drug money or through illicit money that they can get their hands on in some way. . . .

Narrator. Until last year, Jose Blandon was General Manual Noriega's head of political intelligence in Panama. He was a key U.S. government witness for the grand jury that indicted Noriega for drug trafficking. General Noriega was more than ready to support the Reagan administration in the Contra war after Congress cut off funding.[39]

Following is an interview with a reporter from *Frontline* and Jose Blandon:

Frontline: How important was Noriega to the White House in the Contra resupply effort?
Jose Blandon: He play a key role in the supply of arms to the Contras.
Frontline: So when various administration officials like Oliver North met with General Noriega, did they know that he was involved in narcotics trafficking?
Jose Blandon: I think that the United States had information that Noriega is involved in drugs since *at least* eight years.
Frontilne: Eight years?
Jose Blandon: Yes, so they knew about that.
Frontline: Were they just looking the other way on his drug trafficking?
Jose Blandon: The problem is that for the White House, I mean for the administration, the Reagan administration, Nicaragua was so important. The focus of all the foreign policy of the United States in Central America was Nicaragua and the fight against communists, so for them drugs was something in second place.[40]

A respected member of the White House staff, Felix Rodriguez, was an important link in contacting people with underworld connections, people like Ramon Milian Rodriguez. An interview with Blandon continues:

Frontline: Harare, the Israeli, who was working with Noriega, was working with Felix Rodriguez?
Jose Blandon: Yes.
Frontline: And Harare at the same time was involved in drug trafficking?
Jose Blandon: Yes
Frontline: Who was Felix Rodriguez working for, or with, when he approached you?
Ramon Milian Rodriguez: Well the only government mention he made was Vice-President Bush.
Frontline: And what was his relationship with Bush as you understood it?
Ramon Milian Rodriguez: He was reporting directly to Bush. I was led to believe he was reporting regularly to the Vice President.[41]

At the end of the broadcast Judy Woodruff remarked that Vice President Bush declined to be interviewed for the program or to reply to *Frontline's* written questions about his relationship with Felix Rodriguez. Felix Rodriguez is also a name that appears frequently in the memos exchanged between Oliver North and Robert Owen. Both men report that they were unaware that Rodriguez had any drug connections.

THE ENTERPRISE

Perhaps the largest and most financially significant aspect of all the fund-raising efforts in support of the contras was the Enterprise, an organization run by retired General Richard Secord, who had operated behind the scenes in weapons procurement for several years. The Enterprise was a group of companies used to manage weapons sales to Iran and delivery to the contras. It was the organization that controlled secret bank accounts in Switzerland that received contributions from private citizens and friendly governments. It was run like a business, but it was used for political purposes. It came as close as anything might come to CIA Director Bill Casey's dream of an off-the-shelf, self-sustaining, stand-alone entity, which could operate in complete secrecy, and be independent of congressional funds and therefore completely unaccountable to the American people. The Enterprise, as it finally emerged, was a creature of the Reagan administration, but it might well have survived the administration to continue on its own. In reality, such an organization would have no obligation to follow orders from any elected representative of the American people.

General Secord, who headed the Enterprise, was the former head of the Pentagon's foreign military sales program, but his military career had been tarnished by an association with Edwin Wilson, an ex-CIA agent who supplied explosives to Muammar Qaddafi. He was also involved with a company that had overcharged the Pentagon by $8 million for a weapons shipment. He had not been charged in either of these incidents, but they may have contributed to his decision to retire from the Air Force in 1983.[42]

There was considerable conflict between Secord and the contra leaders, who were aware that they were being overcharged by him. Robert Owen was asked by the committee about this in an exchange with Richard Leon, the Deputy Chief Minority Counsel.

Q: Did you discuss with Colonel North the possibility that the contras were being ripped off, defrauded by Secord and other people working down there with Secord?
A: In March of 1986 I made a memo to Colonel North in which I discussed some concerns that people had about the possibility that General Secord was making large profits out of this.
Q: This is, concerns of who?
A: Concerns on the street that I had heard from a variety of sources, and also at one time, I am not sure it was at this point or another point, Adolpho Calero had made mention of it, and at this time in the memo, I put in Tom Clines and several others.[43]

Under questioning by Chief Counsel Arthur Liman and members of the Iran-Contra Committee, it was revealed that $3.5 million in funds had been delivered to the contras, but the Enterprise still retained $8 million. Senator Warren Rudman, vice-chairman of the committee, pushed hard to get Secord to admit that the money belonged to the United States. Secord steadfastly maintained that the money belonged to the Enterprise, but that he might be able to talk his partner, Albert Hakim, into using it to set up a fund to aid the contras. Rudman countered that "in my view . . . that money belongs to the people of the United States, and I will assure you that the Justice Department will make that claim."[44] Senator Sarbanes also pushed Secord on his profiteering. It was revealed that Secord not only kept the lion's share of the profits on the sale of weapons to Iran, but he charged the contras a substantial markup on everything he supplied, including food and medicine.

Senator Sarbanes: If the purpose of the Enterprise was to help the contras, why did you charge Calero a markup that included a profit?
General Secord: We were in business to make a living, Senator. We had to make—we had to make a living. I didn't see anything wrong with it at the time; it was a commercial enterprise.
Senator Sarbanes: Oh, I thought the purpose of the enterprise was to—was to aid Calero's cause.
General Secord: Can't I have two purposes? I did.[45]

Senators William Cohen and George Mitchell, both of whom were members of the committee, were surprised at the way the hearing seemed to play on television. They had assumed the American people would be outraged by the testimony of General Secord. Instead the majority of letters were critical of the Senators who questioned him and particularly of Arthur Liman. The senators reported,

Less than a week into the hearings, thousands of letters, telegrams and phone calls started flooding our offices. They complained about Liman's hair, abrasiveness, and religion. Secord was a patriotic Anglo-American. Liman was a nasty New York lawyer— translate as "New York Jew." . . . The Senate offices of Boren, Trible and Rudman were flooded with angry letters, telegrams and phone calls, berating them for joining forces with "that New York lawyer."[46]

TALKING HIS WAY OUT OF TROUBLE

If General Secord played well on television, Oliver North was the superstar of the hearings. North, like President Reagan, had a unique capacity to triumph over accusations and doubts about his credibility with nothing more than his personality. It wasn't just the words; it was the delivery. Arturo Cruz, Jr. had spotted that charismatic quality in North when they first met. He said that North reminded him of Eden Pastora—a man North hated, but one who had the same capacity for charming others with his words.[47] Many reporters, who are word-smiths themselves, had been struck by North's effective use of words.

The Iran-Contra committee members had already learned that, just because they had the facts on their side, there was no guarantee of public support. The television viewers were reacting very strongly to the physical appearance of the witnesses and to that of the senators and counsel—their accents, their mannerisms. The committee knew that they must not appear to be bullying the witnesses with facts.

North appeared before them, a handsome fellow, in his Marine Corps uniform with a chest full of medals. When he admitted that his operations were kept secret from the American people, John Nields, the Chief Counsel, asked him, "We do live in a democracy, don't we?" When North replied, "Yes, thank God!" there was an emotional quality, a tremor in his voice. This was only the opening salvo, but the Congressmen were aware that they had gotten hold of a phenomenon they could not control.

Despite North's embarrassing admission, during the hearings, that he had lied to General Secord to get him to stay with the project, that he had lied to Congress, and that he had helped to create a false chronology of the events being investigated, he developed a legion of admirers demonstrating for him outside the Russell Senate Office Building. The press reported the total phenomenon—the demonstrations, phone calls, telegrams and letters—as "Ollimania." Surely no one else called before the committee generated such admiration from the public. For this reason he became a difficult witness to question or to prosecute for perjury. After a few days the committee let him have the leash. They allowed him to make lengthy opening statements and to run on at length during his testimony in a blatant display of his ideals and his patriotism, where other witnesses with less public support would have been cut short. He spoke so convincingly that people thought he must be telling the truth—or at least he must believe he was telling the truth.

An excellent example of North's ability to cover the facts with his own convincing display of his virtue and his heroism is seen in the discussion of his home security system. General Secord had paid for the installation of a security system in Colonel North's home. At a later date North typed a bill of sale and backdated it to the time when he was still in the White House, which would indicate that he had paid for it at the time. When Nields asked him if he was aware that Secord had paid for the security system in his home, he gave perhaps his longest answer on record.

I'm going to waffle an answer. I'm going to say yes and no. The issue of the security system was first broached after a threat on my life by Abu Nidal. Abu Nidal is, as I am sure you and the intelligence committees know, the principle foremost assassin in the world today. He is a brutal murderer. . . . (Seven paragraphs later he was still talking without interruption.) I'll be glad to meet Abu Nidal on equal terms anywhere in the world. Okay? There's an even deal for him. But I am not willing to have my wife and my four children meet Abu Nidal on his terms.

He continued on, quoting Abu Nidal from *Der Spiegel* and *Newsweek's* opinion that "For sheer viciousness Abu Nidal has few rivals in the underworld of terrorism." A few paragraphs later he was interrupted by Nields.

Mr.Nields: Wait, before you go to the next—
Lt.Col.North: It is, after all, the answer to your question. It is the answer to your question. You asked me where it came from and I am trying to tell you.
Mr.Nields: I am going to ask you that question, but—
Lt.Col.North: You have already asked me the question. You asked me whether or not the money came from General Secord. I am getting there.
Mr.Nields: All right. Okay.

North continued for another page in the course of which he admitted that the security system was a gift. But he wasn't through yet. His testimony continues.

This April the FBI called and told me that there was another threat on my life. The big difference was this year I was back with a band of brothers that has a long reputation for taking care of its own. And the United States Marine Corps and the Naval Intelligence, Naval Investigative Service of Naval Intelligence, got together and immediately put security on me and my home, where my wife and children are protected.
   I can't tell you how grateful I am for that. The security system that was installed by Mr. Robinette with General Secord's money, or the Enterprise's money, or I don't know whose money, was put in and supplemented enormously by the folks, some of which are sitting in this room right now, some of whom are at my home right now, some of whom drive me around in an armored motorcade that makes it look like a European potentate.
   But the fact is I am grateful for that assistance, beyond measure. Because when you think about what could happen, when somebody like that is out to kill you and doesn't care if he takes out your children with you, you run out of options in a big hurry. I ran

out of options . . . I admit to making a serious, serious judgement error in what I then did to paper it over and I'm willing to sit here and admit to that.[48]

Later he admitted that he lied to Congress, but he implied that it was only because Congress was full of leaks and they could not be trusted with the important information he possessed. He was so deft at the long self-serving speech and the indirect accusation, that Senator Inouye, chairman of the Senate Committee, felt called upon to give his own speech. He defended himself by mentioning that he, too, had a few medals, one of them the highest decoration that can be given to a nonmilitary person. He talked of the fine reputation of the committee in not allowing any leaks. He assured Colonel North that this committee could be trusted. But he, like Colonel North, was actually talking to the cameras.

Bud McFarlane watched the whole show on television. He was recovering from a suicide attempt following the revelation of the Iran-Contra affair and his own role in recommending the initial contact with Iranian leaders. He watched Oliver North shrug off his responsibility for what he had done on the grounds that he was acting under orders. McFarlane was not a man who took responsibility lightly. He had been the only one to testify without immunity. He felt acutely his own responsibility in the affair, but he was even more deeply wounded by the implication that he had approved North's actions.

Watching his performance on television, I felt as though I were being stabbed, over and over again, straight in the heart. Revelation followed revelation until my head was swimming. North's testimony revealed, first of all, that he had lied to me, all through 1984 and 1985. When he had flat-out denied raising money for the contras, he had lied. Willfully and knowingly. He had not only raised money for them, he had set up, without my approval or my knowledge, an off-the-shelf enterprise with Dick Secord to funnel funds and weapons to the contras.

But the worst, the unkindest cut of all, was that he claimed that he had done all this with my knowledge and approval.[49]

Oliver North professed to dislike the glare of publicity. He complained of the public hearings because they revealed the nation's secrets and he said it would have been much better to hold the meetings in private. In reality he made effective use of the hearings and took advantage of the freedom that he would not have had in a court of law or in a private hearing.

There were those who felt North was not really concerned with secrecy and that he enjoyed the public attention. Several memos in the records of the Tower Commission suggest his colleagues on the NSC staff felt he should be more cautious in his conversations. Admiral Poindexter warned him, on May 15, 1986, that he was allowing his operational role to become too public. Arturo Cruz, Jr. suggests that, despite North's care in sending encrypted messages, he may have been a bit too open in private conversations:

Many of us already felt that North was bound to get caught, not because we understood the system better than he did but because North was always willing to sacrifice his body for the sake of the team. I also suspected North wanted everything to unravel. How else would the world ever know of his great conspiracies? The one aspect of his job North disliked was his own anonymity. He feared that no one appreciated his genius."[50]

There was a theatrical quality about both North and Reagan. Both men wanted to do something brave and valiant for their country, whether the country needed it or not. The hearings called on Oliver North's greatest talent, his capacity to play the hero he believed himself to be. When the minority counsel, Mr. Van Cleve, reminded him that the Neutrality Act prohibits the organization of military expeditions from the United States against countries with which we are at peace, North assured him that he was familiar with the act. Then Van Cleve asked North if he and General Secord "scrupulously tried to comply with the Neutrality Act in setting up and running the contra resupply operation," North replied "absolutely." The testimony continues:

Mr.Van.Cleve: Did you ever request, direct or otherwise participate in the shipment of arms from the United States to Central America as part of the covert contra resupply operation?
Lt.Col.North: Never. . . . I will tell you absolutely, categorically, there was never a single bullet, rifle any piece of ordinance that I know of, that was shipped from the United States of America as a part of the covert operation that I was coordinating or managing or directing.[51]

Oliver North's advocates and supporters saw him making that statement before the committee in his Marine uniform with the medals on his chest and the sincere expression in his eyes. They believed every word of it.

IMMUNITY

On March 11, 1988, Robert McFarlane pleaded guilty to charges that he had misled Congress and withheld information. On March 16 Independent Counsel, Lawrence Walsh announced a twenty-three count indictment of North, Hakim, Secord, and Poindexter. They were charged with conspiring to defraud the U.S. by establishing and concealing a plan for illegally supporting the contras. However, since the four men had testified under immunity, none of their testimony could be used as evidence in the trial. It was difficult to prove that other evidence had been developed in complete independence from any knowledge of their previous testimony. None of the men served a long prison term (although Poindexter did get three concurrent six-month sentences). However, the inability to convict them on the major counts gave the impression that they were innocent of some of the more serious charges. For example, Oliver North was found guilty of aiding and abetting an obstruction of Congress, of destroying White House documents, and of receiving an illegal gratuity. He was sentenced to two years probation, fined $150,000, and ordered to perform 1,200 hours community service. A federal court overturned most of the charges against North and Poindexter as well. Of course Poindexter's usurpation of presidential authority, in making the decision to divert funds from the weapons sales to Iran to the support of the contras—a charge to which he freely confessed—was clearly a major crime, but it was made under immunity from prosecution and it could not be proved with independent evidence.

Was it a mistake to grant immunity? Probably not. The willingness of all witnesses (except Robert McFarlane) to take the Fifth Amendment if they were not granted immunity was amply demonstrated before the hearings began. Knowing how the government of the United States had actually been subverted by the president and some of his closest advisors was more important than prosecuting the conspirators. It is highly unlikely that the prosecution could have developed the information without the confession of the participants. And it was important that all the information be made public.

NOTES

1. L. Cockburn, *Out of Control: The Story of the Reagan Administration's Secret War in Nicaragua, The Illegal Arms Pipeline, and the Contra Drug Connection,* (New York: Atlantic Monthly Press, 1987), p. 12.

2. A. Cruz, Jr., *Memoirs of a Counterrevolutionary,* (New York: Doubleday, 1989), p. 180.

3. J. Tower, E. Muskie, and B. Scowcroft, *The Tower Commission Report* (New York: Bantam, 1987), p. 451

4. Ibid., p. 453.

5. R. C. McFarlane, *Special Trust* (New York: Cadell and Davies, 1994), p. 351.

6. Ibid., p. 78.

7. Ibid., p. 68.

8. Ibid., p. 28.

9. O. L. North, *Under Fire: An American Story* (New York: Harper Collins, 1991), pp. 218-221.

10. Ibid., p. 212.

11. McFarlane, *Special Trust,* p. 352.

12. Ibid., p. 460.

13. Ibid.

14. "Carter Pulled Rug from Under Somoza:Buchanan" *Los Angeles Times,* March 4, 1986, p.2.

15. Tower, Muskie, Scowcroft, *Tower Commission Report,* p. 502.

16. *Report of the Congressional Committee Investigating the Iran-Contra Affair,* appendix D, vol. 3, U.S. Senate Select Committee on Securing Military Assistance to Iran and the Nicaraguan Opposition, (Washington, D.C.: US Government Printing Office, 1988), p. 1382.

17. Ibid., p.1370.

18. North, *Under Fire,* p. 192.

19. D. T. Regan, *For the Record,* (New York: Harcourt, Brace, Javanovich, 1988), p. 36.

20. Ibid., p. 37.

21. Ibid., pp. 33-42.

22. *Joint Hearings Before the Senate Select Committe on Secret Military Assistance to Iran and the Nicaraguan Opposition and the House Select Committe to Investigate Covert Arms Transactions with Iran,* One Hundredth Congress, First Session, 100-7, Part I, July 7-10, 1987, testimony of Oliver L. North (Questioning by Counsels), (Washington, D.C.: U.S. Govt. Printing Office, 1988), p. 300.

23. North, *Under Fire,* pp. 12-13.

24. R. W. Reagan, *An American Life,* (New York: Simon and Schuster, 1990), p. 523.

25. North, *Under Fire,* p. 14.

26. *Report of the Congressional Committee Investigating the Iran-Contra Affiar,* appendix D, vol. 4, (Washington, D.C.: U.S. Government Printing Office, 1988), p. 2083.

27. Ibid., p. 2095.

28. *Joint Hearings Before the Senate and House Committees,* First Session, 100-7, Part I, pp. 91-93.

29. Reagan, *An American Life*, pp. 484-485.

30. *Congressional Committee Investigating the Iran-Contra Affair*, Appendix B, Volume 20, p. 863.

31. Ibid., Appendix D, Volume 3, p. 1993, Memo from Robert Owen to Oliver North.

32. Cockburn, *Out of Control*, p.10, ref. note p. 255. Released by Iran-Contra committees.

33. Cockburn, *Out of Control*, p 159. See also her endnote regarding article on the contras bank by Dan Morgan in the *Washington Post*, April 21, 1987.

34. "Contras: Cliff-Hanging." *Economist*, March 14, 1987, p.40.

35. Cockburn, *Out of Control*, p. 154.

36. Cockburn, *Out of Control*, p. 155.

37. Cockburn, *Out of Control*, pp. 172-174.

38. *Frontline* report: "Guns, Drugs and the CIA," produced by Leslie and Andrew Cockburn. May 1988.

39. Ibid.

40. Ibid.

41. Ibid.

42. W. S. Cohen, and G. J. Mitchell, *Men of Zeal*, (New York: Viking, 1988), p. 68.

43. *Congressional Committee Investigating the Iran-Contra Affair*, Appendix B, Volume 20, p. 707. Part of a deposition by Robert Owen.

44. *Joint Hearing on the Iran-Contra Investigation*, 100-1, 1987, p. 266.

45. Ibid. p. 273.

46. Cohen and Mitchell, *Men of Zeal*, p. 75-76.

47. Cruz, *Memoirs*, pp. 178, 226.

48. *Joint Hearings Before the Senate and House Committees*, First Session, 100-7, Part I, pp. 129-133.

49. McFarlane, *Special Trust*, p. 350.

50. Cruz, *Memoirs,* p. 226.

51. *Joint Hearings Before the Senate and House Committees,* First Session, 100-7, Part I, p. 210.

9

LOSING STATURE IN
THE PHILIPPINES

The confusion of statesmanship with personal friendship is one of the major dangers for an American president in the conduct of foreign policy. If he can turn to his secretary of state for an independent opinion, he may find help in the shaping of a policy that is in the best interest of his country. Conversely, if he has a national security advisor in the White House who is more interested in doing his bidding than in providing independent advice on policy, the president is cut off from an important source who might be able to warn him when his personal friendship is getting in the way of policy. This problem developed in the relationship between President Carter and the Shah of Iran. Ronald Reagan had a similar problem in his relationship with President Marcos of the Philippines.

In the Philippines of the late 1980s, for many years a so-called "showcase of democracy," another American-supported dictator, Ferdinand Marcos, was threatened with replacement by a democratic opponent. Considering the embarrassment that Marcos had represented to the United States for so many years, it might have been a relief if he were replaced. But a leading theoretician of the Republican party, Jeane Kirkpatrick, had accused President Carter of losing Nicaragua and Iran because he failed to support an authoritarian regime that was pro-American. Reagan had endorsed this opinion. By the standards of Jeane Kirkpatrick in her famous *Commentary* article[1] it would seem President Reagan, as a good conservative, should stand by his strongman. Marcos was certainly pro-American and violently anti-communist. The problem was that he had developed a system of repression and corruption that rivaled that of Somoza, since he declared martial law in 1972. His army had grown from 60,000 to 200,000 men—all in the name of fighting communism. In 1977 a U.S. State Department report to Congress said the Marcos regime was violating human rights. In that same year the International Commission of Jurists reported the use of torture and denial of free elections, free speech, and habeas corpus. Civil rights organizations failed to find any justification for Marcos's continuation of martial law, except to support his personal power through military control.

That sort of thing had not stopped President Reagan in his support of the government of El Salvador, but in the Philippines the government opponent, Corazon Aquino, had squeaky-clean democratic credentials. Her husband, Benigno Aquino, had been a Philippine senator and the chief democratic opponent of Marcos before he was murdered by government soldiers in 1983. His widow was now seeking public office. Unlike the leaders who had replaced Somoza in Nicaragua and the shah of Iran, she was strongly pro-American and democratic in her political orientation. It should have been an easy choice, but Reagan, remembering his "old friend" President Marcos, found it very difficult.

It was not only the friendship of the two presidents, but the long association between the United States and the Philippines, that seemed to require some kind of response to the developing situation. We have to look back to the Spanish-American war to uncover the many ties that bind us to the politics of the Philippines.

THE UNITED STATES IN THE PHILIPPINES

The Philippines consists of a vast archipelago of over 7,000 islands covering 1,000 square miles. The islands were first "discovered," as far as Europe was concerned, in 1521 by Ferdinand Magellan, who was at the time in search of a southwest passage to Asia through America. Magellan, a Portuguese, was employed by Spain with a crew that was mostly Spanish. He was killed in a conflict and did not return to Seville, but his crew brought back a record of his exploits and his heroism in combat.

King Charles of Spain took possession of Magellan's prize, sending ships, soldiers, and Catholic priests to "pacify" the region. The islands were named after Philip, the Spanish crown prince who was appointed regent at the time. Spanish rule lasted over three centuries, but it was concentrated mainly in the lowland areas of Luzon and the Visayan Islands.

By the nineteenth century, as a result of trade and contact with the outside world, an elite society was organized among the Filipinos, who demanded more native friars in the church and a role in the government. Their group was known by a long and complex Filipino name which is often shortened to *Katipunan* or KKK. They aroused considerable fear among the colonists and, as rumors were circulated about their activities, they were persecuted by the authorities and set upon by Spanish vigilantes. As Spain resisted their demands, the Katipunan began to engage in sabotage, assassination, and printing pamphlets calling for total independence. There were open battles between KKK guerrillas and Spanish troops.

On the Filipino side, Emilio Aguinaldo y Famy emerged as a skilled tactician and became the leader of the Filipino nationalist forces. He was also a member of the KKK. Aguinaldo was aware of the revolutionary movement in Cuba, Spain's major possession in the Caribbean, and the extent to which it had disturbed American commerce in the area. American newspapers were filled with accounts of Spanish brutality in Cuba. Public opinion in the United States was aroused and it was apparent that war was imminent. Aguinaldo sought to take advantage of the situation in hope of securing freedom from Spanish rule, when and if war erupted. Making contact with the American embassy in Hong Kong through his agent, Filipe Agoncillo, he sought help for the cause of Philippine independence. While the United States avoided a direct commitment, government officials used some of Aguinaldo's complaints about Spanish repression as further stimulus to pro-war sentiment.

After the outbreak of the Spanish-American War on April 25, 1898, Aguinaldo and his men were asked to supply intelligence and to aid the Americans in the capture of Manila. Aguinaldo sought assurance from officers under the command of Commodore George Dewey that the United States would support Philippine independence. He was given vague statements to the effect that the Americans would arm them and support their cause. When he asked for the guarantees in writing he was told that the United States was a big country and had nothing to gain by an occupation of the Philippines.

He was also given assurance by E. Spencer Pratt and Rounsevelle Wildman of the U.S. Consular Service that the United States would support Philippine independence. Both men took money from him as a commission on future arms to be sent to Filipino nationalists— arms that were never delivered.   Wildman was later lost at sea and Pratt was scolded by Secretary of State William Day for exceeding his authority.[2] He was later dismissed from his post.

Following a telegram from Dewey to Pratt, urging Aguinaldo to join his squadron in Hong Kong, Aquinaldo boarded ship to meet Dewey. When he arrived, Dewey had already left for his famous victory over the Spanish armada at Manila Bay.   After his celebrated naval victory, Dewey, who needed the support of Aguinaldo and his troops to wipe out Spanish resistance on the land, sent for him and agreed to a talk. The two men met at Manila Bay on May 19, 1898. Aguinaldo was pleased to have the opportunity to fight side-by-side with the Americans against the Spanish, but he wanted to be sure that the United States would support Philippine independence. In later testimony about their meeting Dewey claimed that he gave no assurance of Philippine self-government. As to why Filipinos would fight on the American side if there were no promises of independence, Dewey maintained that the Filipinos really wanted to become American citizens and therefore were quite eager to receive colonial status. Although both men spoke through interpreters, Aguinaldo insisted that he did have Dewey's word that the Filipino nationalists would be in charge once the Spanish were driven out. As evidence, he cited the actions and directives from the nationalist leaders, assuring their followers that the Americans would support independence, as well as news reports at the time of their meeting.[3]

Aguinaldo's troops encircled Manila and attacked Spanish fortifications, interrupting the supply of food and ammunition. He soon discovered that the Americans had made an agreement with the Spanish to keep the Filipino insurgents out of Manila and that they would not participate in a Spanish surrender. As the American forces arrived and forbade Filipino troops from entering Manila it soon became apparent that the Filipinos would not be in control of their own country. Summing up his encounter with the Americans, Aguinaldo remarked,

To us Filipinos, she [America] made studiedly vague verbal offers of friendship and aid and then fairly drowned them with the boom of cannons and the rattle of Gatling guns. I was 29 and, as President of the First Philippine Republic, and Generalissimo of its forces, I was desperately fighting to keep America from occupying my Motherland. We had just liberated her from the tyranny of benighted Spain which had enslaved us for over three centuries. But due to America's intervention our triumph was suddenly becoming our defeat.[4]

After the Spanish had been driven from Manila, Aguinaldo declared Philippine independence on June 12, 1898. But on December 10 the Treaty of Paris between the Spanish and Americans gave the United States full control of the Philippines. American troops were now arriving in force in the area in and around Manila. As they came in direct contact with Filipinos the friction between the two groups was augmented by racism on the part of the Americans. They were contemptuous of the Filipinos, calling them Niggers or Gugus. As the bad feelings intensified there were frequent incidents.

On February 4, 1899, two American privates, William Walter Grayson and Orville Miller, were stationed in a suburb of Manila. In a patrol of their camp they shot three Filipino soldiers from a nearby barracks who failed to respond to their challenge. Private Grayson described it this way:

I yelled "Halt!" . . . The man moved. I challenged him with another "Halt." Then he immediately shouted "Halto" to me. Well I thought the best thing to do was to shoot him. He dropped. Then two Filipinos sprang out of the gateway about fifteen feet from us. I called "Halt" and Miller fired and dropped one. I saw that another was left. Well, I think I got my second Filipino that time. We retreated to where our six other fellows were and I said, "Line up, fellows, the niggers are in here all through these yards."

We then retreated to the pipe line and got behind the water work main and stayed there all night. It was some minutes after our second shots before Filipinos began firing.[5]

Aguinaldo sent a ranking member of his staff to General Otis the next day to tell him that the firing had been against his orders and that he wished to stop further hostilities. According to Aguinaldo, Otis replied, "The fighting, having begun, must go on to the grim end."[6] President McKinley took the position that the firing was started by the Filipinos: "They assailed our sovereignty, and there will be no useless parley, no pause until the insurrection is suppressed and

American authority acknowledged and established."[7]   Said Aguinaldo, "Armageddon was loose—against our desires and in spite of our earnest and sincere efforts to befriend America."[8]

The result of this encounter was a war that lasted over two years and cost the lives of over 4,000 Americans and 16,000 Filipinos. As the situation escalated, the Americans began to lose ground. The local people supported Aguinaldo and the cables from Manila to Washington described an urgent situation for the American troops. In a speech in Boston on February 16, 1899, President McKinley announced that the Filipinos would some day bless the American republic because of all we had done for them. He went on to describe the advantages of an association with the United States.[9] Despite his euphemisms it was clear that the United States was to take charge of the Philippines and create a government managed by Americans.

Aguinaldo was captured on March 23, 1901, but fighting continued until 1903. At the time of Dewey's victory in Manila Bay there was little support in the United States for annexation. We were there as liberators who had come to free the Filipino people from Spanish repression. Even after the battle against the insurgents our occupation authorities took the position that they were preparing the Filipinos for self-government, but the latter were not ready. There is no doubt that the Taft Commission, initiated by McKinley, made major improvements to the educational system in the Philippines installed by the U.S. military. All Filipinos were given an opportunity for public education free of church control. The legal system under the occupation established a version of the American Bill of Rights. But the Americans sought to turn over the reigns of government by coopting the Philippine elite. Wealthy and conservative members of the oligarchy, who could be relied on to go along with the presence of American military bases and trade with American firms, were given positions of authority. This roused considerable resentment among the nationalists. In 1907 the first national election in the Philippines was held, and the Federal party, consisting of American appointees and supporters, was overwhelmingly defeated by the Nacionalista party.

In the United States the Anti-Imperialist League, which had held its first meeting in Boston in November, 1898, took an active role in organizing support for Philippine independence. It included former president Grover Cleveland; Karl Schurz, who had served as Lincoln's envoy to Spain and was prominent in the German Community; George Boutwell, a former governor of Massachusetts; Andrew Carnegie; and other distinguished leaders of public opinion. With the repudiation of the Federalist party they intensified their campaign for genuine Philippine self-government. Various American officials such as Governor General Francis Burton Harrison, appointed in 1913, greatly increased Filipino control of the government, to the extent that he angered the local colonial officials who accused him of being the "plaything and catspaw of the leaders of the Nacionalista Party."[10]   As the Nacionalista party became stronger, the Filipino oligarchy began to invade it and take over positions of power and influence. Corruption and bribery of officials became a problem. In 1934 the Commonwealth of the Philippines was established, with the Philippine Senate replacing the role of the appointed members of the Philippine Commission and a president elected by popular vote.

In the struggle for Philippine sovereignty, the issues of American military bases and the dominance of American firms in Philippine trade became major sticking points. Another thorn in the side of the poor and the tenant middle class was the continued possession of most of the land by the Philippine elite. Luis Quezon, the first president of the Philippine Commonwealth, defeated his rival, Sergio Osmeña, in the election of September 1935, by claiming Osmeña had given the Americans much too favorable trade terms and that he had jeopardized Philippine sovereignty by allowing American bases to remain on Philippine land. In the elections to follow, these two points were obligatory items in a presidential campaign.

Following the Japanese attack on the Philippines, which began directly after Pearl Harbor on December 8, 1941, Americans and Filipinos marched together to Bataan and Corregidor and later, after their surrender, many of them died together in the forced march to prison camps in the north. Later, the Philippine resistance movement was instrumental in limiting Japanese control to only twelve of the forty-eight provinces, reducing the casualties for allied U.S. and Filipino forces in retaking the islands.

INDEPENDENCE

On July 4, 1946, the United States honored its pledge to liberate the Philippines. It was the first time in history that a colonial power had voluntarily relinquished one of its territories. However, the ceremony on the reviewing stand—the speech by General MacArthur, the playing of the American and Philippine anthems, the lowering of the Stars and Stripes followed by the raising of the Philippine flag—was more of a symbolic gesture than a genuine transfer of power. The large land owners of the Filipino oligarchy and several prominent American officials such as United States High Commissioner Paul McNut, had maintained that the Philippines were not yet ready for independence.

From a political standpoint the mechanism for a handover of sovereignty had been in place since the inauguration of the commonwealth. While Philippine politics had always been marred by violence and corruption, there was a two-party system with an elected president and a Philippine House and Senate. However, the Philippine economy was in an appalling state following the war and more dependent on the United States than before the conflict began.

Nevertheless, everyone seemed to realize that the symbolism was extremely important. The Jones Act of 1916 promised that the United States would grant independence as soon as a stable government was established. While no date had been set, the majority of Filipinos had demonstrated their desire for self-government. Filipino resistance groups had played a central role in resistance to the Japanese. Psychologically, this was the dramatic moment. Many Filipino leaders felt that if they did not get independence now, there might not be another opportunity.

The new president was Manuel Roxas, the favorite of General Douglas MacArthur, U.S. commander for the Philippines. Roxas was a member of the Filipino elite, one of the powerful clans that had been prominent in Philippine society before the beginning of U.S. rule. In March 1947, with the approval of the Military Bases Agreement, a U.S. Military Advisory Group was established to supervise and monitor the training of the Philippine armed forces. Just as Somoza sent his contingent of troops to aid Americans in their wars, a Philippine detachment was sent to Korea in 1950.

In many respects American rule of the Philippines continued, much as it had before independence. MacArthur had many friends among the Filipino oligarchy. He awarded them favors and they were compliant and supportive of his policy, just as they had been with the Spanish.   By 1950, living conditions for poor Filipinos had not improved significantly since the beginning of the American occupation, while the members of the oligarchy were consolidating their power and wealth through corruption and outright theft.   Sterling Seagrave, an American reporter, described the post-war corruption:

Everybody was on the make. Millions of dollars worth of consumer goods flowed into Manila just for the maintenance of the U.S. Army. One quarter of these goods ended up on the black market. GIs working with civilians sidetracked trucks, powdered milk, pistols, stockings, typewriters, and cigarettes. Two months after Yamashita's surrender, over $1 million in government-owned goods were seized when police broke up a Manila ring. After that it became serious. . . .

From the turn of the century America's involvement with its pacific colony had been composed of halfway measures—grand designs without adequate follow-through, democratic institutions without checks and balances, permissiveness without restraint, financial aid without accountability, cunning manipulation masked by expressions of virtue—all engineered with the help of agreeable men lacking in principle. America sought out and encouraged a tiny group of leaders who were servile toward their masters, ruthless among their own kind, and contemptuous of all those beneath them. The colonial experiment was doomed by its own hand, a form of suicidal opportunism. After setting such an example for half a century—"fifty years in a brothel"—it is no wonder that corruption had eager understudies waiting in the wings.[11]

The poor peasants and workers could not help seeing the evidence of growing wealth and corruption all around them, while they were cut out of any share of the largess.   As a result, hostility and distrust of the government were on the rise.   The Hukbalahap movement had learned to exploit this feeling to gain new recruits and attack government installations.

Originally the Hukbalahap movement was a small peasant rebellion. It grew because American and Philippine officials ignored the complaints of tenant farmers and the rural poor.   When MacArthur came to the Philippines in 1935 as field marshall for the Philippine forces, the local officials told him that the movement was led by Communists. It is unlikely that this was true at the time. Luis Taruc, the Huk leader, did not join the communist party until four years after MacArthur arrived.[12] As a loosely organized group of peasants that sought to drive out the Americans, the Huk armed themselves as best they could and engaged in sabotage and civil disruption. However, as their movement grew and their political sophistication increased, they soon discovered that the best way to get help in fighting the Americans was to call yourself a Communist and contact the Soviet Union or China. It was inevitable, if the Philippine and American authorities continued to ignore their demands and engaged in brutal repression of their people, that the Huks would soon be led by Communists. Communist states provided not only weapons and financial support, but an ideology that was opposed to capitalism, which had come to represent the United States.

It was impossible to gain a foothold in Filipino politics without American support. Filipinos were avid followers of the American press, and politicians were acutely aware of the importance of a favorable opinion from Washington. Ramon Magsaysay was a hero of the Philippine resistance movement against the Japanese. This, in itself, would seem to provide important credentials for a career in politics. But when Magsaysay sought political power, his first step was a trip to Washington "to seek benefits for Filipino war veterans." There he had a fortunate meeting with Edward Lansdale, a lieutenant colonel in the Air Force on loan to the super-secret Office of Policy Coordination, which later became part of the CIA. Lansdale was impressed with Magsaysay's credentials and took charge of his political career. In 1953, Magsaysay became President of the Philippines with the help of the CIA.

In view of previous CIA candidates, Magsaysay proved to be a fortunate choice. He invited peasants and workers to visit the presidential palace and solicited their comments on his government. He expanded the infrastructure of the country and took military action against the Huk guerilla movement, greatly reducing the threat to his administration. But he roused the anger of the Philippine elite with his proposal for land redistribution. He pressured the legislature to pass the Land Reform Act and set up a program for the purchase of private land and its sale to tenant farmers. In 1955, through a revision of the trade agreement with the United States, he put an end to American authority to control the exchange rate of the Philippine peso. He impressed the Filipino people with his honesty and with his understanding of the problems of social and economic injustice. He restored their faith in government. He was on his way to making further major reforms when he was killed in an airplane crash in Cebu in March 1957.

THE RISE OF MARCOS

Ferdinand Marcos was elected president of the Philippines in December 1965 by a margin of 650,000 votes, after an anticorruption campaign marked by violence, a common feature of Philippine elections. He called for a program of austerity to control the runaway budget and he sought international loans to support the economy. As a member of the Nationalist party he called for a shortening of the ninety-nine-year lease of the American bases. When elected, he negotiated an agreement to reduce the American occupancy to twenty-five years starting in 1966, but he made up for his pressure on the United States by declaring his friendship and his belief in democracy as well as his opposition to communism. To prove his point, he sent a contingent of 2,000 army engineers and other noncombatant security forces to build roads and bridges for the Americans in South Vietnam. However, this time the legislature did not simply rubber stamp the president's support of American foreign policy. Marcos tried to downplay the military nature of his contingent by calling it the Philippine Civic Action Group. Nevertheless, there was intense and heated opposition in the Philippine Senate.

As Marcos continued in power, corruption continued unabated and in 1971 half the wealth in the country was in the hands of 5 per cent of the people. Marcos maintained his strong stand against communism, but he began to use it as a reason for many restrictions on civil liberties. Political rallies were marked by violent bombings and shootings. After a grenade attack on a political rally in Manila in August 1971, which Marcos blamed on the Communists, he suspended *habeas corpus* and threatened to impose martial law if necessary to stop the Communist menace.

The major change in the Philippines occurred in 1972. After a period of popular unrest, street protests, a declining economy, and an increasingly hostile press, President Marcos declared martial law on September 23, 1972. From that point on he ruled by decree, closing down all newspapers and reopening them slowly with strict government censorship, prohibiting all street demonstrations and political rallies. Two months after he declared martial law there were over 6,000 people in detention camps, including students, politicians, journalists, and teachers. Marcos maintained that his reason for declaring martial law was the need to control the Communist insurgency. With such a noble cause there was, of course, no protest from the Nixon administration. However, there was no indication of a date for terminating martial law and it continued through 1985.

Fortunately, the U.S. Department of State had been following the political situation in the Philippines. State's Bureau of Intelligence and Research (INR) was aware of the small, fledgling Communist movement, the NPA (New People's Army), and had concluded that it did not justify a declaration of martial law. In January, 1973 after Marcos had organized a "citizens assembly" with voting by a show of hands while soldiers circulated among the crowds, INR noted that Marcos had "dropped the trappings of constitutionality which had hindered his regime," and concluded, "The present outlook is that the longer he remains in power, the more likely it is that Philippine politics will be characterized by a climate of polarization and disarray which will not be conducive to American interests and the stability of base agreements."[13] This report was a clear refutation, even at this early date, of the notion that American interest consisted of supporting the authoritarian strongman, provided he was pro-American. But the report was published during the Nixon-Kissinger era and nothing was done to try to restrain the Marcos regime.

However, the State Department has a number of career foreign service personnel who followed the Marcos regime over a number of years as he increased his grip on the Philippines and suppressed all political opposition. The Carter administration was critical of his failures in the area of human rights, but the Reagan administration turned things around. George Bush went to Manila in 1981 and delivered a toast to President Marcos, citing his adherence to democratic principles and to the democratic process. By 1985 the Philippines was in a state of severe economic decline. A consensus developed within the U.S. State Department that Marcos could not continue to govern with the extreme autocratic methods that he showed no indication of changing. Despite repression in the Philippines, the country had a strong business class that served as a potential source of support for a more democratic candidate, if Marcos would ever permit elections. The department continued the pressure on Marcos for reforms and for free elections. State also supported the International Monetary Fund, which suspended loans to the Philippines and threatened to cancel a $14 billion rescheduling agreement, if Marcos did not break up the sugar and coconut monopolies of his friends. In late 1985 he called a presidential election for February 7, 1986.

MARCOS IN TROUBLE

Perhaps his first surprise was the support of the business community for his opponent, Corazon Aquino, the wife of a former Philippine senator and vigorous opponent of the Marcos regime. Senator Aquino had been assassinated while in the care of representatives of the Marcos government.

Corazon Aquino put forth many populist proposals, calling for energy taxes and suggesting that she would institute protectionist measures in Philippine trade. Both of these proposals upset her supporters, but they looked upon her as the only way to break out of the years of economic decline that they saw ahead of them if Marcos remained in power. She had many other supporters—students, religious leaders, and journalists—many of whom desperately wanted a change of government and who turned to her as a more reasonable alternative than the Communist NPA.

She also had a great deal of popular support in the United States. But it was the U.S. State Department, rather than the Reagan White House that began to see her as the hope for restoring democracy in the Philippines and thus preventing a successful Communist revolution. Even as Mrs. Aquino was preparing her campaign the State Department was preparing its annual survey of human rights practices around the world. Summary executions and torture were still features of the Marcos administration and they sped up work on the document for an early release. On January 25, 1986 the polls in the Philippines gave her 60 per cent of the vote.

Marcos, perhaps hoping he could count on the Reagan administration for support, asked for American observers of the election process. On January 30, President Reagan announced he would send a delegation from the United States, headed by his conservative friend, Senator Richard Lugar. Aquino, increasingly aware of the importance of American opinion, changed her mind about closing the American military bases and announced that, if she won, they could continue in operation until the lease expired in 1991. On January 2, 1986, she had said she would be pleased by the support of the Communist NPA and might find a way to include them in the government. After this remark set off shock waves among her friends in the United States, she spoke in terms of a cease fire and vowed to fight the Communists with all her resources if they continued their opposition to the Philippine government.

Corazon Aquino had led consistently in the polls, and students of past elections believed that Marcos would have to rig the elections in a very obvious way if he was going to win. The rigging began long before election day. Marcos introduced a new voter registration list five weeks before the election. New voters had to provide four photographs in addition to filling out lengthy forms. Many people who were registered to vote in Manila and other districts where Aquino was strong were simply taken off the list of qualified voters. Other voters were assigned a polling place far from their homes. Nevertheless, when election day arrived, the turnout was heavy. As February 7 came to a close there was blood in the streets, but the count was far from complete. On February 8, 1986, the tally was still not complete, but the evidence of fraud was everywhere. Election clerks were wearing Marcos t-shirts. At a rural polling place, election monitors complained that 4,000 blank ballots had disappeared. In other areas the poll- watchers had been frightened away by government troops. Prominent Aquino supporters were severely beaten. In one place the troops left the local head of Marcos's party in charge of the ballot boxes. Reporters who tried to visit polling places were stopped by troops and some of them were roughed up. As the reports of abuses, beatings, and systematic harassment mounted, Senator Richard Lugar, angered by the open and blatant cheating that he had seen and heard from his observers, accused the Marcos government of fraud. He said the vote count was being deliberately held up.[14]

On February 10 the vote count was still not complete, but President Reagan tried to remain neutral. In an interview with reporters from the *Washington Post* he was pressed to say something about the Marcos fraud, which was now being reported in all the papers, including the remarks of Senator Lugar, his own personal representative.

Q: You called for free and fair elections. How does the United States respond to these reports of fraud from our observers, and can Marcos ever again make a claim to legitimacy after this?

The President: Well, I'm going to wait until I have a chance to talk to our observers. I'm sure you know, even elections in our own country—there are some evidences of fraud in places and areas.[15]

His response was very much like Jimmy Carter's comment when he was told about human rights violations in Iran. Yes, said Carter, "but we have human rights violations in this country too." In fact, there is a remarkable parallel between the way Carter handled the fall of the shah and Somoza and the way President Reagan dealt with the demise of Marcos. American presidents have traditionally resisted any change in authoritarian regimes—even in dictatorships—if the leadership favors American economic and military relationships. As I have already indicated, the U.S. State Department, as a result of a long-term study of the situation, had already concluded that a continuation of the Marcos regime would not be in the best interest of the United States. Secretary of State George Shultz had been trying to pave the way for major political change in Manila for several years. As the dictatorial nature of the regime became more obvious, Americans were perceived as the supporters of Marcos and many of his acts were blamed on "American Imperialism."

On February 11, 1986, the vote count was still far from complete and it was now obvious that it was being held up to give Marcos a chance to rig it further. One can judge, from this long delay, how overwhelming must have been the initial vote for Corazon Aquino, despite the new registration requirements and voting district changes. Senator Lugar had returned to the Unites States and reported his findings to the president, but Reagan still could not bring himself to condemn Marcos. He made a cautious announcement that, since the votes were not yet counted, it would not be appropriate for him to render a judgement.

Even Senator Lugar had been hushed up by the president after his return. When questioned by reporters, he cautioned that we did not know, just yet, who won the election and he did not want to make any comments that might give Marcos a chance to say we had scuttled him. Privately, members of his delegation said Lugar was angered by Reagan's statements, which suggested there was still a two-party system in the Philippines and that Mrs. Aquino might work within the Marcos government. Within a few days Lugar became an outspoken advocate of U.S. support for Aquino. Members of Congress were also getting ahead of the president. Representative Thomas Foley predicted there would be a move by Congress to cut off foreign aid funds if Marcos persisted in holding up the vote.

Finally, President Reagan decided to send Ambassador Philip Habib to Manila to investigate once again. He was still refusing to pass a final judgment on the election. Later that day he made the impromptu remark in a news conference, regarding the election fraud, that "it could have been that all of that was occurring on both sides."

CORIZON AQUINO FIGHTS BACK

Corazon Aquino was becoming distressed by the President Reagan's hesitation to condemn the obvious fraud by Marcos and by Reagan's suggestion that she might be just as guilty. Marcos was now reported as being ahead in the vote count and she was fearful that Reagan would allow him to steal the election from her. She said, "I would wonder at the motives of any friend of democracy who chose to conspire with Mr. Marcos to cheat the Philippine people of their liberation." She threatened to lead a campaign of civil disobedience if she was cheated out of her victory and Philippine church leaders said fifty bishops were holding a meeting to consider joining her.[16] John Chancellor on NBC news remarked, "President Reagan is sending the wrong message to the Philippines who have shown how desperately they want change. The Communists have said that the U.S. can do nothing about Marcos and Reagan is proving them right."

Finally, on February 14, although the vote was still not yet official, it appeared that Marcos was far ahead. The protest, which had been organizing for several days, was now overwhelming. The bishops of the Catholic Church declared the fraud unparalleled and urged support for a campaign of nonviolent resistance against the Marcos government. An independent tally declared Corazon Aquino the winner. Labor unions planned one national strike per week. Mrs. Aquino began holding prayer meetings in different cities, and Marcos accused her of pushing the country toward civil war.

On February 15, Marcos declared himself the winner of the election, but this was clearly only the beginning of the battle against him. On that day the *Economist* of London carried an editorial on Marcos entitled "Now Go," in which it remarked, "The burden of removing Mr. Marcos from power will have to rest on Filipino shoulders, prayer books, and, if necessary, rifles. It will rest easier when President Reagan grasps that Mr. Marcos is the depth-charge that could sink America's Pacific fleet."[17] Several European ambassadors declared that they would boycott the inauguration. West Germany and Spain recalled their ambassadors. At this point President Reagan was virtually alone in his support for Marcos. Not only foreign leaders, but even congressmen from his own party were urging him to drop his "old friend" and accept political reality.

On February 22, Marcos's defense minister, Juan Ponce Enrile and the acting chief of staff of the armed forces, General Fidel Ramos announced their resignations from his government. They cited the many instances of fraud and called on Marcos to step down. That day, through his deputy press secretary, President Reagan announced that the Philippine elections were marred by fraud "perpetuated overwhelmingly by the ruling party." His statement also read that Ambassador Habib was returning from the Philippines and would soon report on his findings.

On February 24, after learning that Marcos was planning an attack on a camp held by forces loyal to Aquino, Reagan made a call (again through his deputy press secretary), this time urging Marcos to stop the violence and adding, "A solution to this crisis can only be achieved through a peaceful transition to a new government." In all of his pronouncements our president had managed to avoid mentioning the name of Corazon Aquino, nor did he say anything positive about her heroic fight against the dictator.

On February 25 it fell to Secretary of State George Shultz to announce the recognition of the Philippine government of Corazon Aquino. Speaking of her struggle, Schultz said, "We pay special tribute to her for her commitment to nonviolence, which has earned her the respect of all Americans. The new government has been produced by one of the most stirring and courageous examples of the democratic process in modern history."[18]

Marcos still tried desperately to find some role for himself in the new government. His only hope in such a move would be some shred of official support from the United States. He called Senator Paul Laxalt, who had visited him the previous October. Laxalt consulted the president and telephoned back to tell Marcos, that any role for him in the Aquino government would be impractical. "I'm so very, very disappointed," said Marcos.

About a month later, on March 21, Mr. Reagan still had not called Mrs. Aquino to personally congratulate her. When asked by a reporter why he had waited so long, the president replied, "I don't think there's been any occasion to, and I don't think that we can say that she's through with the process or the business of getting her government underway and going. And we've maintained contact with her through our ambassadors and others."[19] Perhaps the president was still miffed at Mrs. Aquino for her sharp remarks about him in public, regarding his procrastination in recognizing the legitimacy of her movement. He may also have been a bit embarrassed. Having accused President Carter of undermining the shah of Iran and Somoza in Nicaragua, he now found himself forced to go along with the replacement of his friend, Ferdinand Marcos. In all three cases the impetus for change came from the people and there was little that even such a powerful world figure as the American president could do about it unless he was prepared to order in the Marines.

If the United States had been prepared for a proactive rather than a reactive approach to foreign policy, we might have decided that it would be much better for the advancement of American interest, in both the moral and the practical sense, if the shah, Somoza, and Marcos had all been "undermined" at a much earlier date. In the cases of the shah and Somoza we might have provided encouragement to democratic movements which could replace the authoritarian regimes and short-circuit an antiAmerican revolution. In the Philippines we were fortunate to have Corazon Aquino.

NOTES

1. J. Kirkpatrick, "Dictatorships and Double Standards," *Commentary*, vol. 68, no. 5, November 1979, pp. 34-45.

2. S. Karnow, *America's Empire in the Philippines* (New York: Random House, 1989), pp. 106-138.

3. E. Aguinaldo with V. A. Pacis, *A Second Look at America* (New York: Robert Speller and Sons, 1957), pp. 49-55.

4. Ibid., p. 13

5. Ibid., pp.93-94.

6. Ibid., p. 94.

7. Ibid, p. 94.

8. Ibid., p. 94.

9. Karnow, *America's Empire*, pp. 139-160.

10. F. M. Bunge, ed., U.S. Department of the Army, *Philippines: A Country Study,* Foreign Area Studies, American University, 1983 (Washington, D.C.: U.S. Govt. Printing Office, 1984), p. 31.

11. S. Seagrave, *The Marcos Dynasty* (New York: Harper and Row, 1988), pp.127-28.

12. Ibid., p. 122.

13. Quoted from R. Bonner, *Waltzing with a Dictator* (New York: Random House, Times Books, 1987), p. 136.

14. M. Fineman, "Fraud Widespread in Philippine Vote," *Los Angeles Times*, February 8, 1986, p. 1.

15. Interview with Lou Cannon and David Hoffman of the Washington Post, February 10, 1986, *Public Papers of the Presidents of the United States* (Washington, D.C.: U.S. Government Printing Office, 1986), p. 195.

16. Reuters dispatch, February 12, 1986.

17."Now Go," *Economist*, February 15, 1986, p. 12.

18. Statement of Secretary of State Shultz Announcing United States Recognition of the Philippine Government of President Corazon C. Aquino. February 25, 1986, *Presidential Papers,* 1986, p. 251.

19. Interview with R. W. Apple, Jr., G. M. Boyd, and B. Weintraub of the *New York Times,* March 21, 1986, *Presidential Papers,* 1986, p. 386.

10

THE CIA AND THE NSC

In the previous chapters we have examined a number of crisis situations in American intervention in which the long term interest of the United States was not well-served. I have described this style of intervention as a product of the American character. This does not mean there is nothing we can do about the problem. It might be useful to step back and take a look at some of our government institutions to see if changes could be made which might help to establish a more coherent foreign policy. We also need to have a look at more effective means of monitoring American policy with the goal of keeping it on a single coherent course and avoiding sudden changes due to the whim of a single powerful individual within the administration.

Members of the congressional committee investigating the Iran-Contra affair were shocked to hear National Security Advisor John Poindexter tell them that he had, on his own authority, approved the covert actions of Iran-Contra directed by Oliver North. He did not tell the president what was being done in his name. However, this is not the first time that one or more members of the National Security Council has acted without presidential knowledge or authority. In 1976, the Select Committee to Study Intelligence Operations, chaired by Senator Frank Church, found the NSC had used the concept of "plausible denial" to protect the president. Further, it found that "one means of protecting the President from embarrassment was not to tell him about certain covert operations, at least formally."[1] Bromley Smith, an NSC staffer from 1958 to 1969, told the committee, "the government was authorized to do certain things that the president was not advised of."[2]

The danger of such a policy was clear in the Iran-Contra investigation. The policy of "plausible denial" is intended to be used against foreign accusations or accidental revelations of covert actions. It is not intended for use against a U.S. congressional investigation. The president is accountable to the people who elected him and Congress is the collective representative of the people. Therefore, "plausible denial" should not shield the president from his responsibility to notify Congress of any covert operation. A National Security Decision Directive issued by President Reagan would seem to preclude such action. It states that all covert actions must be approved by the president personally and in writing. How, then, did it happen?

There are two basic problems. First, the Central Intelligence Agency is nominally under the National Security Council, which is part of the Executive Branch of government. However, the full NSC, with all the cabinet-level officers, is convened only by the president. It does not meet on its own and therefore it cannot perform such day-to-day functions as directing and controlling the CIA. Hence, the CIA functions as an independent agency, operating in secret with little direct control except from the director of central intelligence. Congress has created more than one oversight committee in an effort to keep track of CIA activity. But the CIA, a secret organization, generally decides, within its own ranks, what it will tell Congress. The second problem lies within the NSC itself. To understand it in detail, one must understand its origin.

The NSC was established by the Truman administration in 1947. It was seen by President Truman as an aid in the unification of the armed forces and as a single, high-level, agency that could be used in the development and coordination of policy. It consisted of the leadership of various departments of government in addition to the secretaries of the Army, Navy, and Air Force. In 1949 the service secretaries were dropped and represented on the NSC by the secretary of defense. At that time the NSC consisted of the president, the vice-president, the secretaries of state and defense, and the chairman of the National Security Resources Board. The president often deliberated with the members of the NSC, and sometimes they were asked to prepare memo recommendations for him. It was Truman's policy that no recommendations were to be activated until the memo had his signature.

As organized by Truman, the secretary of state was an integral part of the NSC. He advised the president on foreign policy and provided much-needed information on the attitudes of world leaders as well as basic political and economic history of a particular country under discussion. He was also a source of foreign intelligence. However, since 1949, the NSC has been used by some presidents to formulate policy without consulting the State Department. It has become a miniature State Department without the resources of that agency. The NSC has sometimes created tension between the White House and the State Department, to the detriment of both.

President Truman organized a competent NSC staff, which consisted of career government service people without strong political connections.[3] It was his intention that the staff would serve as a continuing organization, not unlike the Civil Service, regardless of what administration was in power. But he did not make it a part of the Civil Service, thus leaving to each succeeding administration discretion to mold and use the NSC staff as the president desired.

At one time the staff had an executive director, but succeeding administrations also appointed an advisor for national security affairs. In certain administrations this position was separate from the director of the NSC staff and at times it replaced the director.

In talking about the NSC, it is important to differentiate between the full NSC, in which the principals are meeting (president, vice-president, secretaries of state, defense, etc.) and the NSC staff, which is there to provide support services. Often the term NSC is used interchangeably. Oliver North, for example, was a member of the staff, but it is clear that in his zeal to implement policy he came close to making policy.

THE CIA

The Central Intelligence Agency was created in 1947 as part of the National Security Act, the same act that gave birth to the NSC. Truman intended the CIA to be under the control of the NSC and to report to that agency according to the intelligence needs levied on it. James F. Byrnes was secretary of state at the time. He agreed to the creation of the CIA over the explicit protest of his undersecretary, Dean Acheson. Acheson was concerned that the State Department had muffed several opportunities to create its own intelligence department. In September 1945 the State Department was augmented by the Research and Analysis branch and the Presentation Branch of the Office of Strategic Services (OSS). It was the beginning of an intelligence collection function within State. But, according to Acheson, this function died almost at once. By 1947 when the CIA was proposed, State had already abdicated its leadership in the field of intelligence.[4]

When George Marshall became secretary of state, Undersecretary Acheson tried again to develop a center for intelligence activities in State. One of his first steps was to urge Marshall to reverse Byrnes's "deplorable decision" to split up the intelligence work among the geographic divisions. Marshall prepared an order on February 6 centralizing the administration of all research and intelligence units, including the regional research divisions in the office of the special assistant to the secretary of state. Acheson's memoirs indicate that he was not satisfied:

Thus a year too late my recommendation to Secretary Byrnes was put into effect and his own unhappy action of the preceding April undone. A year too late because in the meantime events had passed us by. Pressure had developed to strengthen the newly created National Intelligence Authority. This was done in July, 1947 by the creation of the Central Intelligence Agency. I had the gravest forebodings about this organization and warned the President that, as set up, neither he, the National Security Council, nor anyone else would be in a position to know what it was doing or to control it.[5]

Acheson was proved right. Under Eisenhower, Allen Dulles, as director of central intelligence, controlled the CIA on his own authority. From 1953 to

1955 Dulles strayed from the control of the NSC and coordinated project approvals with the Psychological Strategy Board or the Operations Coordination Board.[6] However, he coordinated his work with his brother, John Foster Dulles, who was Eisenhower's secretary of state. The informal controls were effective.

In the early days of the Kennedy administration, Allen Dulles was still DCI and able to dominate U.S. policy on Cuba through his experience with the invasion plans of the previous administration and his knowledge of the CIA. President Kennedy later admitted that he had been intimidated by Dulles's knowledge of the situation and continued with the invasion plans for Cuba against his own better judgement.

However, the CIA is not a warlike monolith that dominates US policy. Like any other organization, its leadership looks for positions of strength. CIA is strongly influenced by the perceived policy and inclination of the administration. President Johnson, desperate for certainty, wanted to know how to end the war in Vietnam by any means possible. But in his desperation, he was drawn by any convincing argument. Having little confidence in political or moral opinions and formal briefings, his Tuesday lunch group was dominated by Defense Department and CIA experts with well-planned statistical presentations. In retrospect, it is clear that Johnson's personality shaped the character of the decision group that surrounded him. It was an in-group in the sense described by Irving Janis, in which members showed their loyalty to Johnson by supporting his Vietnam policy. There was pressure on dissenters to come into line.[7]

Another factor at this time was the personality of Robert McNamara, secretary of defense. McNamara was a strong believer in "hard data," the kind of information that could be supplied by the statisticians from the CIA. The close Defense Department-CIA alliance was a potent influence on Johnson. Vice-President Humphrey tried to offer an alternative to the bombing policy and the sending of additional troops to Vietnam. But in the summer of 1965 he admitted to E. J. Hughes the futility of his efforts:

It is a vain exercise—and an unequal struggle between the State Department and the Defense Department. The boys from State come into the NSC supposedly representing the *political* viewpoint; but the bulk of their arguments in favor of caution are generalities or theories. The fellows from Defense come in armed to the teeth. They have charts and graphs and maps and neat flags to plant all over them. Everything is concrete and specific. "Attack here, bomb there, and we promise this exact result." It is all confident and brisk and overwhelming. And it overwhelms any President looking for hard data to support a decision.[8]

Intelligence organizations are normally cautious. However the CIA contains both an intelligence-gathering function and covert military capabilities. When the military wing of the CIA is strengthened, it tends to dominate the intelligence function. This happens whenever the administration decides on covert military action.

Intervention in Vietnam began with Eisenhower. *The Pentagon Papers* reveals that both the National Intelligence Estimate of August 3, 1954, as well as the recommendation of the Joint Chiefs of Staff, were opposed to American military involvement in Vietnam under prevailing conditions. Eisenhower chose to ignore these warnings and take a chance with limited resources because the potential gains seemed worth the small risk.[9] This proved to be the thin edge of a wedge. Once the Eisenhower administration and the Kennedy and Johnson administrations had committed themselves to intervention in Vietnam, the CIA was fully aboard. Intelligence reports reflected the view of opinion leaders within the administration. The CIA understood that further negative reports about the prospects for a military solution in Vietnam were detrimental to the agency's welfare.

This is only one example in which the CIA gave way to an administration intent on a wrong course of action, shaping its intelligence reports to conform to the president's views. The same thing happened in our adventures in Iran. In this case, however, the involvement of the military wing of the CIA in placing the shah on his throne began a period in which intelligence reports were influenced markedly by the CIA's own covert actions and by its role in the training of SAVAK, the secret police organization of the shah. Despite this initial bias, there was a period during the Kennedy administration when the CIA (reflecting the instructions of President Kennedy) began to make contact with dissident groups and to provide a more objective assessment of the long-range prospects for survival of the Pahlavi regime. There was another change in CIA policy when it picked up on Carter's Christmas speech in praise of the shah and shaped its reports to conform with what it perceived as administration policy.

This is not to say that the CIA has a deliberate and cynical policy of "give the administration what it wants." Within the CIA there are a variety of analyst reports. CIA leadership must summarize these reports and present a single consistent view of a particular situation. One of the factors that influences the decision of the CIA leadership is U.S. policy at the time. High-level government officials do not want to take a position in direct opposition to the president. In this regard the director of central intelligence is no different from other officials. He wants to present a report that will make sense to the administration. Thus, when he sifts through the various reports of his agency looking for the "truth," his view is also shaped by what might be perceived as true. He wants to present an intelligence summary that is not only factual but credible. In this case, "credible" actually means something that is close enough to what the administration already believes so it will not be discarded or ignored. The DCI might describe this as just being practical.

Another factor in shaping CIA reports is the personality of the individual who is appointed DCI. Kissinger describes Richard Helms, a career CIA man, promoted from the ranks to DCI:

Disciplined, meticulously fair and discreet, Helms performed his duties with the total objectivity essential to an effective intelligence service. . . . I respected Helms . . . because of his professional insight and unflappability. He never volunteered policy advice beyond the questions that were asked him, though never hesitating to warn the White House of dangers even when his views ran counter to the preconceptions of the President or of his security adviser. He stood his ground where lesser men might have resorted to ambiguity. . . .

CIA analyses, were not, however, infallible. Far from being the hawkish band of international adventurers so facilely portrayed by its critics, the Agency usually erred on the side of the interpretation fashionable in the Washington Establishment. In my experience the CIA developed rationales for inaction much more frequently than for daring thrusts.[10]

The DCI position was at first downgraded under Nixon because of his suspicion that the CIA was full of liberal intellectuals who opposed him.[11] He did not like Helms, his DCI, and wanted to replace him, but Kissinger objected. Then he tried to keep Helms out of meetings of the National Security Council. Secretary of Defense Melvin Laird objected to this, and Helms eventually joined the NSC meetings as a full participant. On February 17, 1970, a committee was created by National Security Defense Memorandum 40 to specify the conduct of intelligence activities. It was named the 40 Committee after the memorandum. It assigned the DCI responsibility for coordinating and controlling covert operations. His responsibility was to plan these operations while consulting with other "interested agencies or officers on a need-to-know basis."[12]   This gave Helms a wide latitude which he evidently did not abuse.

When president Nixon took office he consolidated the NSC staff under his special assistant for national security affairs, Henry Kissinger. Nixon had little confidence in the State Department and he selected William P. Rogers for the job of secretary of state because he was confident Rogers would not attempt to advise the White House on foreign policy. When Nixon interviewed Rogers, the latter assured him he knew little about foreign affairs. He accepted a subordinate role to Kissinger even before he came to office.[13] Kissinger and Nixon (with the help of Kissinger's hand-picked NSC staff) made foreign policy in the White House with little contact with the other departments of government. Later Kissinger formally took over the position at State as well as his special assistant title and Rogers was ousted from his job.

THE NSC VERSUS THE STATE DEPARTMENT

Kissinger clearly saw that the conflict between national security advisor and secretary of state was a product of the overlapping responsibilities and authority in the two positions. This potential conflict was inherent in the positions regardless of who occupied them. It is demonstrated by the conflict between Zbigniew Brzezinski, President Carter's national security advisor and Cyrus Vance, his secretary of state. The two men began as friends, Brzezinski having recommended Vance for the post at State. The president tended to use his national security advisor as a means of controlling foreign policy from the White House. Brzezinski saw himself as providing tough-minded advice on foreign policy as opposed to the idealistic view from the State Department.[14] There was the usual bickering between Brzezinski and Secretary of State Cyrus Vance. in which Vance accused Brzezinski of sending cables to his ambassadors and undercutting his advice to the president. Even in their arguments Brzezinski always regarded Vance as a gentleman, a man he could respect. But the conflict was intensified by the press, which would seize upon areas of disagreement and portray one of the two men as victorious. Even if they were inclined to agree Brzezinski found that members of his staff urged him to stand up for his rights and not let Vance tread on his turf. He assumed the same thing was happening with Vance and the State Department staff.[15] In a sense, both men had been given the same job and the world was watching to see which one emerged on top.

At no time was the inborn conflict between the position of secretary of state and that of national security advisor more evident than in the Reagan administration. Both of President Reagan's secretaries of state (Alexander Haig and George Shultz) were prominent, decisive men, experienced with command, before they came to the office. Neither was inclined to tolerate another primary foreign policy advisor located in the NSC with immediate access to the president.

The first advisor for national security affairs was Richard Allen, a right-wing Republican noted for his anticommunism, who had been active in the Nixon campaign and served on the NSC staff under Kissinger. When he was given the top position under President Reagan he was in constant conflict with Secretary of State Alexander Haig. Haig saw him as a potential competitor and did not trust him. Allen finally resigned and was replaced by Bill Clark, who had been Haig's deputy. Clark, a former judge and friend of the president, had been a county chairman in Reagan's first political campaign. He was essentially a political appointee. Except for his tour of duty under Haig, he was without extensive education or experience in the field of international relations. The NSC staff consisted of men who did not have broad political education and experience. An exception was Robert McFarlane, who followed Clark as national security advisor. During his tour of duty in the Marine Corps, McFarlane was sent to study international relations at the prestigious Institut de Hautes Etudes in Geneva. He later caught the eye of Kissinger and worked under him at the Nixon NSC. In that position he distinguished himself by his capacity for working long hours and by his tact and discretion in working with Congress. Kissinger appreciated his quiet, unobtrusive style.

The other members of the NSC staff were men used to taking orders. They were mostly military or ex-military. They were not oriented toward acting as staff to the NSC principals, but saw their job as serving the needs of the president.

George Shultz, the secretary of state who followed Haig, was a professor of economics who also had wide experience in business and politics, having served as secretary of labor and secretary of the treasury under Nixon. His experience as an executive with Bechtel Corporation gave him a strong background in international relations. However, Bill Clark, the NSC advisor in 1982 when Shultz was appointed, regarded himself as *the* foreign policy expert in the White House. He began at once to take issue with foreign policy advice coming from the secretary of state.

The DCI was Bill Casey, an old friend of President Reagan. He was older and more experienced than most of the NSC staff and clearly was able to dominate that body. Casey's attitude was, as the president's personal friend and confident, he did not need formal approval for much of what he did. This seems to have included his plans for an off-the-shelf, financially self-sustaining, stand-alone covert intelligence entity that could operate free of both the need for congressional funds and the requirement to report to Congress. Such an organization could remain from one administration to the next, provided it continued to make money.

Casey was not the first DCI to seek to conduct the affairs of government without the awareness or participation of Congress or the American people. Marchetti and Marks maintain that a secret cult of intelligence, composed of an American aristocracy, has existed for many years. This secret fraternity "recognizes no role for a questioning legislature or an investigative press. Its adherents believe that only they have the right and obligation to decide what is necessary to satisfy the national needs."[16]

The history of the CIA lends some support to this assertion. Various directors of the CIA have sought to escape the control of Congress by finding other sources of funds, thus avoiding financial accountability. Top CIA officials generally have been wealthy men of high social standing with an elitist attitude toward the control of society. In 1948, CIA leaders sought funds by asking their wealthy friends in New York's Brook Club. The Granary Fund and the Rubicon Fund were conduits for CIA money to private groups. Oveta Culp Hobby, secretary of health, education and welfare in the Eisenhower administration allowed the CIA to use the Hobby Foundation as a conduit. Countless wealthy and socially prominent people have been solicited for funds to support the CIA. The agency apparently had no intention of restricting its activity to foreign countries. Contrary to the intent of Congress it began a small domestic operation in 1949; in 1964 this was considerably expanded to the Domestic Operations Division.[17]

THE CIA MAKES POLICY

Long before the Iran-Contra affair Secretary of State Shultz became aware that the president was not being well served in the area of foreign policy. He felt that Bill Clark was too hard-line, lacking in awareness of the importance of negotiation and lacking in knowledge of foreign affairs.[18]   Under President Reagan there was a striking tendency for the NSC staff to become involved in covert activities. They were essentially "staff people" with all the implications of that term, but many of them longed for line authority. As a group, they were intensely competitive with the State Department and sought some basis for initiating foreign policy decisions on their own.   Oliver North felt the State Department was full of idealistic and well-meaning liberals, whereas the NSC staff were mostly military men whom Reagan had hired to replace the political appointees of the previous administration. North accepted the mutual hostility between State and the NSC staff as a given, but he felt his boss,   Robert McFarlane (head of the NSC and national security advisor), would not "stand up to Shultz or Weinberger."[19]   He soon developed a personal relationship with the Bill Casey, director of central intelligence, who was quite outspoken in his desire to influence foreign policy. The fears expressed by Acheson in 1944, regarding the CIA, were realized during the Reagan administration in the person of Bill Casey, who took control of foreign policy in the area that interested him and made decisions that were the prerogative of the President of the United States.

Shultz wanted to advise the president on foreign policy, but he found first Bill Clark and then Bill Casey always blocking his access and opposing his advice. Bill Casey, who considered himself an authority on foreign policy, had a regular morning intelligence briefing with the NSC and the president. The briefing was supposed to be factual, but Casey's "facts" always came with his own ideological implications. Shultz remarked in his memoirs,

Someone, I said, needed to be preeminent in managing the president's foreign policy—as John Foster Dulles had been under Eisenhower and Kissinger had been under Nixon and Ford. One central person has to orchestrate things on behalf of the president.

I was determined to do this job. There were two inherent problems, however, that I knew I could never resolve. The president was terribly reluctant to discipline or fire anyone: when people know that, they are ultimately impossible to control. I was also increasingly uneasy about CIA director, Bill Casey. He had very strong policy positions which were reflected in his intelligence briefings. He claimed he was objective, but his views were so strong and so ideological that they inevitably colored his selection and assessment of materials. I could not rely on what he said, nor could I accept without question the objectivity of the "intelligence" that he put out, especially in policy-sensitive areas.[20]

Another problem was Reagan himself. It was difficult to raise caveats or propose contrary ideas to the president. He found reasoned and forceful objections difficult to handle and would rather avoid the discussion altogether. When Shultz offered strong opposition to Iran-Contra, he found that "State was cut out of the cable traffic." Reagan began to isolate him. He often failed to discuss policy with Shultz if he sensed that Shultz might object. Nevertheless, Reagan's diary and his memoirs indicate that he was impressed by Shultz and appreciated his style of quiet diplomacy.   When some of his conservative supporters urged him to fire his secretary of state on the grounds that Shultz was soft on the Russians, Reagan told them this was nonsense.[21]

FINDINGS AND RECOMMENDATIONS

After the Iran-Contra affair the problem of the conflict between the State Department and the NSC staff came under congressional investigation. The Tower Commission and the Iran-Contra Congressional Committees both looked into this area as well as the problem of controlling the CIA. Both bodies had a number of suggestions for improvement. Only the most significant recommendations need be reviewed here.

The Tower Commission, which was the president's special review board, was less drastic in its findings and recommendations. It said the president was not well served by his advisors and it was not sure whether any laws had been broken. There was a movement underway, in the Carter administration, to make the position of NSC advisor subject to Senate confirmation. After his experience in that position, Brzezinski made this recommendation himself.[22] However, despite the fact that the Tower Commission described the NSC staff as led by "reckless cowboys off on their own on a wild ride," it specifically recommended *against* making the national security advisor accountable to Congress by the process of confirmation.

In some ways, the role of the NSC was actually strengthened by the commission. The members recommended that the national security advisor chair the full meetings of the National Security Council and that his staff prepare an agenda for the meetings, thus increasing the role of the NSC staff in policy formulation. They emphasized the importance of "maintaining the integrity and objectivity of the intelligence process," but made no recommendations as to how this objectivity might be assured.[23]

The report of the joint Congressional Iran-Contra Committees was much more severe in its criticism of all parties involved in Iran-Contra. It censured Casey for his "manipulation of intelligence findings to affect decisions of elected officials," pointing out that he had become a "single-minded advocate of policy" and that he created intelligence reports to support the policy he was promoting.[24] Casey was also castigated for his influence on Oliver North, "giving him direction, and promoting the concept of an extra-legal covert organization."[25] Casey was held directly responsible for the Enterprise and the illegal activities of that organization.

In regard to the role of the president, the congressional report stated "the question whether the President knew of the diversion is not conclusive on the issue of his responsibility. The President created or at least tolerated an environment where those who did know of the diversion believed with certainty that they were carrying out the President's policies." The report was highly critical of the attitude of NSC staff members, suggesting they saw themselves as working for the president and that any actions they took were in response to the needs of their boss.

Finally the report quoted Justice Brandeis who said, "Our Government is the potent, the omnipresent teacher. For good or ill it teaches the whole people by its example. Crime is contagious. If the Government becomes a law-breaker, it breeds contempt for law, it invites every man to become a law unto himself, it invites anarchy." "The Iran-Contra Affair," said the report, "resulted from a failure to heed this message." [26]

Among the recommendations were a prohibition against the NSC becoming involved in covert activities, a requirement that the president make regular reports to Congress on the number and activities of the NSC staff, with particular attention to the "number and tenure of uniformed military personnel assigned to the NSC." Another significant recommendation, based on the tendency for military officers to look for a single line of command and to follow orders of their commanding officer, was that the national security advisor "should not be an active military officer and that there should be a limit placed on the tour of military officers assigned to the staff of the National Security Council." It was also recommended that the CIA have an independent statutory inspector general confirmed by the Senate.[27]

In the executive summary of the report it was suggested that the role of intelligence and policy functions be separated, but no recommendation was put forth describing how they were to be separated. Another problem touched upon by the committee was the incompatibility between intelligence and covert operations. These two capabilities have been combined in the CIA almost from the time of its origin. While both functions are needed, they should not be under the same director of central intelligence. Clearly, a separate agency is needed to perform covert actions, but there were no formal recommendations to this effect.

ADMINISTRATIVE CHANGES

None of the committees or the Tower Commission faced up to the problem of the conflict between the national security advisor and the secretary of state. It is essential to combine these two positions in a formal and statutory manner. Unless this is done there will remain a built-in source of conflict and stress around the president. Kissinger recognized the inevitable competitiveness of these two positions. His recommendation was that the president should make the secretary of state his principal adviser and use the national security adviser to coordinate discussions in the NSC meeting and make sure each point of view is heard. This might have been a good solution if the position of NSC advisor were a new position. Unfortunately the history of this appointment would have a strong influence on anyone in this role.

Also the president needs an advisor on foreign affairs who will spend part of his time in the White House. If this proves to be too much for the many duties of the secretary of state, he may have to appoint a deputy with authority to supervise the cable traffic and communicate with ambassadors. The State Department is a great bureaucracy. Dean Rusk, who was secretary of state for Kennedy, remarked that many of the ancient time-honored procedures of the department seemed designed to evade responsibility for any decision. An important cable would sometimes take three weeks to go from the country desk to the secretary's office on the seventh floor. Kennedy used to dream of creating a secret office of a few experts to run foreign policy "while maintaining the state department as a facade in which people might contentedly carry papers from bureau to bureau."[28]

No one is more capable of advising the president on foreign policy than the secretary of state. He has the staff and the Bureau of Intelligence and Research (INR) within the State Department to help him do the job. He simply needs more direct access to the White House. Kissinger saw the need for combining these two positions. He held both of them at the same time. However, the combined position was never formalized. This new and more influential position would not prevent the president from seeking advice from any other agency or person, but it would reduce an important source of stress and diffusion of purpose within the administration.

Lastly, something needs to be done about the CIA. As Acheson foresaw, it has become a rogue elephant, out of control and responsible to no one. Of course it can be tamed by a DCI who is a career professional and understands the limits of his mission. But the DCI may be a political appointee, without the professional discipline required for the job. There is no formal administrative control of the CIA. The NSC, which has the authority to control it, does not have the means or the centrality of purpose.

What is needed is single line authority, under the president, who is responsible to interpret the mission and set limits for the CIA. It should be someone of cabinet rank who is not part of the CIA, and someone who is accountable, that is, subject to confirmation by Congress. Possibilities are the secretary of defense, secretary of state (in his new, augmented role) or the vice-president. As the advisor to the president on foreign policy, the secretary of state is in the best position to control the CIA. If the CIA is split into two functions (the so-called black operations or covert military activity and the pure information-gathering function), it would be quite feasible for the military function to come under the authority of the chairman of the Joint Chiefs of Staff, who is himself subject to the control of the secretary of defense. The separation of the CIA into two organizations would help to prevent unauthorized covert operations. It would mean that intelligence agents assigned to gather information would be forbidden to engage in assassination, sabotage, falsification of documents, drug running, or training the secret police of a foreign power. While these activities are not acknowledged by the current CIA, they do occur.[29] It will remain difficult to control such activity, but it will be easier if the operational and intelligence functions are performed by two separate agencies.

NOTES

1. *U.S. Senate Foreign and Military Intelligence: Book I, Final Report of the Select Committee to Study Governmental Operations with Respect to Intelligence Activities* (Washington DC: US Govt. Printing Office, 1976), p. 46.

2. Ibid.

3. H. S. Truman, *Memoirs, Vol. 2, Years of Trial and Hope* (Garden City: Doubleday, 1956), p. 60.

4. D. Acheson, *Present at the Creation: My Years in the State Department* (New York: W. W. Norton. 1969), pp.127-130.

5. Ibid., p. 214.

6. *U.S. Senate, Foreign and Military Intelligence: Final Report,* p. 49-50.

7. I. L. Janis, and L. Mann, *Decision Making: A Psychological Analysis of Conflict, Choice, and Commitment* (New York: The Free Press, 1977), p. 130. See also I. L. Janis, *Victims of Groupthink* (Boston: Houghton Mifflin, 1972).

8. E. J. Hughes, *The Living Presidency: The Resources and Dilemmas of the American Presidential Office* (New York: Coward McCann, 1972), p. 264, EJH interview of HHH August 1965.

9. N. Sheehan, H. Smith, E. W. Kenworthy, and F. Butterfield, *The Pentagon Papers* (New York: Bantam, 1971), pp. 14-15.

10. H. A. Kissinger, *The White House Years* (Boston: Little Brown, 1979), p. 37.

11. Ibid., p. 36.

12. *U. S. Senate, Foreign and Military Intelligence: Final Report,* p. 53.

13. S. M. Hersh, *The Price of Power: Kissinger in the Nixon White House* (New York: Summit Books, 1983), p. 32.

14. Z. Brzezinski, *Power and Principle* (New York: Farrar Straus and Giroux, 1983), p.13.

15. Ibid., p. 37.

16. Marchetti, V. and J. D. Marks, *The CIA and the Cult of Intelligence* (New York: Knopf, 1980) pp. 4-5.

17. D. Wise, and T. B. Ross, *The Espionage Establishment* (New York: Random House, 1967), pp.140-146.

18. G. P. Shultz, *Turmoil and Triumph: My Years as Secretary of State*, (New York: Charles Scribner's Sons, 1993), p. 305.

19. O. North, *Under Fire: An American Story* (New York: Harper Paperbacks, 1991), p.181-182, 222-223.

20. G. P. Shultz, *Turmoil and Triumph*, p. 691.

21. R. Reagan, *An American Life*, (New York: Simon and Schuster, 1990), pp. 605, 617, 642, 673.

22. Z. Brzezinski, *Power and Principle*, p. 536.

23. J. Tower, E. Muskie, and B. Scowcroft, *The Tower Commission Report* (New York: Times Books, 1987), pp. 94-99.

24. *Report of the Congressional Committee Investigating the Iran-Contra Affair, House Rept. No. 100-433, Senate Rept. No. 100-216, 100th Congress, First Session.* (Washington DC: US Government Printing Office, 1987), p. 382.

25. Ibid. p.20.

26. Ibid., pp. 3-22.

27. Ibid., pp. 423-427.

28. A. M. Schlessinger, Jr. *A Thousand Days: John F. Kennedy in the White House* New York: Fawcett Crest, 1965, pp. 382-383.

29. *Foreign and Military Intelligence: Final Report*, 1976; P. Agee, *Inside the Company: CIA Diary* (New York: Bantam Books), 1973; L. Cockburn, *Out of Control: The Story of the Reagan Administration's Secret War in Nicaragua, the Illegal Arms Pipeline, and the Contra Drug Connection* (New York: Atlantic Monthly Press, 1987; E. Hollman and A. Love, *Inside the Shadow Government* (Washington, DC: Christic Institute, 1988; R. W. McGehee, *Deadly Deceits: My Twenty-Five Years with the CIA* (New York: Sheridan Square Publications, 1983); N. Sheehan, H. Smith, E. W. Kenworthy, and F. Butterfield, *The Pentagon Papers* (New York: Bantam Books, 1971).

11

"THE NEW WORLD ORDER"

The improvement of government administration, as briefly suggested in the previous chapter, is one step toward controlling excessive American intervention. However, we will need to have continuing American *involvement* in world affairs. The nature of this involvement must change from neocolonial domination to cooperation.

Following World War II a standard reason for United States intervention into a region was to save the people from the threat of communism. There were either communists in the government or the danger of a communist takeover of a democratic government. The notion of an expanding communist threat has vanished with the fall of the Soviet Union and the retreat of communist governments from eastern Europe. Neocolonialism is declining as well. Subject peoples are becoming politically more alert. They are no longer content to have their economy and their government managed by a foreign power. As the British Commonwealth has gradually become a group of independent nations, so the colonial empire of the United States is shrinking. If we Americans really want to contribute to the development of a democratic world, we will have to change our goals as well as our slogans. We will have to be prepared to encourage the development of independent—and sometimes competitive —democratic states instead of developing a ring of resentful subject nations.

The United States is at the stage of historical development that Toynbee[1] described as the universal military state. The military option will not be available much longer. We no longer have the financial resources or the national will to support it We must work out some other means for establishing a stable world environment that is compatible with American policy. This means a more proactive, flexible policy that is developed in cooperation with the other major powers of the world. Given the American character, this will not be an easy task. Pride, selfishness, greed and sheer inertia will impede our understanding and our growth. In this chapter we will examine what steps can be taken to build a new approach to world problems and some of the ridgidities of character that stand in the way of our achieving peace in the modern world. ͻ

THE MILITARY OPTION

On August 2, 1990, Saddam Hussein led the forces of Iraq in a one-day conquest of the nation of Kuwait. President George Bush responded immediately by organizing world opposition and in December he had 300,000 troops in the region. He secured promises of financial and/or military support from most of the major world powers and many of the Arab states. In the total engagement, which lasted six weeks, 450,000 U.S. troops joined an allied army of mainly European and Arab nations. The Iraqi army was estimated at a million men. In the final conflict on the ground the Iraqi army was routed in 100 hours.

President Bush called the total operation the beginning of a new world order. He did not spell out what this new world order was going to do. Presumably it would manage world affairs to reduce the level of aggression by one state against another.

The Gulf War was a great victory for the allied forces and for President Bush. While it made the president the hero of the moment, it did not get him reelected. The war was presented as an effort to restore the legitimate rulers of Kuwait. But there were many established governments being toppled by stronger military powers at the same time. Why Kuwait? What was in it for the United States?

The Gulf War began, not because we wanted justice for Kuwait, but because the West had become dependent on Middle East oil and our industrial society could not continue at full capacity without it. An important stated goal of the war—the overthrow of Saddam, destruction of his chemical and biological weapons, and putting an end to his program to develop a nuclear bomb—was ignored during the victory celebrations. The full mission was not accomplished although some biological and chemical weapons were destroyed. In any event, we were soon back in the Gulf (with air power alone) trying to stop Saddam from his brutal suppression of the northern Kurds and the Shiite Moslems in the south. Despite the enormous cost, the victory did not solve the major problem, simply because Saddam Hussein knew he could thumb his nose at us as soon as we brought our massive forces out of the region.

The Gulf War was followed by the "saving" of Somalia in 1992-93. Both military operations involved the use of forces from several nations. Yet neither problem was resolved by the use of military force. Future historians may well view the massive troop deployments of the Gulf War, as one of the last grand adventures in world-wide military missions.

As to the intervention in Bosnia-Hercegovina, we probably would not have gone there if it had been only a U.S. decision. It is one of the difficulties of having a "new world order" that intervention becomes not only a joint operation but a joint decision. While several other nations joined us in the Gulf War, the major support for our operation (both military and moral) came from Europe. This made it very difficult to opt out of the problems of Europe when the remains of Yugoslavia began erupting into violence. Serbs and Croats, Moslems and Christians have been murdering each other in that region long before the assassination of the Archduke Ferdinand brought that territory to world attention in 1914. The ancient hatreds in that part of central Europe are so deep and pervasive and so little understood by Americans that the prospect of an American military solution to the problem is very remote.

If our new world order is to be nothing more than military joint ventures, it appears we will spend our time trying to combat some current emergency without tackling the real problems facing world society. It is always much more difficult to reach international (or even national) agreement on what constitutes a "real" problem, but it is clear that any long term solution to the three regional conflicts mentioned above will have to involve a change of attitude on the part of the people involved. That takes time. It requires a longer attention span than our world leaders have demonstrated thus far. As long as we must promise Congress that the troops will be home in a year or the boys will be home by Christmas there is little prospect that anything significant will be accomplished.

To ask if military intervention is necessary is almost always to raise the wrong question. The right question is, "What might have been done to take early action on the problem to avoid military involvement?" It is clear that the Gulf War was "necessary," given the situation that we had allowed to develop. President Bush was right when he said sanctions would not work. It was already years too late for sanctions. What of the first troop movement in response to the invasion of Kuwait? Were there other options besides war? It depends on how far back in time we look to answer that question. It is only when we wait until the actual invasion of Kuwait that it appears there was no other option except the military one. The waiting and refusal to face a problem has its rewards. There is no need to plan ahead. Weapons firms can make lots of money and oil companies can raise the price when they are threatened with a shortage.   A genuinely new world order should involve coordinated action by other than military means. This is not to say that a military solution is never justified. It does point up the importance of learning to spot international problems earlier and, if force is necessary, it can be used earlier when less of it is required.

The nonmilitary solution to the problem posed by Saddam Hussein's invasion comprises two essential elements, each supplementing the other.   First, an international system of arms control. Second, a system for energy conservation and development of new energy resources.   Saddam was able to create his formidable military power because Western nations fell over each other trying to sell him weapons and provide him with advice.   This is one of the great defects of international capitalism.   A true capitalist will not only sell a refrigerator to an Eskimo, but a knife or gun to a murderer. He recognizes no morality but the art of the deal. Emerging capitalists must be restrained if the world is to maintain even a modicum of safety. Iraq was armed, in large part, by Great Britain, Germany, France, the Soviet Union, and the United States.

THE CONTROL OF WEAPONS

The need for a system of international cooperation in weapons sales has been recognized for some time. Such a system has never been developed because each nation sees the other as a potential competitor. Control is also impaired by the mutual fear that others will cheat.

George Shultz, who was secretary of state for the Reagan administration, saw the need for an international system to control chemical weapons. In late 1983 he discovered that Iraq had employed chemical weapons on the front lines in its war with Iran. Intelligence reports identified the Soviets as possible suppliers, but there was also evidence that Iraq had developed its own production capacity with assistance from West German companies. Shultz made use of his contacts in the German government to consider possible means of control including disciplining offending companies. In his memoirs he says, "I found a profound lack of enthusiasm for my views. The West German government seemed singularly indifferent and incurious about what their private companies were shipping to Iraq."[2] In 1988 the U.S. developed evidence that a chemical weapons plant was being built in Rabat, Libya. Says Shultz, "The Japanese were building a metal-working plant nearby that could readily be adapted to the production of canisters of one kind or another. We raised the issue with the Japanese, and they replied that their investigation showed that no Japanese laws had been broken."[3] When he sought some kind of international agreement on the limitation of chemical weapons, Shultz found as much resistance from his fellow Americans. "Within the 'National Security Community' in Washington there was strong opposition to the prohibition of chemical weapons production. A principal and important argument was the formidable problem of verifying compliance with such a treaty. The United States would comply, the argument went, but others would cheat, thereby leaving us at a disadvantage."[4]

The same problems arise in the control of other types of weapons. In the effort to get a jump on the competition the capitalist wants to be the first to get a developing country to adopt his weapon system so he can follow up with training and sales of replacement parts. We had spectacular international cooperation in the Gulf War regarding the *use* of weapons, but we cannot generate anything like that level of cooperation in their *control*. An arms control system, which could have prevented the war, would be far less expensive than the war itself, but it would require the full recognition of the danger of unrestrained competition.

Very briefly stated, an effective system of arms control would involve supervision of weapons sales and a willingness to use military force, if necessary, at an early stage to prevent the development of unauthorized weapons as well as the build-up of chemical, biological, and nuclear weapons in military dictatorships. An example is the preemptive strike by Israel against the Osirac-type, French-supplied, nuclear reactor near Baghdad on June 7, 1981. But the Israeli strike was not the decision of an international arms control organization. Further, no cooperative effort was made to prevent the French from selling the reactor to Iraq or (once the sale was completed) to interdict shipment of parts. There is still no international organization, including the UN, that is capable of taking forceful action, in advance, to prevent the buildup of nuclear weapons. Reaching and implementing such an agreement would not be easy. Witness our attempt to prevent the development of nuclear weapons in North Korea.

The result of the lack of a system of arms control is an each-man-for-himself situation, in which those developing nations that feel they need nuclear weapons will find the means and the material to develop them. Those nations that feel threatened by these weapons will seek international intervention and, if this fails and they have the capability, they will conduct preemptive military strikes against the offending nations to prevent this nuclear buildup.

Despite the diplomatic outrage leveled at Israel by the United States and the major industrial powers (and the offers by France to rebuild the reactor), without the action of Israel the allied powers might have faced an Iraq with nuclear arms in the 1990-91 Gulf War.

In all likelihood, the world does not have the collective resolve to control nuclear, chemical, and biological weapons. The use of poison gas in World War I and the many returning soldiers with horrible wounds and ravaged lungs had a sufficient effect on world opinion to prevent the further use of chemical weapons through the end of World War II. The exception, of course, is Mussolini's use of poison gas in Ethiopia, which was never acknowledged by either side in the conflict. While the British and French knew about it, they chose to keep quiet. Today there is clear evidence that several nations are developing chemical weapons and some have already used them against their own populations and against enemy soldiers. Based on this experience, we may have to undergo several instances of battlefield use of nuclear, chemical, or biological weapons or terrorist incidents against our cities before we develop the determination to control weapons on an international scale and to conduct preemptive strikes against nuclear, chemical, or biological weapons development. The quandary remains that, when we finally get around to doing something about the problem, a nuclear capability may be spread throughout the less developed nations and several terrorist groups.

ENERGY CONSERVATION

Weapons control is not the only consideration in the management of the troubled areas of the world. There is also the heavy reliance of all the industrial powers on fossil fuels as an energy source. The failure to conserve fossil fuels and develop alternate sources of energy makes it possible for a single dictator to exploit the scarcity of world oil resources. It is important to note here that there is no current scarcity of world energy, but there is a scarcity of *cheap* energy. The terrorism of Saddam's act and his threat to world energy supplies would not have been possible without years of increasing world oil consumption and a reluctance to develop alternative sources of energy.

There is a myth that the oil shortage is "not real," that it is a scam created by the oil companies in order to justify high prices. Whenever the oil companies hike the price, motorists protest that there is no real oil shortage. It is an artificial shortage created by "Big Oil." While it is true that oil companies may use an international crisis as an excuse to raise prices, the total supply of available oil is decreasing at a steady rate, despite discovery of new fields. Again, there is no shortage of oil in the ground, but the methods of extracting it are becoming increasingly costly. It is not as though the tap will be shut off suddenly. It is more economically feasible to extract oil from the larger fields. As oil exploration proceeds, the larger fields are discovered first and the average size of the fields discovered decreases thereafter. With smaller fields, more drilling is required per barrel of oil extracted. At some point, even though there will still be plenty of oil in the ground, it will no longer be economically feasible to continue the search for or the extraction of oil from smaller fields. Other sources of energy will become more economical than the light to medium oil now in use.

It is the limited availability and increasing cost of oil, and not a physical shortage, that has brought on a series of oil crises. Our determination to have cheap fuel increases the rate of consumption and further diminishes the world oil supply, making it possible for a small power with a strong army to threaten the rest of the world with a denial of control of an important energy resource. There is a direct line of causation between the consumption of world energy and the vulnerability of a nation. A nation that becomes dependent on nonrenewable energy sources for a vast array of electrical appliances such as blenders, slicers, grinders, microwave ovens, dishwashers, clothes washers, toasters, refrigerators, freezers, central heating, air conditioning, sprinkler systems, security systems, CD players, television sets, VCRs, personal computers, and children's games—not to mention the various forms of military and personal transportation such as jeeps, jet planes, missiles, automobiles, private planes, dirt bikes, speed boats, motor scooters and recreation vehicles—such a nation has a vast energy need simply in order to maintain its ordinary way of life. The more "civilized" Western nations are the more vulnerable to a shortage of nonrenewable sources of energy.

If a people want to maintain their standard of living, there is an increasing likelihood they will either have to pay heavily for it or fight for it. Further, the more inflexible they become in their insistence that they deserve cheap energy, the easier it will be for a smaller, oil-rich power to push them into a state of crisis.

As a nation, the United States needs a system of energy and resources conservation, and an active program for the development of alternate sources of energy. Gasoline can be made from coal, tar sands, shale, or heavy oil, but the processes are not currently economically feasible. There is a need for capitalists who will spend the money for research and development in this area, even if it requires partial government subsidy. Currently there is an attitude in this country that prevents the United States from implementing a system of resource conservation and development of new potential sources of energy. To a limited extent the world has already begun to conserve energy, with a heavy tax on gasoline in Europe, Japan, and many parts of Asia and Africa, but the United States has always been a laggard when it comes to energy conservation.

It is characteristic of Americans that we are proud of having big cars, big houses, and lots of appliances, and that we do not see the connection between this consumption of the lion's share of energy and an act of aggression. In his Christmas Tree speech for 1969, President Nixon exemplified this attitude. He said,

There are 85 million television sets, there are 80 million automobiles, there are 300 million radios in America, and 150,000 airplanes. . . . today America is the richest nation in the world, we are the strongest nation in the world . . . So I say to you that as we enter the decade of the seventies, America will continue to be rich, America will continue to have more of the worlds goods, there will be more television sets and more radios and more automobiles . . .[5]

Yet this bellicose speech was entitled "The Pageant of Peace." It was the same speech in which he told his fellow Americans that we were the first power to be the major power in the world without asking for it. From the words of Nixon it would appear that all of this power and all of these worldly goods came to us because we are a good, hard-working people. So we deserve it and we're not about to give it up.

Cheap energy is a part of our culture, particularly cheap gasoline for cars. In 1952, the cost of a gallon of gasoline was 28 cents. By 1962, it was 30 cents. In Europe at that time the price ranged from 45 cents to 60 cents for an American gallon, but an American living in Europe and working for the U..S. government could drive into a gas station on any U.S. military base in West Germany and buy gasoline for 11 cents a gallon.

The first oil shock occurred in 1973 with the Yom Kippur War and the Arab oil embargo. The United States had no effective response to this move except to ration gasoline. This produced long lines at the pumps, a slowdown of economic activity and, a major inflation. When gas was available again the price ranged as high as $2.50 per gallon in some parts of the U.S., but it gradually settled back down to about $1.20.

The oil embargo was still ripe in the memory of President Jimmy Carter, who was perhaps the first American president to see clearly the link between energy conservation and world peace. In addition to his more substantive proposals, he tried to set an example by turning down the thermostat in the White House and appearing on television in a sweater. But Carter's symbolism and his proposals flew directly in the face of a century of profligate energy use. In 1980, President

Carter called dependence on foreign oil a clear and present danger to national security, and announced he would limit oil imports to a maximum of 8.2 million barrels a day. Using his presidential authority, he imposed a fee of over $4 a barrel on imports of both crude oil and gasoline.

A congressional resolution removed the president's authority for the action. Although Carter vetoed the resolution, his veto was overridden by both houses of Congress. It was the first time in twenty-eight years that a president suffered a defeat of his veto when his own party was in control of Congress. Many of his other proposals for energy conservation suffered a similar fate.

Ronald Reagan learned from Carter's mistake. When Reagan told us this austerity was not really necessary, everyone relaxed again. It was what we wanted to believe. By 1990, the price of gas had come down to $1.06, only to rise again following Iraq's invasion of Kuwait. George Bush brought an end to that nonsense with the Gulf War, the loss of 234 American lives, and 479 wounded. The costly task of putting out the fires in the oil wells of Kuwait was to take another year. By 1993 the price of gasoline was back down to a little over a dollar a gallon, proving that we Americans could have cheap and plentiful gasoline for our cars for as long as we wanted it. However, if an American tourist pulled into a West German gas station to fill his tank in 1993, it would cost him over $4 for an American gallon of gasoline, sold by the liter. Many other nations have raised gas prices comparably.

ENERGY DEVELOPMENT

There is not, as yet, a world organization responsible for the distribution of energy. At the present time every nation uses and prices its oil as it pleases. The United Nations does not have the status or the capability of managing the distribution of world energy. Waste, inefficiency, nepotism, a bloated bureaucracy, and political corruption are endemic at the United Nations.[6] However, for purposes of energy conservation and weapons control it would appear that some kind of world organization will be necessary. We need an organization of responsible nations with the power to enforce its decisions. At the present time it appears that, if they are not to be held hostage, an alliance of Western nations with some of their Asian allies will have to take over these functions. Lacking a more comprehensive body, perhaps NATO could serve as a beginning for such an organization—an augmented NATO, staffed with some civilian administrative personnel.

Fossil fuels (oil, bitumen, natural gas and coal) supply 90 per cent of the energy in use today. Most of this energy comes from the light oil in general use, but our total oil reserves are declining. Today, 70 per cent of the unconsumed oil comes from the Eastern Hemisphere, so the West will become more and more dependent on the great Al-Ghawar field of Saudi Arabia, the world's largest, and the Arabian-Iranian basin, which includes Kuwait's Al-Burqan field, the second largest in the world. The area of the former Soviet Union contains a total oil reserve almost as large as Saudi Arabia's.

World oil production now appears stabilized, but there is no control on oil use. If world oil production continues to be stabilized and if the estimate of the total undiscovered oil is accurate, it is estimated current oil production volume could be sustained until the year 2035, at which time a shortage of oil resources will force a production decline.[7] While this figure is debatable, it is clear that production will begin to decline at some point in the next century.

Western nations might make greater use of natural gas. While 79 per cent of the remaining natural gas is believed to be located in the Eastern Hemisphere, it is much more abundant.   The natural gas fuel cell uses chemistry, not combustion, to convert natural gas into electricity and heat. The installation of this new technology has just begun in the United States. Electricity can also be produced by natural gas-fired turbine power generation.

Heavy oil is another alternative. This oil is more expensive to process, but 65 per cent of it is believed to be in the Western Hemisphere. There is also the possibility of processing coal into oil. This is an expensive operation, but western nations have an abundant source of coal.   Only 2.8 per cent of the world's coal reserves have been exploited, and it is estimated that the remaining supply will last from a few hundred to a few thousand years, depending on the rate of consumption and the extent to which coal becomes the primary source of energy.

At some point, photoelectric cells will be used commercially to produce energy. For fixed facilities such as heating and lighting, solar power will become economically feasible as the cost of oil and natural gas becomes excessive. While swift acceleration may continue to require fossil fuels, solar power or natural gas may be used to supplement more conventional fuels in transportation.

As a fixed source of energy the conventional nuclear fission reactor has many problems including safety and the storage of spent, but still active, nuclear fuel—the so-called atomic waste. Public fears of nuclear power, the escalating cost for plant construction, and the sharp decrease in the expected production level of electricity from these plants have all slowed the building of nuclear fission reactors in most of the developed nations, with the exception of a few countries which do not have adequate supplies of fossil fuels.

The clean-burning fusion reactor represents a potential alternative to the fission reactor. Right now fusion is only on the horizon, but it may be available by the time oil is in short supply. While fusion reactors represent a great increase in efficiency, the heat required and the difficulty of confining the hot plasma generated by such reactors could present problems. We have not yet made an adequate assessment of the dangers of the development of these advanced nuclear reactors.

One thing is clear from all of this. Heavy oil, natural gas, coal, photoelectric, and nuclear energy can all be developed from sources available to the West, and the sooner we begin working on these energy sources, to make them safe and economically feasible, the more rapidly we will develop energy independence. This independence is necessary to maintain our economic strength in the face of an increasingly competitive world. But it will also mean that we will no longer be at the mercy of petty tyrants who can force us to move masses of troops halfway across the world to protect our source of cheap energy. The money used to finance the Gulf War could sponsor a massive alternative energy program that would lead us toward energy independence.

There appears to be a growing consensus that the economic leadership in the world is shifting from North America to Asia. In light of this change, it will be important for us to establish a close relationship with those democratic powers which will be influential in Asia.

THE THREAT OF FAMINE

The situation in Somalia was another problem that we chose to solve by military force, although it represents an example of a larger problem that is facing the world as a whole. Every year the total arable land in the world decreases. Outbreaks of famine have haunted the less-developed nations for the last two decades.

United States involvement in Somalia, with the help from other members of the new world order, seemed, at first, to be a characteristic example of American generosity. On December 4, 1992 President Bush announced our mission to Somalia. It was a speech filled with all the great glittering generalities. The president spoke of easing suffering, America was going to "answer the call" of the UN, although it was at Bush's suggestion that the UN made the request for American aid. The operation, called Restore Hope, would be undertaken by "America's finest," who would "perform their mission with courage and compassion."

The people of Somalia and especially the children of Somalia need our help. We're able to ease their suffering. We must help them live. We must give them hope. America must act. . . . When we see Somalia's children starving, all of America hurts. We've tried to help in many ways. And make no mistake about it, now we and our allies will ensure that aid gets through. . . . And let me be very clear. Our mission is humanitarian, but we will not tolerate armed gangs ripping off their own people, condemning them to death by starvation. . . . And so, to every sailor, soldier, airman and Marine who is involved in this mission, let me say you're doing God's work. We will not fail. Thank you, and may God bless the United States of America."[8]

After these fine words he handed the mission over to President Bill Clinton.

One must ask the question, why was Somalia selected to receive the benefit of our generosity? At the time U.S. troops were landing in Mogadishu, Angola was starving in the midst of civil war. The UN's World Food Program was active in the region but the starvation continued. Police were needed to beat back the mobs of people whenever food was handed out. Jonas Savimbi"s UNITA party had been defeated at a UN-supervised election, but he had not accepted the verdict of the people and was using his armed forces to recapture territory. Those who did not die of starvation were blown up by the land mines that ringed several settlements or they died of cholera, which was widespread. The UN estimated that 1,000 people died each day in Angola.[9]

A similar problem faced Nigeria, and millions were starving in Southern Sudan, a situation that had grown steadily worse since the Sudan's civil war flared up again in the 1980s. Now it was aggravated by drought. Rwanda was in peril due to late planting of crops for the 1993-94 season. Food scarcity was evident everywhere in Rwanda and a major problem of genocide soon emerged in that nation. Kenya's corn crop was meager due to drought. Military clashes kept farmers from their fields in Sierra Leone. Drought from the previous year had devastated Zimbabwe. Sub-Saharan Africa had the largest and fastest-growing concentration of undernourished people, where the population was expected to grow by 3.2 per cent every year.[10]

Why, then, Somalia? The public is not privy to the secret discussions that took place before President Bush made the decision to send in the troops. But it is a safe bet that—as more than justice for Kuwait was involved in the decision to move into the Persian Gulf—there were more than humanitarian considerations involved in our decision to intervene in Somalia. The old colonial powers took what they wanted without apology. They marched in with their armies, seized territory, knocked heads together, and set up their viceroys to command the local princes and satraps. It was a brutal policy but honest. When the United States intervenes, it is always behind the facade of benevolence.

Somalia is strategically located at the Horn of Africa, with access to the Indian Ocean, the Red Sea and hence the Suez Canal. Off-shore the Gulf of Aden is estimated to have abundant oil resources. The Somali people are divided into six clans, but there are many subclans and factional groups motivated by a spirit of intense rivalry. Islam is the dominant religion. Control of this region has been sought since before World War I by the British, the French, and the Italians, each nation creating its own small protectorate. They were called British Somaliland, French Somaliland, and Italian Somaliland. The shape and size of these territories have changed over the years, but not the lust of the major European powers for command of this important region of Africa. On July 1, 1960, the Republic of Somalia was created from British Somaliland and the Italian trust territory of Somalia. Since the end of World War II, the United States and the Soviet Union had been searching for a good reason to get their hands on the region. As both nations prided themselves on not being a "colonial power," they sought to dominate the region without taking possession of territory. They tried to gain influence and establish a dependent relationship by "helping" the various clan leaders. As the clans were constantly at war, what better way to help than to supply weapons?

After a coup in 1969, Major General Mohammad Siad Barre took over the country as president and organized a Marxist regime. In principle the new regime was to do away with clan politics, which was a threat to national unity. There was to be one nation of the Somali people without clan or tribal divisions. In reality, the clan of Siad Barre and his family dominated the government.

The Ogaden war of 1977-78 between Somalia and Ethiopia increased the need for modern weapons, and the United States and the Soviet Union began supplying weapons to both sides. Over the years the size and firepower of the weapons escalated. If the United States supplied cartriges, the Soviet Union countered with automatic rifles. If the U.S. made a gift of troop carriers and C-5 fighter-bombers, the USSR replied with land mines and shoulder-mounted missiles. Soon both Somalia and Ethiopia were armed with the most lethal modern weapons.

When the Soviet Union seemed to favor Ethiopia, Siad Barre sought help from the United States. He even agreed to modify his policy of summary arrests, jailings and torture if we would give him a handout. But his oppressive style continued. He angered the farmers by inviting them to bring their harvest to market and then setting a price for the sale of their crops that was often below cost. Food became scarce as farmers refused to harvest more than enough crops to feed their own relatives. By his policies, Siad Barre lost the countryside to his enemies and retreated to the control of Mogadishu. Even in this last stronghold he was faced with riots and protests and he resorted to his old policy of jailings, torture, and the massacre of civilians. On July 9, 1989, Bishop Salvador Colombo, a critic of the regime, was murdered in his church and it was rumored that the order for his assassination came from the presidential palace. At this point Siad Barre retreated from Mogadishu and the city was in the hands of warring clans.

Meanwhile, the clan wars had resulted in a neglect of agriculture and a drought in central and southern Somalia left hundreds of thousands starving. There was a massive movement of refugees into all the neighboring states of the region. As famine threatened the population, food became one of the weapons of the warlords. They swept down upon convoys from international aid missions, who were powerless to resist their superior firepower, and attempted to corner all the supplies for themselves. The people were starving and, although the international community had spent millions of dollars sending food, it was never distributed.

The leadership in the United States, not surprisingly, felt a sense of responsibility for this growing disaster. After visits to the region by U.S. officials and an order from President Bush for a food airlift in August, the UN mandate followed.

When the order came to send in the American forces there were many initial indications of success. Just the word that the Americans were coming brought two of the clans to the conference table, but no agreement was achieved. The Americans arrived in December, and by late March they had confiscated 5,000 small arms, 90 heavy machineguns and more than 1.3 million rounds of ammunition, plus assorted tanks and personnel carriers.[11] They had begun to undo the initial mistake of arming the local people with murderous weapons, but only a fraction of the job was completed. Soon they began to encounter resistance from General Mohammad Farrah Aideed, the largest and most elusive clan leader in the region, who toured the area with his own band of armed thugs and struck at the allied forces when and where he pleased.

It soon became apparent that the U.S. forces might have to shoot people and risk being shot themselves if they were to continue the disarmament. After consultation, the new American position was that disarming the combatants was not part of the U.S. mission. Following the ambush and murder of twenty-three Pakistani troops we sought the capture of General Aideed. But when he escaped several attempts to trap him and gave a public radio broadcast in which he incited his people to violence against us, we declared that we did not want to take him prisoner after all. When the Somalis killed several Americans and dragged their bodies through the streets, we ran into stiff protests from the home front. Several congressmen began to wonder what we were doing in Somalia. We declared victory and left the task of disarmament to the UN force, less than half our size and not as well equipped.

After seizing several rifles and stores of ammunition, the UN also made a public announcement that their mission was not disarmament. There seemed to be confusion as to just why any military force was in Somalia. Certainly the UN, which had less capability than the U.S., could not continue to guard every convoy indefinitely. If there was to be free passage for food convoys there must be a very sharp reduction if not elimination of the modern weapons in possession of the warring factions.

Somalia was clearly one of the places where a strong military response could have helped in the distribution of food. And the United States had a strong military force. But disarming the roving bands of thugs was absolutely essential, as a first step. The first stories in the American press suggested that this would be the approach—take the weapons away from the warring clans so they could not cause such disruption. However, it soon became apparent that the task would require more force than was available and much higher casualty figures among American troops than we were prepared to accept. The possession of a powerful military tempts us to use that force, but the loss of life for American soldiers rouses protests in Congress and causes us to abandon the proposal. The result is a sense of failure and the appearance that we lack resolution and decisiveness.

In the case of Somalia, it was the product of an overambitious mission and an unwillingness to think through the consequences of what we were undertaking. This unwillingness applies to Congress as well, for they were among the most vociferous complainers that "American boys" were being killed. If we are not prepared for war, we should not send a military force, for there is no essential difference between a war and a police action. Policemen get shot too.   Better, then, not to use the military option in those situations where we cannot justify loss of life for our forces.

An alternative course might be diplomatic contacts with the clan leaders by American officials who are experts in the region, followed by a program to purchase the most lethal weapons. The funds for such a program could be raised by the international community. Both General Mohammad Farrah Aideed and his chief opponent, Ali Mahdi Mohammad, have shown themselves to be very flattered by some form of diplomatic contact. A small contingent of troops might be required to guard the weapons after they were purchased and while they were being destroyed, but no more than the force that was sent by President Bush. It is conceivable that vigorous efforts to work out a peace settlement between the warring clans might prove effective in getting them to agree to safe passage for food convoys.

As to the problem of famine, in general, the solution is much more complex. Most aid workers agree that simply ladling out the grain from Western harvests is not a solution. Clearly, in the face of immediate starvation, food distribution and medical measures to prevent dehydration and disease are necessary first steps. But external imports of food can become a devastating blow to farmers in the region if it is continued beyond the point where the edge is taken off starvation.   The hopelessness of the farmer following a dictated price for his crops by the president is continued by the arrival of cheap foreign grains. The *Economist* reported on the economics of starvation even before the American troops arrived in Somalia. Citing *African Rights,* a London publication, it pointed out that the price of cereals in Somali markets had begun to fall even before the arrival of American troops:

By March this year the price of Sorghum, wheat and maize in local markets had been depressed so far that farmers were complaining. One farmer told the authors [of *African Rights]* that . . . he would not start planting again unless prices rose. Pushing down the high price of food during famine is desirable. But if prices continue to drop, because food aid continues to be pumped in, the fragile livelihoods of farmers can be harmed.

One logical solution recommended in the report would be to stop shipping in western grain and start buying Somali farmer"s crops instead. Yet this would bump up against the western world's self-serving policy of subsidized farming, which explains a lot of its enthusiasm for shipping grain to Africa.[12]

The use of modern Western farming techniques may only make the problem worse. Chemical fertilizer can poison the local water supply and contribute to the exhaustion of the land. The problem of famine can be solved by the avoidance of large fields of single crops, which are extremely vulnerable to insects that eat only one crop. Other omnivorous insects can be controlled by allowing spaces of open land between stands of crops. The teaching of organic farming techniques, the restoration of traditional farming practices using drought and insect-resistant native plants—all these practices tend to stabilize the agriculture of the region and make it less vulnerable.[13]

Projects to save a region must begin long before the television images of starving children with bloated bellies are flashed across the screen in our Western cities. Most of the people seen in these sensational broadcasts are already beyond help. Much of the food sent on an emergency basis never reaches the people who are hungry and much of the money is wasted due to the "wartime" atmosphere in which these efforts operate. The goal should be not just famine relief, but famine prevention. Famine relief unbalances the economy. Famine prevention teaches people to develop their own sources of food and water. In short, feeding the hungry may be an essential first step, but if it is done prior to our departure, without providing the methods for achieving self-sufficiency, it can be very harmful to the long-range development of the region. It fosters dependency and encourages a passive waiting for help from abroad. It generally takes a year for the economy to recover after the well-meaning efforts of these emergency aid workers.

THE INCREASING WORLD POPULATION

Population control is another crucial aspect of famine prevention, but it also cuts across all the other problems we have examined. Food for the hungry is only one aspect of the problem. World energy use is directly related to world population as is acid rain, stripping of forests for farm land, and environmental pollution in general. However, few people make the connection. The problem of world population, like the energy problem, seems to have generated a series of urgent warnings of world catastrophe and, when the catastrophe does not occur, we relax as though population presents no problem at all.

In 1798, Thomas Robert Malthus published his book, *An Essay on the Principle of Population as it Affects the Future Improvement of Society.* He saw an inevitable rise in human misery due to the tendency for population to increase faster than the means of subsistence. He demonstrated, by means of the statistics in vogue in his time, that population, when unchecked, increases in a geometrical ratio while, subsistence increases only in an arithmetic ratio. In his first essay he went so far as to approve crowding and unsanitary conditions for the poor and complained the poor law in England made conditions worse by the dole and various other aids. Without these forms of support, he argued, the poor would be forced to limit the size of their families. After the storm of protest following his work, he learned to be more diplomatic in later editions.

In 1972 the Club of Rome published *The Limits to Growth,* in which it maintained that the growth of world population is rapidly reaching a point where it will no longer be sustainable.[14] The club proposed the development of a system for the transition from growth to world equilibrium. Several objections were made to the note of urgency in this study and the suggestion of imminent world collapse. Also there was the claim that *Limits* was an elitist statement in which the haves were asking the have-nots to limit their growth and consumption. In 1974 the Club of Rome followed up with a more optimistic picture of the use of world resources. In *Mankind at the Turning Point* they employed a more sophisticated computer analysis than that used in *Limits* and treated the world by regions rather than as a monolithic whole.

Among those who warn of the dangers of population pressure, there seems to be a tendency to estimate an early date for world collapse. Since the time of Malthus world population has more than tripled and living conditions have greatly improved. This does not mean that Malthus was wrong in principle. It does mean that he was too specific in his prediction of an urgent population crisis and in his focus on food shortage as the primary consequence.

Paul Ehrlich, who is an authority on population studies, has published several informative books that outline the development and future course of the population crisis.[15] Ehrlich's works breathe the same note of urgency, but he paints the future with a broader brush. He points out the vast implications of overpopulation for world food distribution, immigration, refugee problems, pandemic disease, riots, genocide, and various forms of environmental degradation. He takes the position that voluntary means of population control are still possible. His books urge the organization of action groups to bring about population control by political means. Ehrlich's *The Population Bomb* lists organizations to contact and offers sample letters that can be sent to public figures to make the world more aware of the population crisis.

It is doubtful that even widespread awareness of the problem will be enough to halt the expansion of world population. The urge to reproduce is as strong as, or stronger than the sex drive. One has only to look at a mother hovering over her children or a father handing out cigars following the birth of a child. Unlike sex, reproduction is still quite respectable in our society. If one talks about the dangers of sexual promiscuity or second-hand cigarette smoke one can find support from several quarters, but to point to an innocent child as a danger to our society would be regarded as reprehensible.

We have from five to six billion people on the planet at the present time. What is the carrying capacity of the planet? Ehrlich has indicated that, at the average American standard, the world could temporarily support between 500 million and a billion people.[16] On a vegetarian diet we could support more, but our system of distribution is often ineffective. There are periods of famine in which millions starve to death. There are also instances of genocide which are an indirect result of competition for food and resources. According to Ehrlich, "since 1968, more than 200 million people—mostly children—have perished needlessly from hunger and hunger-related diseases."[17] This suggests that we are already beyond the carrying capacity of the planet, considering food alone and not the depletion of natural resources. Yet the stabilization level of world population has been variously estimated at between ten and fifteen billion people. We will not know the answer until we reach that supposed level of stabilization. But if we do stabilize on such a high level, the energy required to prevent catastrophe somewhere in the world will be much greater.

It would seem that the human race, as the only species capable of reasoning, should be able to limit its total population and not be subject to a massive die-off, as occurs with certain animal species when the population density within an area becomes excessive. But it is not reason that will determine our future birth rate. It will be the shock of an insupportable world population that will bring about some form of mandatory control. It does not seem likely that mankind will do it voluntarily.

The most serious aspect of the population problem is *perception*. If most of the world does not see what is happening or, worse yet, finds evidence in the new techniques of agriculture, that the world can support a much higher level of population than we have today, we are faced with a political problem.

Popularizers of the green revolution are enthusiastic. Robert Katz tells us, "Powered by varied and sometimes conflicting intentions scientists are engaged in highly diverse tasks, which seem to foreshadow a golden age of food culture for all mankind, whatever its numbers may be."[18] In contrast to Ehrlich, Katz seems to feel that the population problem has only one consequence and that if we can feed everyone, even if we limit them to a vegetarian diet, we will enter the golden age.

People are not content with subsistence. They want to eat well. They will continually strive and compete to get eggs, milk, cheese, meat, and other products. As they gain in prosperity they will want running water in their homes, electricity, appliances, automobiles, cement highways, and many of the other accouterments of civilization. In studies designed to feed larger populations one cannot take it for granted that the new arrivals will be content to live at the subsistence level. One must assume that when their bellies are full they will look around to see what else they might want. They will want more of the enjoyment of life and will do what they can to provide these pleasures for themselves and their families. Simply providing food for the newborn is not enough. In fact, allowing unrestricted growth of population is one way of being sure they will not be well fed or educated. Further, if we make no attempt to restrain population, we will finally bump up against the limits of even the most extensive and well-planned food production program. There is a limit to growth, even though it cannot be specified exactly.

THE FUTURE COURSE

In this chapter we have examined four alternatives to military intervention as a means of resolving crisis situations in the world: weapons control, energy conservation, agricultural aid for developing nations, and population control. All of them would require long-range planning and voluntary cooperation.

There is another alternative to the systematic effort to solve global problems. Let nature take its course. In short, do nothing. If things get bad enough the problem will solve itself. For example, if there are too many people in the world we may control excessive populations by failing to intervene in massive regional famines and in genocidal attacks by one race or tribe against another. It would reduce world population and save a lot of money at the same time. There is a strong tendency, among a large segment of our society to solve the problem this way. It is not expressed openly, but in the complaints about using our resources abroad when "we should be helping our people right here at home" one finds the unspoken assumption that we can separate ourselves from the rest of the world.

Every year the world gets smaller and it becomes more apparent that we are all part of one global community. Like the man who looks out his window to find that a woman is being beaten and raped on the sidewalk, we are discovering that there are no innocent bystanders. To observe is to be involved, whether or not we accept that involvement.

Even "scientific objectivity" cannot keep us out of trouble. The physical scientist used to believe that it was possible to observe, measure, and even predict the outcome of events without affecting these events or changing the outcome. But physicist Werner Heisenberg learned some time ago that there was a limit to his ability to remain outside the situation he was observing. He discovered it was not possible to determine both the position and velocity of subatomic particles because of the influence of his measuring instrument. In short, he found that by observing an event he had an effect on one of the two aspects he wanted to measure (that is, position or velocity). Concerning the results of his experiments and the later "Copenhagen interpretation" of quantum theory that followed, Heisenberg remarked,

To what extent, then, have we finally come to an objective description of the world? In classical physics science started from the belief—or should one say from the illusion?—that we could describe the world or at least parts of the world without any reference to ourselves. . . . quantum theory reminds us, as Bohr has put it, that when searching for harmony in life one must never forget that in the drama of existence we are ourselves both players and spectators.[19]

Every day, with every act, we all help to make our world. We cannot shift the responsibility to elected leaders—or even to nonelected leaders. We will be forced to live with the consequences of our benign (or malevolent) neglect. We may not be able to do enough. We may make mistakes. But we must (and will) do something, simply because the decision to do nothing is doing something.

To some extent we will have to limit the extent of our intervention because we do not have the resources or the resolve to manage the world as a whole. At the present time we cannot prevent our own and other nation's capitalists from selling weapons wherever they can. The American people are not prepared for the sacrifice of their comfort and, at present, they will not willingly conserve their use of energy. They want the freedom to drive large powerful cars and control their indoor climate with the temperature control set just the way they like it. But the total energy in the world is limited, as is the food and the natural resources. If we will not admit this, there are those who will say, "if there is food enough to feed the world, why am I so hungry? If there is plenty of energy, why are we left behind in cold and darkness? I want a share of what you have!"

The poor of the world are no longer cut off from our society. They may live in slums, but the vivid pictures of the world media have pressed their nose to the glass and they can look in on all of us and see us eating at a well-provided table. They are no longer content to wait passively for their fate, but they cry out in rage and seek some means to take by force what they do not have. With the vast proliferation of weapons, more and more of them have the fire power to try it.

The rapid growth of world population means the spilling over of desperate refugees into adjacent lands. Whether they are fleeing hunger or oppression makes little difference. They will come and they will flood the resources of the developed nations. Population control is essential. However, not every nation will develop this control at the same time. For this reason the world will have to go through a period where immigration will be opposed by stringent, sometimes violent and unjust measures. This may give way to a system of free trade in which we realize the only way to keep out the hordes of the poor is to remove trade barriers and give all nations a chance to develop their economies and feed their people.

Compassion is a wonderful thing. It *was* wonderful when the United States was a rich nation, able to support everyone who could not work and to talk of ending hunger throughout the world. It is an uncomfortable fact that we no longer have—if we ever had—the resources to support all the poor and disabled in the United States and go half way around the world to prevent some perceived catastrophe. Population in the United States—and particularly the number of aged, disabled, and otherwise unemployable Americans who cannot contribute to productivity—is reaching a point where financial resources are insufficient to cover their needs. Both political parties recognize that we will have to do something to reduce entitlements, but neither has the will to act. This does not mean that everyone must struggle for his own survival, but we must take another look at the way we are distributing our resources. For example, the very wealthy can collect Social Security as well as the very poor, and the entitlements of the wealthy are usually higher because they have worked longer at a higher salary.

Inequality between the rich and poor has been increasing in this country since 1969. The rich are getting richer and the poor are getting poorer, despite our efforts to provide entitlements to the disadvantaged.[20] On the other hand, it has been demonstrated that those nations with the greater equality of income also have a greater productivity of labor.[21] The political-economic system in the United States today is not working, and if we do not learn to revise it, it will break down altogether.

As a result of these internal pressures, intervention to prevent world hunger and to aid population control will be selective, based in large measure on political considerations. We will work more vigorously to influence the economy and population of those nations that are pressing on our border and that threaten to flood our resources with a mass of illegal immigrants. We are already witnessing some of the desperate measures to stem the flow of people into the United States. Proposition 187, which passed in the 1994 California elections sought to deny all but emergency medical care and all education to illegal immigrants. We are picking up others at sea and placing them in various prison camps on islands outside our borders. There is much injustice in these measures for the very reason that they are measures of desperation and because we do not fully understand the reasons why these masses are overwhelming our border defenses. Runaway population is clearly an important reason. A booming economy can support many more people than a depressed one. But even booming economies reach the point where population pressures diminish the quality of life. The world refugee problem becomes greater every year as the battle for living space erupts into genocide around the globe.

Calhoun, in his studies of rats, has demonstrated that aggressive and socially destructive behavior increases as the density of rat population reaches a certain level.[22] This phenomenon is not limited to rats. It occurs, even in the cities of developed nations, as population pressures mount. The rate of violent crimes is much higher in metropolitan areas than in small cities and rural areas. For both black and white teenagers the relationship of murder to population density is striking.[23] There is as yet no general recognition of the extent to which mounting world population is contributing to immigration pressures, mass murder, and genocide.

Ideally, a responsible citizen of this planet would limit his energy use and food consumption to accommodate others. He would limit reproduction so as not to crowd others. He would limit pollution to improve the health and comfort of himself and others. That is, he would do these things if he truly understood the extent to which we are all interdependent. As things stand, the history of mankind and our development as a species has not prepared us for voluntary accommodation. Man achieved his toehold on this planet by fighting other competing forms of life, by accumulating food and energy for himself and his immediate relatives, and finally for his tribe and his nation. His very success in this struggle for survival has shaped his nature to that of an intensely competitive, accumulating, consuming, procreating individual. He is not inclined to limit his reproductive urge or his personal comfort and possessions. Why should he? His concept of himself ends at the boundry of his own ego. He is unable to perceive the extent to which a shrinking planet has coalesced our possibilities so that we must cooperate if we are to survive.

Occasionally, nations will cooperate with one another in an emergency to crush another nation, but most nations are reluctant to cooperate for some future goal that will benefit the planet as a whole. There is no reason to expect that they will until each individual has some experience—probably some physical experience—that changes his perception of the world. We see things the way we do because of a long history in which we slowly learned to cope with what we thought was the real world. As a result we are limited by our perception of the outside world as a dangerous, combative place where other life forms are enemies. This view of life will not be changed by an intellectual understanding of the cause of acid rain or climate change. It does no good to describe spaceship Earth, or to talk about the need to share the remaining space, food, and energy with other creatures. Nor can it be changed by a sudden emotional conversion to the belief that we must love one another. We cannot change the result of a million years of evolution by logic or emotional exhortation.   To make a change in our behavior there must be an alteration of the way we perceive what we call "reality."   It may well take a major shock of some kind to change our perception of the world. Until that time comes, things may get worse before they get better.

NOTES

1. Toynbee, A. J. *A Study of History* (New York and London: Oxford University Press, 1947).

2. G. P. Shultz, *Turmoil and Triumph: My Years as Secretary of State*, (New York: Charles Scribner's Sons, 1993), p. 238.

3. Ibid., p. 244.

4. Ibid., pp. 238-239.

5. R. M. Nixon, "The Pageant of Peace Ceremony." *Weekly Compilation of Presidential Documents*, 1969, vol. 5, no. 51,1757-1758.

6. W. Dowell, M. Michaels, A. Purvis, and E. Wallace, "Draining the Swamp." *Time*, October 28, 1995, pp. 74-76.

7. *Encyclopedia Britannica*, (Chicago: Univ Chicago Press, 1990), vol 19, pp 588-611.
"Proven reserves are now enough to supply the world for 43 years at current rates of production, compared with less than 35 years during the 1970s, according to BP, one of the oil giants. Proven reserves of naural gas now stand at more than 66 years' worth of current production, up from 44 years in 1970. Coal reserves will stubbornly last for 235 years of production at current levels.
Of course rates of production will not stay unchanged. The world's demand for energy could more than double by 2025, as populations soar and poor countries industrialise. But, even given the growth in demand, the proven reserve figures probably underestimate the longevity of fossil fuels." *The Economist*, December 7, 1995, pp. 23-26.

8. G. Bush, *Public Papers of the Presidents of the United States*, 1992-1993 (Washington D.C.: U.S. Government Printing Office, 1993), pp. 2174-2176

9. "A Slow Death." *Economist*, September 18, 1993, p. 46.

10. "Events of the Year: Agriculture and Food Supplies," *Britannica Book of the Year,* 1944, Encyclopedia Britannica, 1944, pp. 83-84.

11. "A Touch of Spring." *The Economist,* March 27, 1993, p. 57.

12. "Overstuffing Africa." *The Economist,* May 8, 1993, p. 50.

13. R. Rodale, *Save Three Lives: A Plan for Famine Prevention* (San Francisco: Sierra Club Books, 1981, pp. 3, 27, 33-34.

14. D. H. Meadows, D. L. Meadows, J. Randers, and W. W. Behrens, *The Limits to Growth: A Report for the Club of Rome's Project on the Predicament of Mankind* (New York: Universe Books, 1972.

15. P. R. Ehrlich, *The Population Bomb* (New York: Ballantine Books, 1968); P. R. Ehrlich, and A. H. Ehrlich, *The Population Explosion* (New York: Simon and Schuster, 1990).

16. P. R. Ehrlich, and A. H. Ehrlich, "The Population Crisis," *Britannica Book of the Year* (London: Encyclopedia Britannica, Inc., 1971), pp. 605-607.

17. Ehrlich and Ehrlich, *The Population Explosion,* p. 9.

18. R. Katz, *A Giant in the Earth* (New York: Stein and Day, 1973), p. 47.

19. W. Heisenberg, *Physics and Philosophy* (New York: Harper and Row, 1962), pp. 55-58.

20. "Inequality: For Richer, for Poorer." *Economist,* November 5, 1994, pp. 19-21.

21. Ibid.

22. J. B. Calhoun, "A Behavior Sink," in E. L. Bliss, ed., *Roots of Behavior* (New York: Harper, 1922), pp. 322-336.

23. L. A. Fingerhut, D. D. Ingram, and J. J. Feldman, "Firearm and Non-Firearm Homicide Among Persons Fiften Through Nineteen Years of Age." *Journal of the American Medical Association,* June 10, 1992, vol. 267, no.22, pp. 3048-3053.

SELECTED BIBLIOGRAPHY

Acheson, D. *Present at the Creation: My Years in the State Department*. New York: Norton, 1969.

Agee, P. *Inside the Company: CIA Diary*. New York: Bantam, 1973.

Aguinaldo, E. with V. A. Pacis, *A Second Look at America*. New York:Robert Speller and Sons, 1957.

Avrigan, T. and M. Honey, eds. *La Penca: On Trial in Costa Rica*. Printed in Costa Rica. San Pedro: Montes de Oca, 1988.

Ball, G. *The Past Has Another Pattern*. New York: Norton, 1982.

Baraheni, R. *Crowned Cannibals: Writings on the Repression in Iran*. New York: Vintage, 1977.

Blanchard, W. H. *Aggression American Style*. Santa Monica, Calif. Goodyear, 1978.

Bonner, R. *Waltzing with a Dictator*. New York: Random House, Times Books, 1987.

Boorstin, D. J. *An American Primer*. Chicago: University of Chicago Press, 1966.

Brzezinski, Z. *Power and Principle*. New York: Farrar, Straus and Giroux, 1983.

Bunge, F. M. *Philippines: A Country Study* Department of the Army Washington: U.S. Government Printing Office, 1984.

Calhoun, J. B. "A Behavior Sink," in *Roots of Behavior,* edited by E. L. Bliss. New York: Harper, 1922.

Carter, J. *Keeping Faith*. New York: Bantam, 1982.

Chamorro, E. *Packaging the Contras: A Case of CIA Disinformation*. New York: Institute for Media Analysis, 1987.

Cockburn, L. *Out of Control: The Story of the Reagan Administration's Secret War in Nicaragua, the Illegal Arms Pipeline, and the Contra Drug Connection*. New York: Atlantic Monthly Press, 1987.

Cohen, W. S. and G. J. Mitchell, *Men of Zeal*. New York: Viking, 1988.

Cottam, R. W. *Nationalism in Iran*. Pittsburgh: University of Pittsburgh Press, 1964.

Cruz, A. J., Jr. *Memoirs of a Counterrevolutionary*. New York: Doubleday, 1989.

Douglas, W. O. *The Douglas Letters: Selections from the Private Papers of Justice William O. Douglas*, edited by Melvin I. Urofsky. Bethesda: Adler and Adler, 1987.

Ehrlich, P. R. *The Population Bomb.* New York: Ballantine Books, 1968.

Ehrlich, P. R. and A. H. Ehrlich, *The Population Explosion.* New York: Simon and Schuster, 1990.

Fischer, M. M. J. *Iran: From Religious Dispute to Revolution* Cambridge: Harvard University Press, 1980.

Glad, B. *Jimmy Carter in Search of the Great White House.* New York: Norton, 1980.

Hall, E. T. *The Hidden Dimension.* Garden City: Doubleday Anchor, 1969.

Hersh, S. M. *The Price of Power: Kissinger in the Nixon White House.* New York: Summit Books, 1983.

Hollman, E. and A. Love, *Inside the Shadow Government.* Washington D.C.: Christic Institute, 1988.

Hoveyda, F. *The Fall of the Shah.* New York: Wyndham, 1979.

Hughes, E. J. *The Living Presidency: The Resources and Dilemmas of the American Presidential Office.* New York: Coward McCann, 1972.

Janis, I. L. *Victims of Groupthink.* Boston: Houghton Mifflin, 1972.

Janis, I. L. and L. Mann, *Decision Making: A Psychological Analysis of Conflict, Choice and Committment.* New York: The Free Press, 1977.

Johnson, H. *In the Absence of Power: Governing America.* New York: Viking, 1980.

Jordan, H. *Crisis: The Last Years of the Carter Presidency.* New York: Norton, 1982.

Karnow, S. *America's Empire in the Philippines.* New York: Random House, 1989.

Katz, R. *A Giant in the Earth.* New York: Stein and Day, 1973.

Kissinger, H. *The White House Years.* Boston: Little Brown, 1979.

McFarlane, R. C. *Special Trust.* New York: Cadell and Davies, 1994.

McGehee, R. W. *Deadly Deceits: My Twenty-Five Years with the CIA.* New York: Sheridan Square Publications, 1983.

Meadows, D. H., D. L. Meadows, J. Randers, and W. W. Behrens, *The Limits to Growth: A Report for the Club of Rome's Project on the Predicament of Mankind.* New York: Universe Books, 1972.

Millspaugh, A. C. *Americans in Persia.* New York: DeCapo Press, 1976.

Nirumand, B. *Iran: The New Imperialism in Action.* New York: Monthly Review Press, 1969.

North, O. L. *Under Fire: An American Story.* New York: Harper Paperbacks, 1991.

Petrov, V. *A Study in Diplomacy.* Chicago: Henry Regnery, 1971.

Reagan, R. W. *An American Life.* New York: Simon and Schuster, 1990.

Regan, D. T. *For the Record.* New York: Harcourt, Brace and Javanovich, 1988.

Rodale, R. *Save Three Lives: A Plan for Famine Prevention.* San Francisco: Sierra Club Books, 1981.

Rosset, P. and J. Vandermeer, eds. *The Nicaraguan Reader.* NewYork: Grove, 1983.

Rudolph, J. D., ed. *Nicaragua: A Country Study.* Washington, D.C.: US Government Printing Office, 1982.

Saikal, A. *The Rise and Fall of the Shah.* Princeton: Princeton University Press, 1980.

Seagrave, S. *The Marcos Dynasty.* New York: Harper and Row, 1988.

Schlesinger, A. M., Jr. *A Thousand Days: John F. Kennedy in the White House.* New York: Fawcett Crest, 1965.

Schumpeter, J. *Social Classes and Imperialism*. New York: World Publishing, Meridian, 1966.

Shalom, S. *The United States and the Philippines: A Study of Neocolonialism*. Philadelphia: Institute for the Study of Human Issues, 1981.

Sheehan, N., H. Smith, E. W. Kenworthy, and F. Butterfield, F., eds. *The Pentagon Papers*. New York: Bantam, 1971.

Shultz, G. P. *Turmoil and Triumph: My Years as Secretary of State*. New York: Charles Scribner, 1993.

Sick, G. *All Fall Down: America's Tragic Encounter with Iran*. New York: Random House, 1985.

Tower, J., E. Muskie, and B. Scowcroft, *The Tower Commission Report*. New York: Times Books, 1987.

Truman, H. S. *Memoirs, Volume 2: Years of Trial and Hope*. Garden City, N.Y.: Doubleday, 1956.

Walker, T. W. *Nicaragua in Revolution*. New York: Praeger, 1982.

Wilson, W. *Messages and Papers of Woodrow Wilson*. New York: George H. Doran, 1924.

Wise, D. and T. B. Ross, *The Espionage Establishment*. New York Random House, 1967.

INDEX

About the Author

WILLIAM H. BLANCHARD has held positions with the Rand Corporation and the Planning, Analysis, and Research Institute. He is the author of *Aggression American Style* (1978), *Rousseau and Revolt* (1967), and *Revolutionary Morality* (1984).

ISBN 0-313-30013-5

HARDCOVER BAR CODE